T000606?

Learning
Hindi

How to Stream the Audios and Flash Cards of this Book.

1. Make sure you have an Internet connection.
2. Type the URL below into your web browser.
   https://www.tuttlepublishing.com/learning-hindi

For support, you can email us at info@tuttlepublishing.com.

A LANGUAGE GUIDE FOR SELF-STUDY

Learning Hindi

Speak, Read and Write Hindi with **Manga Comics**!

Brajesh Samarth, PhD

Professor and Language Coordinator in Hindi-Urdu,
Emory College of Arts and Sciences, USA

TUTTLE Publishing

Tokyo | Rutland, Vermont | Singapore

Contents

Namaste! Welcome to Hindi!

First of all, congratulations for deciding to learn Hindi. This book will take you on an exciting journey where you will learn not only the language, but also about the culture of the people who speak it.

HINDI IN POPULAR CULTURE

The rich culture of India is perhaps most commonly associated with Bollywood (a portmanteau of Bombay and Hollywood), the popular term used for the Hindi film industry based in Mumbai or Bombay. The first Hindi film was the silent *Raja Harishchandra* made by Dadasaheb Phalke in 1913, while the first Hindi movie with sound was *Alam Ara,* made by Ardeshir Irani in 1931. Bollywood films are famous for their music and dancing. About 800 movies are made in India each year, giving you a wide variety of shows to watch to improve your listening comprehension and widen your vocabulary.

Among the list of famous people from India are Vivekanada, Mother Teresa and Gandhi, political figures like Jawahar Lal Nehru and Indira Gandhi, cricketer Sachin Tedulkar, actors Amitabh Bachchan and Shahrukh Khan, and the poet Rabindranath Tagore.

DIFFERENCES BETWEEN ENGLISH AND HINDI

Hindi differs from English in several ways. Hindi has many more terms to describe kinship and relationships, as family and relationships are very important to Indian society that the language developed around them. For example, there are three different words for the second person pronoun "you," each conveying a different degree of formality. People are very careful to choose the right pronoun (although it's always safe to use **aap**) in conversation.

Hindi has many phonetic variations for the same English letter, sometimes up to four sounds for one letter (e.g., the consonant "t.") Making all these sounds will give your lips, tongue, and muscles of your face quite a workout. You will enjoy learning and producing these sounds—following along with the native speakers on the audio recordings. While this takes some practice, the good news is that most of the time, the pronunciation of written letters is always the same, unlike "rough" and "though" in English.

USING THIS BOOK

Each lesson of this book contains several sections, starting with a dialogue that you can memorize and use in your daily conversations. Try to commit the entire dialogue to memory and mimic the native speakers' pronunciations from the recordings that can be found online. The dialogue is followed by a vocabulary list, grammar notes to explain the unique features of Hindi grammar, as well as cultural notes to help you avoid cultural missteps. Pattern Practices and Exercises are included to test your understanding of what you've read in the lesson. Finally, read through the checklist at the end of the lesson and see if you have managed to accomplish all the goals.

An English-Hindi and Hindi-English dictionary has also been added at the back of the book, enabling you to find 1,500 of the most common words in either language in either direction, so you can easily look up the Hindi version of the word you're trying to convey, or vice versa.

Multi-ethnic students having a project discussion

LESSON 1

An Introduction to the Hindi Language and Writing System

Hindi has several different names: "Khari boli," "Hindi-Urdu," or "Nagari Hindi." These are related to the language's history and its relationship to its sister language Urdu. At the level of grammar and colloquial speech the languages are mostly the same, but Urdu has more vocabulary from Persian and Arabic, and is written in an Arabic-derived script. The term "Hindi-Urdu" underscores this relationship, while "Nagari Hindi" emphasizes that Hindi is written in the Indic (Deva)nagari script originally developed to write Sanskrit. "Khari boli" or "upright speech" is the name of the dialect spoken traditionally in and around Delhi forming the basis for the standard forms of both Hindi and Urdu. The word "Hindi" itself is originally a Persian word that simply meant "Indian (language)." Whatever name we use, it is by far the most commonly used and understood language in modern India.

Apart from being one of the official languages of the Indian Republic as a whole—the other being English—it is an official language in the Indian states of Rajasthan, Madhya Pradesh, Uttar Pradesh, Uttarakhand, Himachal Pradesh, Bihar, Chattisgarh, Jharkhand, Delhi and Haryana.

THE HINDI WRITING SYSTEM

The Hindi script is called Devanagari. It is written from left to right, and has a horizontal line running above each letter to join the syllables forming a word. The Devanagari script is also used to write other languages like Bhojpuri, Nepali, Marathi, Sanskrit, Marwari and Maithili. It is not difficult to learn to read and write Hindi. The script is phonetic, which means you read it as it is written. There are no silent letters, and there is a direct correspondence between the written symbols and their pronunciation.

The Hindi Alphabet (01–01)
Hindi Consonants

	Non-Voiced Non-Aspirated	Non-Voiced, Aspirated	Voiced, Non-Aspirated	Voiced, Aspirated	Nasal
Velar	क ka	ख kha	ग ga	घ gha	ङ nga
Palatal	च cha	छ chha	ज ja	झ jha	ञ nya
Retroflex	ट Ta	ठ Tha	ड Da	ढ Dha	ण Na

	Non-Voiced Non-Aspirated	Non-Voiced, Aspirated	Voiced, Non-Aspirated	Voiced, Aspirated	Nasal
Dental	त ta	थ tha	द da	ध dha	न na
Labial	प pa	फ pha	ब ba	भ bha	म ma
Semi Vowels	य ya	र ra	ल la	व va/wa	
Sibilants	श sha	ष shha	स sa		
Conjuncts	क्ष ksha	त्र tra	ज्ञ jna/gya		
Flapped Gutturals	ड़ Ra	ढ़ Rha			

The letter र **ra** is written in a special way when it is added to other consonants. For example, to write **kra** we put a diagonal stroke on the left of क to form क्र. Thus, **pra** is written प्र, **bra** is written ब्र, and **mra** is written म्र.

Consonants Used only in Loanwords:

क़ qa   ख़ <u>Kha</u>   ग़ gha   ज़ za   फ़ pha

Hindi Vowels

Short	अ a	इ i	उ u	ए aye	ओ oe
Long	आ aa	ई ii	ऊ oo	ऐ aiye	औ ouv
	अं añ	अः ah	ऋ ree		

Explanations of the Terms Used:

Aspirated: A puff of air is expelled when pronouncing the sound
Voiced: The throat resonates when the sound is produced
Nasal: Sounds produced using the nose

The Hindi Consonants (01–02)

There are 28 consonants, but some have a second version with a dot that represents a related but slightly different sound. It's best to listen to the audio recordings carefully and practice pronouncing each letter as accurately as possible. When the consonants are read on their own, an "**a**" sound follows each consonant. Hence the letter "**k**" is pronounced "**ka**." If there's a dot below the letter, as in ख़ **kha**, the sound should be pronounced deeper in the throat, like a "ch" sound (which is also how Urdu speakers would pronounce it), but most Hindi speakers would say this letter as ख **kha**. Below is a list of the full forms of the consonants. In the transliterations, when a letter is capitalized, that indicates it is retroflex, meaning it is pronounced with the tongue curled back against the roof of the mouth.

Velar Consonants

These consonants are all pronounced at the very back of the mouth, in the throat. English equivalents are the letters "k" and "g," but Hindi has many more.

Consonant	Sounds Like	Examples
क ka	like "k" in "king" and "kind"	काम **kaam** "work"
क़ qa	like "q" in "queen," but further back in the throat	क़लम **qalam** "pen"
ख kha	like "k" but aspirated	खोलना **kholnaa** "to open"
ख़ kha	like the Scottish and German "ch" in "Loch" and "Bach"	ख़ुश **khush** "happy"
ग ga	like "g" in "go," "get"	आग **aag** "fire"
ग़ gha	between "g" and "r," like a French "r"	ग़लत **ghalat** "incorrect"
घ gha	like "g" but aspirated	घड़ी **ghaRii** "watch, clock"
ङ nga	like "ng" in "sing," where the "ng" is shown with a dot	रंग **rang** "color"

Palatal Consonants

These consonants are all pronounced at the top of the mouth—the "palate" is the roof of the mouth.

Consonant	Sounds Like	Examples
च cha	like "ch" in "chair," "church"	चावल **chaaval** "rice"
छ chha	like "ch" but aspirated	छुरी **chhurii** "knife"
ज ja	like "j" in "jungle" or "jail"	जल **jal** "water"
झ jha	like "j," aspirated	झंडा **jhanDa** "flag, banner"
ञ nya	like "nee," with less emphasis on the "ee" sound, used in Sanskrit loanwords and shown with a dot	रंजित **ranjit** "colored"
ज़ za	like "z" in "zest"	ज़िंदगी **zindagii** "life"

Retroflex Consonants

These consonants are all pronounced with the tongue curled back against the roof of the mouth.

Consonant	Sounds Like	Examples
ट **Ta**	like "t" but stronger	टांग **Taañg** "leg"
ठ **Tha**	similar to **Ta** but aspirated	ठंडा **ThanDaa** "cold"
ड **Da**	like "d" but stronger	डर **Dar** "fear"
ढ **Dha**	similar to **Da** but aspirated	ढकना **Dhaknaa** "to cover"
ण **na**	like "n" but stronger	कारण **kaaran** "reason"

Semi–Vowels

These are consonants that sound similar to vowels, e.g., "year" and "why" in English where the sounds made by "y" and "w" are similar to "ee" and "oo."

Consonant	Sounds Like	Examples
ल **la**	like "l" but lighter, e.g., "like" and "light"	लाल **laal** "red"
र **ra**	like "r" in "rose" and "right"	रानी **raani** "queen"
व **va**	in between the "v" and "w" in "victory" and "water"	वायु **vaayoo** "air"
य **ya**	like "y" in "young" and "youth"	या **yaa** "or"

Dental Consonants

These consonants are pronounced with the tongue striking the upper teeth. Its English equivalents are "t" and "d."

Consonant	Sounds Like	Examples
त **ta**	like "t" in "Taj Mahal"	ताज़ा **taazaa** "fresh"
थ **tha**	similar to **ta** but aspirated	थूकना **thuuknaa** "to spit"
द **da**	like "th" in "there"	दिल **dil** "heart"
ध **dha**	similar to **da** but aspirated	धूप **dhuup** "sunshine"
न **na**	like "n" in "now"	नाक **naak** "nose"

Labial Consonants

These sounds are made using both lips.

Consonant	Sounds Like	Examples
प pa	like "p" in "papa" or "parrot"	पानी **paanii** "water"
फ pha	similar to pa but aspirated	फल **phal** "fruit"
फ़ fa	like "f" in "fan" or "first"	फ़ालतू **faalatoo** "useless"
ब ba	"b" in "boy" or "bus"	बकरी **bakari** "goat"
भ bha	similar to ba but aspirated	भालू **bhaaloo** "bear"
म ma	like "m" in "mother" or "mouth"	मछली **machhalii** "fish"

Sibilant Consonants

These consonants are produced with a hissing sound.

Consonant	Sounds Like	Examples
श sha	like "sh" in "shut," "shave"	शब्द **shabd** "word"
स sa	like "s" in "sound" and "side"	सब्ज़ी **sabzii** "vegetable"
ष shha	like the shushing sound "shh!"	षट **shhat** "six"

Glottal Consonant

Consonant	Sounds Like	Examples
ह ha	like "h" in "Hindi" or "high"	हंस **hans** "swan"

Conjunct Consonants

Consonant	Sounds Like	Examples
क्ष ksha	like "cush" in "cushion" with less emphasis on the "u"	कक्षा **kakshhaa** "class"
त्र tra	like "thr" in "through" with a rolled "r"	त्रिशूल **trishool** "trident"
ज्ञ gya	like "gear" with less emphasis on the "r"	ज्ञानी **gyaanii** "learned person"
र ra	like "r" in "rose" and "right"	रानी **raani** "queen"

Flapped Gutturals

These are similar to a rolled "r," produced by flapping the tongue.

Consonant	Sounds Like	Examples
ड़ **Ra**	a combination of "l," "r" and "d"	पेड़ **peRh** "tree"
ढ़ **Rha**	similar to **Ra** but aspirated	पढ़ना **paRhnaa** "to read"

HALF AND FULL CONSONANTS

In Hindi, there are both half and full consonants. To mute the "a" sound in the full consonant, a special mark or क् **viraama** (विराम) is added below the consonant, so कम **kam** becomes क्म **km**. This mark is rarely shown in writing though, usually replaced with the half consonant, which resembles the left half of the consonant. Here's what the consonants become when paired with म (**ma**) and muting the "a" sound.

ब ba → ब्म bm	भ bha → भ्म bhm	च cha → च्म chm
छ chha → छ्म chhm	द da → द्म dm	ध dha → ध्म dhm
ड Da → ड्म Dm	ढ Dha → ढ्म Dhm	ग ga → ग्म gm
घ gha → घ्म ghm	ह ha → ह्म hm	ज ja → ज्म jm
झ jha → झ्म jhm	क ka → क्म km	ख kha → ख्म khm
ल la → ल्म lm	म ma → म्म mm	न na → न्म nm
ण Na → ण्म Nm		

ङ nga → ङ्म ngm (only occurs before **ka/kha/ga/gha** and is almost always contracted to a dot, e.g., ग्ङ्म)

ञ nya → ञ्म nym (only occurs before **cha/chha/ja/jha** and is almost always contracted to a dot)

प pa → प्म pm	फ pha → फ्म phm	र ra → र्म rm
स sa → स्म sm	श sha → श्म shm	ष sha → ष्म shm
त ta → त्म tm	थ tha → थ्म thm	ट Ta → ट्म Tm
ठ Tha → ठ्म Thm	व va → व्म vm	य ya → य्म ym

THE HINDI VOWELS (01–03)

There are eleven vowels, including three long vowels.

Vowel	Sounds Like	Examples
अ **a**	"a" in "apply," "available"	अब **ab** "now"
आ **aa**	a long "a" sound, like in "Father"	आग **aag** "fire"
इ **i**	"ee" in "pit" or "hit"	इतवार **itvaar** "Sunday"
ई **ii**	a longer "ee" sound, like "wee" or "feed"	ईख **Eekh** "sugarcane"
उ **u**	"u" in "put" or "full"	उठना **uThnaa** "to rise, get up"
ऊ **uu**	a long "u" sound like in "food"	ऊपर **uupar** "above"
ए **e**	"ay" in "may"	एक **ek** the number "one"
ऐ **ai**	"eh" in "pen" and "men"	ऐसा **aisaa** "such"
ओ **o**	"oh" in "domain"	ओझल **ojhal** "hidden"
औ **au**	"aw" in "awesome" or "awful"	और **aur** "and"
ऋ **ri**	"ri" in "riddle"; considered to be a vowel in Hindi, usually used with words of Sanskrit origin	ऋषि **rishi** "sage, seer, wise man"

There are two other vowels derived from a combination of **a** and the final consonants **m** and **h**. These are अं (**añ**—the **ñ** is a nasal consonant pronounced like "n" in "nine") and अः **ah**.

COMBINING VOWELS WITH CONSONANTS

When vowels come after consonants in a syllable, they are represented by shortened forms or **maatraa**. Thus when writing the word का **kaa**, rather than writing कआ, it becomes का **kaa**, where the vowel आ **aa** is shortened to ा. Similarly, if you wanted to write **Ti**, it should be ट **Ta** + इ **i**. But using the **maatraa** इ **i**, the word becomes टि **Ti** instead.

Only अ **a** doesn't have its own **maatraa** since it is inherent in the consonants. This inherent "a" can be silenced by applying the क् **viraama** (विराम) as discussed on page 14 and the vowel "a" is usually automatically silent at the end of a word.

The other **maatraa** forms are shown in the table below:

Vowel	Maatraa	Combination with ka + maatraa
अ **a**	none	क + no **maatraa** = क **k(a)**
आ **aa**	ा	क + ा = का **kaa**
इ **i**	ि	क + ि = कि **ki**
ई **ii**	ी	क + ी = की **kii**
ऋ **ri**	ॢ	क + ॢ = कृ **kri**
उ **u**	ु	क + ु = कु **ku**
ऊ **uu**	ू	क + ू = कू **kuu**
ए **e**	े	क + े = के **ke**
ऐ **ai**	ै	क + ै = कै **kai**
ओ **o**	ो	क + ो = को **ko**
औ **au**	ौ	क + ौ = कौ **kau**
अं **añ**	ं	क + ं = कं **kañ**
अः **ah**	ः	क + ः = कः **kaH**

NOTE: र **ra** is the only consonant where the **maatraa** for उ **u** or ऊ **uu** is placed inside the letter, rather than under it: रु **ru** and रू **ruu**. If a word starts with a vowel sound or has a vowel sound independent of a consonant, it is written with a vowel and not a **maatraa**. For example, America starts with अ **a** and is written अमेरिका **Amerika**.

WRITING EXERCISE 1
Write the following sounds using the Hindi script:

1. gaa
2. bi
3. lii
4. ku
5. puu
6. me
7. tai
8. jo
9. mau
10. kri
11. fañ
12. maH

WRITING EXERCISE 2

Write in Hindi the following sounds on a piece of paper:

1. **pa**	**paa**	**pi**	**pii**	**pu**	**puu**
2. **pe**	**pai**	**po**	**pau**	**pañ**	
3. **paa**	**paamaa**	**pimaa**	**piimaa**	**puma**	**puumaa**
4. **pemaa**	**paimaa**	**pomaa**	**paumaa**	**pañbaa**	
5. **lala**	**laalaa**	**lilaa**	**liilaa**	**lulaa**	**luulaa**
6. **lelaa**	**lailaa**	**lolaa**	**laulaa**	**lañbaa**	
7. **tata**	**taataa**	**titaa**	**tiitaa**	**tutaa**	**tuutaa**
8. **tetaa**	**taitaa**	**totaa**	**taitaa**	**taañbaa**	
9. **kiila**	**kilaa**	**maami**	**maamii**	**maamu**	**maamuu**
10. **maame**	**maamai**	**mamo**	**mamau**	**jañbo**	

EXERCISE 1

How should this sentence be read in Hindi?

मेरा नाम माया है। इसका नाम लीला है।

Pattern Practice 1

Read these words in Hindi:

a) क   का   कि   की   कु   कू   के   कै   को   कौ   कं

b) कल   काला   किला   कीला   कुल   कूल   केला   कैला   कोला   कौला   कंज

c) मन   माना   मिना   मीना   मुन   मून   मेना   मैना   मोना   मौना   मंज

d) जल   जाला   जिला   जीला   जुल   जूल   जेला   जैना   जोना   जौना   जंच

e) सम   समा   समिना   सनीमा   समुल   समूल   समेल   समैल   समोना   समौना   संट

The magnificent Taj Mahal, in Uttar Pradesh, India

LESSON 2
Introducing Yourself

In this lesson, Maya meets her Hindi language teacher for the first time. We will learn how to introduce ourselves in Hindi and practice some of the basic greetings. After this lesson you should be able to:

- **Greet someone**
- **Introduce yourself**
- **Tell the listener where you are from**
- **Ask how others are**
- **Say thank you**
- **Say goodbye**

🎧 ┊ DIALOGUE ┊ **GREETINGS** (02–01)

Maya is an American student studying in India. In this dialogue, she meets Kabir, her Hindi language teacher and greets him.

Maya:	Hello. What's your name?
	Namaste jii. Aap kaa naam kyaa hai?
	नमस्ते जी ! आपका नाम क्या है?
Kabir:	My name is Kabir. What's your name?
	Jii, meraa naam Kabir hai. Aapkaa naam kyaa hai?
	जी, मेरा नाम कबीर है। आपका नाम क्या है?
Maya:	My name is Maya.
	Jii, meraa naam Maya hai.
	जी, मेरा नाम माया है।
Kabir:	Greetings Maya! I'm your Hindi teacher.
	Namaste Maya! Maiñ aapkaa Hindi adhyaapak huuñ.
	नमस्ते माया। मैं आपका हिंदी अध्यापक हूँ।
Maya:	How are you?
	Aap kaise haiñ?
	आप कैसे हैं?
Kabir:	I am well. Thank you. How are you?
	Maiñ Thiik huuñ. Shukriyaa! Aap kaisii haiñ?
	मैं ठीक हूँ। शुक्रिया ! आप कैसी हैं?
Maya:	I am well too. Thank you.
	Maiñ bhii Thiik huuñ. Shukriyaa!
	मैं भी ठीक हूँ। शुक्रिया !

Kabir: Where are you from?
         Aap kahaañ se haiñ?
         आप कहाँ से हैं?

Maya: I'm from America. And you?
         Maiñ Amerika se huuñ. Aur aap?
         मैं अमेरिका से हूँ। और आप?

Kabir: I'm from India. Jaipur in India.
         Main Bharat se huuñ. Bharat meiñ, Jaipur se.
         मैं भारत से हूँ। भारत में, जयपुर से।

Maya: Glad to meet you.
         Aap se milkar baRii khushii huii.
         आपसे मिलकर बड़ी ख़ुशी हुई।

Kabir: Me too.
         Mujhe bhii.
         मुझे भी।

Note on Hindi Punctuation

Hindi and English share several punctuation marks, for e.g., the comma, the question mark and the exclamation mark. The symbol l at the end of a sentence has the same function as the English period or full stop.

Vocabulary List (02-02)

परिचय (m)	**parichay**	introduction
नमस्ते !	**Namaste!**	Greetings!
जी	**jii**	politeness marker
आप	**aap**	you (formal)
कैसे/कैसी/कैसा	**kaise/kaisii/kaisaa**	how
ठीक	**thiik**	fine, OK
शुक्रिया	**shukriyaa**	thank you
और	**aur**	and
नाम (m)	**naam**	name
मेरा/मेरे/मेरी	**meraa/mere/merii**	mine
आपका/आपके/आपकी	**aapkaa/aapke/aapkii**	your
कहाँ	**kahaañ**	where
से	**se**	from
में	**meñ**	in

आप से मिल कर बड़ी खुशी हुई	**Aap se milkar baRii, khushii huii.**	Glad to meet you.
मुझे भी	**Mujhe bhii.**	Me too.
यह	**yah** (usu. pronounced **ye**)	this, she, he, it
वह	**vah** (usu. pronounced **ve**)	that, she, he, it
ये	**ye**	these, they
वे	**ve**	those, they
मैं	**maiñ**	I
हम	**ham**	we
हिंदी	**Hindi**	Hindi
हिंदुस्तानी	**Hindustaanii**	Indian
अमेरिका	**Amerika**	America
भारत	**Bhaarat**	India
जयपुर	**Jaypur**	Jaipur
अध्यापक (m)	**adhyaapak**	teacher
विद्यार्थी	**vidyaarthii**	student

Supplementary Vocabulary

बच्चा (m)	**bachchhaa**	child (male)
अच्छा/अच्छे/अच्छी	**achchhaa/achchhe/achchhii**	good, well
पिता	**pitaa**	father
किताब (f)	**kitaab**	book
हाँ	**haañ**	yes
नहीं	**nahiiñ**	no
फिर मिलेंगे।	**Phir mileñge.**	See you again.
हिंदी में X क्या है?	**Hindi meiñ X kyaa hai?**	What is the Hindi word for X?
यह क्या है?	**Yah kyaa hai?**	What is this?
यह कितने का/की है?	**Yah kitne kaa hai?**	How much does it cost?

CULTURAL NOTE Thank You and You're Welcome

There are two common ways to say "Thank you" in Hindi: **Shukriyaa** and **Dhanyavaad**. **Shukriyaa** is colloquial and **Dhanyavaad** is a little more formal. There is no Hindi equivalent of "You are welcome!" Hindi speakers instead say **Koii baat nahiiñ** ("There is nothing to thank.").

CULTURAL NOTE Greeting Someone with **Namaste** (02-03)

Namaste is the most common greeting in India. As you say this, hold your palms together and bow towards the person you are greeting. The word comes from Sanskrit and is made up of two words, **namas** "to bow" and **te** meaning "to you." Thus, the meaning of **namaste** is "I bow to you."

GRAMMAR NOTE Personal Pronouns (02-04)

The words for "I" and "we" are मैं **main** and हम **ham** respectively. For the other pronouns, there are two or three variations in Hindi, as shown in the table below.

English	Hindi	Use This with
you (formal)	आप **aap**	people older than you or whom you are meeting for the first time
you (informal)	तुम **tum**	people that you know, those younger than you and friends
you (informal)	तू **tuu**	small children, close friends, younger siblings
this, she, he, it	यह **yah**	a thing or person near you
that, she, he, it	वह **vah**	a thing or person far from you
these, they	ये **ye**	things, animals or people near you
those, they	वे **ve**	things, animals or people far from you

GRAMMAR NOTE Hindi Word Order

The sentence word order in Hindi differs from the word order in English. In English the order is Subject + Verb + Object, for example, *I* (subject) + *ate* (verb) + *an apple* (object). In Hindi, however, the word order is Subject + Object + Verb, e.g., *I* (subject) + *an apple* (object) + *ate* (verb).

GRAMMAR NOTE The Verb "to be" (02-04b)

In Hindi, the verb "to be" has a different conjugation for each person, just as in English. For example, when the subject is मैं **main** or "I," the verb form is हूँ **huuñ** or "am." Here are the conjugations for each personal pronoun.

मैं हूँ	**main huuñ**	I am
हम हैं	**ham haiñ**	we are
आप हैं	**aap haiñ**	you (formal) are
तुम हो	**tum ho**	you (informal) are
तू है	**tuu hai**	you (informal) are
यह है	**yah hai**	he is, she is, it is, this is (nearby)
ये हैं	**ye haiñ**	they are, these are
वह है	**vah hai**	he is, she is, it is, this is (far away)
वे हैं	**ve haiñ**	they are, those are

GRAMMAR NOTE Masculine and Feminine Nouns (02-05)

All nouns are either feminine or masculine. While it's easy to tell whether some nouns are feminine or masculine, e.g., "girl," "boy," "father," "mother" and "brother," others are a little more perplexing. A very rough guide is that words ending in आ **aa** are usually masculine and words ending with ई **ii** are feminine, but this does not apply for all nouns. It is a good idea to memorize the gender of each noun as you learn it. Here is a list of some common nouns:

अध्यापक (m)	**adhyaapak**	teacher
बच्चा (m)	**bachchhaa**	child (male)
डॉक्टर (m)	**daktar**	doctor
गोश्त (m)	**gosht**	meat
इंजीनियर (m)	**injiiniyar**	engineer
कर्मचारी (m)	**karmcaarii**	employee
मैनेजर (m)	**maineja**	manager
नाम (m)	**naam**	name
पानी (m)	**paanii**	water

पिता (m)	**pitaa**	father
पुलिस अधिकारी (m)	**pulis adhikaarii**	police officer
रसोइया (m)	**rasoiyaa**	cook
साल (m)	**saal**	year
सीना (m)	**siinaa**	chest
सूअर का मांस (m)	**suuar ka maañs**	pork
विद्यार्थी (m)	**vidyaarthii**	student
वाइन का ग्लास (m)	**waain kaa glas**	glass of wine
बियर (f)	**biyar**	beer
कॉफी (f)	**kaafii**	coffee
चिकन (f)	**chikan**	chicken
किताब (f)	**kitaab**	book
मछली (f)	**machhlii**	fish
नर्स (f)	**nars**	nurse
शिक्षिका (f)	**shikshikaa**	teacher
वाइन (f)	**waain**	wine

Nouns

In Hindi, nouns are classified as masculine or feminine nouns. Both masculine and feminine nouns have two forms: singular and plural. However, for many nouns, their singular and plural forms are the same.

Here is a short introduction to the formation of singular and plural masculine and feminine nouns, based on their vowel or consonant endings:

I.   Masculine Nouns

	Singular	**Plural**
aa ending:	कमरा **kamaraa** "room"	कमरे **kamare** "rooms"
	यह मेरा कमरा है।	ये मेरे कमरे हैं।
	yah meraa kamaraa hai.	**yeh mere kamare hain.**
	This is my room.	These are my rooms.
ii ending:	भाई **bhaaii** "brother"	भाई **bhaii** "brothers"
	यह मेरा भाई है।	ये मेरे भाई हैं।
	yah meraa bhaaii hai.	**yeh mere bhaii hain.**
	He/This is my brother.	These are my brothers.
oo ending:	भालू **bhaaloo** "bear"	भालू **bhaaloo** "bears"
	भालू कहाँ है?	भालू कहाँ हैं?
	Bhaaloo kahaan hai.	**bhaaloo kahaan hain.**
	Where is the bear?	Where are the bears?

	Singular	**Plural**
Consonant ending:	शहर **shahar** "city"	शहर **shahar** "cities"
	यह सुंदर शहर है।	ये सुंदर शहर हैं।
	yah sundar shahar hai.	**yeh sundar shahar hain.**
	This is a beautiful city.	These are beautiful cities.

II. Feminine Nouns

	Singular	**Plural**
aa endng:	माता **maataa** "mother"	माताएँ **maataaen** "mothers"
	यह मेरी माता है।	ये उनकी माताएँ हैं।
	yah merii maataa hai.	**yeh unkii maataaen hain.**
	She/This is my mother.	These are their mothers.
ii ending:	खिड़की **khiRhkii** "window"	खिड़कियाँ **khiRhiyaan** "windows"
	यह खिड़की है।	ये खिड़कियाँ हैं।
	yah khiRhkii hai.	**yeh khiRhkiyaan hain.**
	This is a window.	These are windows.
oo/u ending:	अच्छी वस्तु **vastu** "thing"	अच्छी चस्तुएँ **vastuen** "things"
	यह अच्छी वस्तु है।	ये अच्छी वस्तुएँ हैं।
	yah achchhii vastu hai.	**Yeh achchhii vastuen hain.**
	This is a good thing.	These are good things.
Consonant ending:	मेज़ **mez** "table"	मेज़ें **mezen** "tables"
	यह मजबूत मेज़ है।	ये मजबूत मेज़ें हैं।
	yah mazboot mez hai.	**yeh mazboot mezen hain.**
	This is a strong table.	These are strong tables.

Postpositions

In English, prepositions are words that show the relationship between different words in a sentence, and they usually come *before* the nouns to which they relate. However, in Hindi such words are placed *after* nouns and they are then known as **postpositions**. These words are में **meñ** ("in"), पर **par** ("at, on"), को **ko** ("to"), etc. Depending on the ending of certain nouns based on their gender and number, the placement (position) of such postpositions may be different.

I. Masculine Nouns + Postpositions

aa ending:

यह मेरा झोला है। **yah meraa jholaa hai.**   This is my bag.

इस झोले में कुछ नहीं है।   **is jhole mein kuchh nahien hai.**

    There is nothing in my bag.

ये अच्छे छाते हैं। **yeh achchhe chhaate hain.** These are good umbrellas.

इन छातों के दाम क्या हैं? **in chhaaton ke daam kyaa hain?**

    What are the prices of these umbrellas?

ii ending:

मेरा हाथी कहाँ है? **meraa haathii kahaan hai.** Where is my elephant?

हाथी का रंग भूरा है। **haathii kaa rang bhooraa hai.**

    The color of an elephant is brown.

मेरे भाई यहाँ हैं। **mere bhaaii yahaan hain.**

    My brothers are here.

मेरे भाइयों के दोस्त यहाँ हैं। **mere bhaaiyon ke dost**

    yahaan hain.

    My brothers' friends are here.

oo ending:

यह भालू काला है। **yah bhaaloo kaalaa hai.** This is a black bear.

इस भालू का नाम कालू है। **is bhaaloo kaa naam Kaloo hai.**

    This bear's name is Kaloo.

ये भालू भारत से हैं। **yeh bhaaloo Bhaarat se hain.**

    These bears are from India.

इन भालुओं को माँस पसंद है। **in bhaaluon ko maans**

    pasand hai.

    These bears like meat.

Consonant ending:

यह मेरा शहर है। **yah meraa shahar hai.** This is my city.

इस शहर का नाम जयपुर है। **iskaa naam Jaipur hai.**

    The name of this city is Jaipur.

ये भी सुंदर शहर हैं। **yeh bhii sundar shahar hain.**

    These are also beautiful cities.

इन शहरों में जीवन शांत है। **In shaharon mein jeevan shaant hai.**

    The life in these cities is peaceful.

II. Feminine Nouns + Postpositions

aa ending:

यह मेरी कक्षा है। **yah merii kakshaa hai.** This is my class.

इस कक्षाएँ में कुछ विद्यार्थी हैं। **is kakshaa mein kuchh vidyaarthii hain.**
There are few students in this class.
ये उनकी कक्षाएँ हैं। **yeh unkii kakshaaen hain.** These are their classes.
इन कक्षाओं बहुत में विद्यार्थी हैं। **in kakshaaon mein bahut vidyaarthii**
hain. There are many students in these classes.

ii ending:
यह लड़की सुंदर है। **yah sundar laRhkii hai.** This/She is a beautiful girl.
इस लड़की का नाम नूतन है। **is laRhkii kaa naam Nutan hai.**
The name of this girl is Nutan.

ये लड़कियाँ भारत से हैं। **yeh laRhkiyaan Bharat**
se hain.
These girls are from India.
इन लड़कियों के नाम क्या हैं। **in laRhkiyon ke**
naam kyaa hain.
What are the names of these girls?

oo ending:
यह झाड़ू किसकी है? **yah jhaaRhoo kiskii hai.** Whose broom is this?
इस झाड़ू का रंग पीला है। **is jhaaRhoo ka rang piilaa hai.**
The color of this broom is yellow.
ये किसकी वस्तुएँ हैं? **yeh kiskii vastuen hain.** Whose things are these?
इन वस्तुओं के दाम बहुत ज़्यादा हैं। **in vastuon ke daam bahut zyaadaa**
hain. The prices of these things are too much.

Consonant ending:
यह मेज़ बहुत सुंदर है। **yah mez sundar hai.** This is a beautiful table.
इस मेज़ का दाम क्या है? **is mez kaa daam kyaa hai.**
What is the price of this table?
ये बहुत अच्छी किताबें हैं। **yeh baut achchhii kitaaben hain.**
These are good books.
इन किताबों को पढ़िये। **in kitaabon ko paRhiye.** Please read these books.

For pronouns, the postpositions cause a change in the pronouns depending
on the type of pronouns (1st person, 2nd person, 3rd person), and their forms
(singular or plural).

	+ का	+ में, पर, को
यह **yah** this	इसका **iskaa** his/her/its	इसमें, इस पर, इस को (इसे) **Ismein** in this, **is par** on this, **isko (ise)** to this

	+ का	+ में, पर, को
वह **vah** that	उसका **uskaa** his/her/its	उसमें, उस पर, उसको (उसे) **usmein** in that, **us par** on that, **usko** (use) to that
ये **yeh** these	इनका **inkaa** of these/their	इनमें, इन पर, इनको (इन्हें) **inmein** in these, **in par** on these, **inko** (**inhen**) to these
वे **ve** those	उनका **unkaa** of those/their	उनमें, उन पर, उनको (उन्हें) **unmein** in those, **un par** on those, **unko** (**unhen**) to those
मैं **main** I	मेरा **meraa** mine	हम में, हम पर, हम को (हमें) **ham mein** in us, **ham par** on us, **ham ko** (**hamein**) to us
हम **ham** we	हमारा **hamaaraa** our	हम में, हम पर, हमको (हमें) **ham mein** in us, **ham par** on us, **ham ko** (**hamein**) to us
तुम **tum** you (informal/friendly)	तुम्हारा **tumhaaraa** your	तुम में, तुम पर, तुम को (तुम्हें) **tum mein** in you, **tum par** on you, **tum ko** (**tumhe**) to you
तू **tuu** you (informal)	तेरा **teraa** your	तुझमें, तुझ पर, तुझ को (तुझे) **tujh mein** in you, **tujh par** on you, **tujh ko** (**tujhe**) to you
आप **aap** you (formal)	आपका **aapkaa** your	आप में, आप पर, आप को **aap mein** in you, **aap par** on you, **aap ko** to you

GRAMMAR NOTE Possessive Pronouns (02-06)

In Hindi, the possessive pronoun can be either masculine or feminine. Choose the pronoun that co-relates to whether the *item* is male or female, rather than whether its owner is female or male. Please refer to the table below for the forms.

Meaning	Masc., sing.	Masc., pl.	Fem., sing. & pl.
my	मेरा **meraa**	मेरे **mere**	मेरी **merii**
our	हमारा **hamaraa**	हमारे **hamaare**	हमारी **hamaarii**

Meaning	Masc., sing.	Masc., pl.	Fem., sing. & pl.
its/her/his	इसका **iskaa**	इसके **iske**	इसकी **iskii**
its/her/his	उसका **uskaa**	उसके **uske**	उसकी **uskii**
their/(formal) his/her	इनका **inkaa**	इनके **inke**	इनकी **inkii**
their/(formal) his/her	उनका **unkaa**	उनके **unke**	उनकी **unkii**
your (formal)	आपका **aapkaa**	आपके **aapke**	आपकी **aapkii**
your (less formal)	तुम्हारा **tumhaara**	तुम्हारे **tumhaare**	तुम्हारी **tumhaarii**
your (informal)	तेरा **teraa**	तेरे **tere**	तेरी **terii**

Thus, Kabir or Maya would both say मेरी किताब **merii kitaab** "my book" using the feminine form of **merii** "my" because the item **kitaab** ("book") is female.

Similarly, if they were talking about their glasses of wine, they would both say मेरा वाइन का ग्लास (m) **meraa waain kaa gla**, that is, "my glass of wine" because a "glass of wine" is masculine. If you wanted to say "our glasses of wine," you would then say हमारे वाइन का ग्लास (m) **hamaare waain kaa gla** "our glasses of wine" using the plural masculine form.

Pattern Practice 1

Match the Hindi terms below with their English meanings.

- नमस्ते ! **Namaste!**
- आप कैसी हैं? **Aap kaisii haiñ?**
- मैं ठीक हूँ **Maiñ Thiik huuñ.**
- और आप? **Aur aap?**
- आप कैसे हैं? **Aap kaise haiñ?**
- शुक्रिया ! **Shukriyaa!**

Thank you.
How are you? (asking a woman)
And you?
Greetings!
How are you? (asking a man)
I am fine.

Pattern Practice 2

Imagine you are traveling on a local train in India. Turn to your fellow passenger and greet her or him in Hindi and imagine how he or she will respond.

You: Greetings! How are you?
Passenger: Greetings! I'm fine, thank you. And you?
You: I'm fine. Thank you.

Pattern Practice 3

Practice saying the following phrases in Hindi.

1. Name
2. How are you?
3. Thank you.
4. Where are you from?
5. I am from America.
6. Glad to meet you.
7. Me too.

Pattern Practice 4

Read the dialogue above again and complete the sentences.

1. आप _____ हैं? (asking a woman how she is)

   Aap_____ haiñ?

2. मैं _____ हूँ। _____ (I am fine. Thank you.)

   Maiñ _____ huuñ. _____

3. मैं _____ से हूँ। (I am from America.)

   Maiñ _____ se huuñ.

4. आप _____ से हैं? (Where are you from?)

   Aap_____ se haiñ?

5. आप से _____ बड़ी खुशी हुई। (Glad to meet you.)

   Aap se_____ baRii khushii huii.

6. _____ भी। (Me too!)

   _____ bhii.

Pattern Practice 5

Please write down two sentences about yourself in Hindi.

1. My name is_____

2. I am from_____

Pattern Practice 6

Translate the following from Hindi to English.

Question: यह कौन है?   **Yah kaun hai?**
Answer: यह मायकल जैक्सन है।   **Yah Michael Jackson hai.**

Question: _____?
Answer:_____.

Pattern Practice 7

Using the table on pages 27–28, identify the personal pronouns as well as the conjugated form of the verb "to be" in the following situation.

1. मेरा नाम माया है।   **Meraa naam Maya hai.**
2. आपका नाम क्या है?   **Aap kaa naam kyaa hai?**
3. आप कहाँ से हैं?   **Aap kahaañ se haiñ?**
4. आप कैसे हैं?   **Aap kaise haiñ?**
5. मैं अमेरिका से हूँ।   **Maiñ Amerika se hooñ.**
6. ये हिंदुस्तानी हैं।   **Ye Hindustaanii haiñ.**
7. वे अमेरिकन हैं।   **Ve American haiñ.**
8. तुम कैसी हो।   **Tum kaisii ho?**
9. तू बच्चा है।   **Tuu bachchaa hai.**
10. हम हिंदी विद्यार्थी हैं   **Ham Hindi vidyaarthii haiñ.**

GRAMMAR NOTE Hindi Adjectives

In Hindi, adjectives are placed before nouns they modify, just as in English (e.g., अच्छा कमरा **achchhaa kamaraa** "good room"); however, they need to agree with the gender and number of the noun they modify. For example, the masculine singular form of the word "small" is छोटा लड़का **chhoTaa**. However, when it is applied to masculine plural, feminine singular and feminine plural nouns, it has different endings added to agree with the noun modified. Here's how to change the masculine singular to the other forms.

Masc., sing.	छोटा लड़का	**chhoTaa la<u>R</u>kaa**	"small boy"
Masc., pl.	छोटे लड़के	**chhoTe la<u>R</u>ke**	"small boys"
Fem. sing.	छोटी लड़की	**chhoTii la<u>R</u>kii**	"small girl"
Fem. pl.	छोटी लड़कियाँ	**chhoTii la<u>Rkiyaañ</u>**	"small girls"

Pattern Practice 8

Choose one of the words in the parentheses to fill in each blank.

1. यह _____ भाई (brother) है। (मेरा/मेरे/मेरी)
   Yah _____bhaaii hai. **(meraa/mere/merii)**

2. वह _____ बहन (sister) है। (मेरा/मेरे/मेरी)
   Vah_____behen hai. **(meraa/mere/merii)**

3. यह _____ किताब (f) है। (अच्छा/अच्छे/अच्छी)
   Yah _____ kitaab hai. **(achchha/achchhe/achchhii)**

4. _____ नाम क्या है? (आपका/आपके/आपकी)
   _____ **naam kyaa haai? (aapkaa/aapke/aapkii)**

5. ये _____ हिंदी अध्यापक हैं। (आपका/आपके/आपकी)
   Ye_____ **Hindi adhyaapak hain. (aapkaa/aapke/aapkii)**

GRAMMAR NOTE Question Words

All question words in Hindi start with the consonant क **ka**. In order to answer a question, which usually takes the form Subject + Question Word + Verb, e.g., **You** + **how** + **are** = How are you?, replace the question word with the answer word phrases. For example:

Question: यह क्या है? **Yah kyaa hai?** What is this? (lit., This what is?)
Answer: यह किताब है। **Yah kitaab hai.** This is a book. (lit., This book is)

Yes or No questions normally begin with क्या **kyaa** or "what." For example:

Question: क्या यह किताब है? **Kyaa yah kitaab hai?**
   Is this a book? (lit., What this book is?)
Answer: जी हाँ, यह किताब है। **Jii haañ, yah kitaab hai.**
   Yes, this is a book. (lit., Yes, this book is).
   जी नहीं, यह किताब नहीं है। **Jii nahiiñ, yah kitaab nahiiñ hai.**
   No, this is not a book.

EXERCISE 1

Answer these questions in Hindi.

1. आपका नाम क्या है?   **Aapkaa naam kyaa hai?**
2. आप कहाँ से हैं?   **Aap kahaañ se haiñ?**
3. आप कैसे/कैसी हैं?   **Aap kaise/kaisii haiñ?**
4. क्या आप अमेरिकन हैं?   **Kyaa aap American haiñ?**

EXERCISE 2

Write the Hindi equivalent of these words.

1. Father   2. I   3. we
4. book   5. Yes

A busy street in Calcutta with cars, bikes, buses and pedestrians

EXERCISE 3

Select the correct translation for these words.

1. Those, they
   - a. ये ye
   - b. वे ve
   - c. स se
   - d. वह vah
2. Child (male)
   - a. किताब kitaab
   - b. बच्चा bachchhaa
   - c. परिचय parichay
   - d. नाम naam
3. From
   - a. से se
   - b. ये ye
   - c. वे ve
   - d. आप aap
4. And
   - a. और aur
   - b. ठीक Thiik
   - c. में meñ
   - d. मैं maiñ
5. Me too.
   - a. मुझे भी mujhe bhii
   - b. शुक्रिया shukriyaa
   - c. नमस्ते! Namaste!
   - d. बच्चा bachchha

A street with roadside stalls and Diwali festival decorations in Rishikesh

EXERCISE 4

Read the statements below and then circle the correct answer.

1. में **meñ** = In		True	False
2. नहीं **nahiiñ** = No		True	False
3. आप **aap** = You (formal)		True	False
4. अच्छा/अच्छे/अच्छी **achchaa/**			
achchhe/achchhii = Good, well		True	False
5. नाम **naam** = Yes		True	False

EXERCISE 5

Match the Hindi words below with their English meanings.

- कैसा/कैसे/कैसी **kaisaa/kaise/kaisii**   Fine, OK
- विद्यार्थी **vidyaarthii**   Introduction
- ठीक **Thiik**   Mine
- परिचय **parichay**   How
- मेरा/मेरे/मेरी **meraa/mere/merii**   Student

CHECKLIST

Can you do these things in Hindi now?

- **Greet someone**
- **Introduce yourself**
- **Tell someone where you are from**
- **Ask how others are**
- **Say thank you**
- **Say goodbye**

LESSON 3
Asking Directions

In this lesson, Maya loses her way when going to the railway station, and she asks someone on the road for directions. After this lesson, you should be able to:

- **Tell someone you are lost**
- **Ask someone for directions**
- **Give simple directions**
- **Thank someone and show appreciation**

🎧 ┊ DIALOGUE ┊ **GETTING TO THE TRAIN STATION** (03–01)

Maya is trying to get to the train station but she has lost her way. She asks a passerby for help.

Maya:	Excuse me sir.
	Suniye bhaaiisaahab.
	सुनिये भाई साहब।
Passerby:	Please say.
	Jii, kahiye.
	जी, कहिये।
Maya:	I've lost my way. Please help me.
	Maiñ raastaa bhuul gayii huuñ. Aap kii madad chaahiye.
	मैं रास्ता भूल गयी हूँ। मुझको आपकी मदद चाहिये।
Passerby:	Yes. Please tell me, where do you want to go?
	Jii haañ, bataaiye, aapko kahaañ jaanaa hai?
	जी हाँ, बताइये, आपको कहाँ जाना है?
Maya:	I have to go to the railway station.
	Mujhko *Railway-station* jaanaa hai.
	मुझको रेल्वे स्टेशन जाना है।
	Do you know where the railway station is?
	Kyaa aap ko maaluum hai, *Railway-station* kahaañ hai?
	क्या आपको मालूम है, रेल्वे-स्टेशन कहाँ है?

Passerby:	Yes, the railway station is not far from here.
	Jii haañ, *Railway-station* yahaañ se duur nahiiñ hai.
	जी हाँ, रेल्वे-स्टेशन यहाँ से दूर नहीं है।
Maya:	How many minutes will it take on foot?
	Paidal kitne *minute* kaa raastaa hai?
	पैदल कितने मिनट का रास्ता है?
Passerby:	It will take about 15 minutes.
	Lagbhag pandrah *minute* kaa raastaa hai.
	लगभग पंद्रह मिनट का रास्ता है।
Maya:	Good!
	Achchha.
	अच्छा !
Passerby:	You go straight from here. Please turn left from the traffic light, till (you reach) the cinema hall.
	Aap yahaañ se siidhe jaaiye. *Traffic light* se baayeñ muRiye, aur *cinema-hall* tak jaaiye.
	आप यहाँ से सीधे जाइये। ट्रैफ़िक लाइट से बायें मुड़िये, और सिनेमा-हाल तक जाइये।
Maya:	Okay. After that?
	Thiik hai. Uske baad?
	ठीक है। उसके बाद?
Passerby:	After that, please turn right. There is a taxi stand. The taxi stand is just opposite the railway station.
	Uske baad daayeñ muRiye. Vahaañ ek *taxi-stand* hai. *Taxi-stand* ke saamne hii *Railway-station* hai.
	उसके बाद दायें मुड़िये। वहाँ एक टेक्सी-स्टैंड है। टेक्सी-स्टैंड के सामने ही रेल्वे-स्टेशन है।
Maya:	Thank you very much for the help.
	Jii, madad ke liye bahut bahut shukriyaa.
	जी, मदद के लिये बहुत बहुत शुक्रिया।
Passerby:	There is nothing to thank.
	Koii baat nahiiñ.
	कोई बात नहीं।

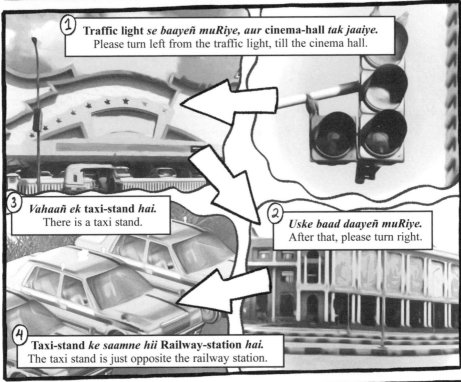

Vocabulary List (03-02)

सुनना	sunnaa	to listen to, to hear
सुनिये	suniye	please listen
भाई साहब	Bhaaiisaahab	Sir
कहना	kehnaa	to say
कहिये	kahiye	please say
भूलना	bhuulnaa	to forget
भूल गयी	Bhuul gayii	I forgot (for woman)
भूल गया	Bhuul gayaa	I forgot (for man)
मुझको/मुझे	mujhko/mujhe	to me
मदद	madad	help
चाहिये	chaahiye	needed
मुझको मदद चाहिये	Mujhko aap kii madad chaahiye	I need help
बताना	bataanaa	to tell
बताइये	bataaiye	please tell (me)
कहाँ	kahaañ	where
यहाँ	yahaañ	here
वहाँ	vahaañ	there
जाना	jaanaa	to go
जाइये	jaaiye	please go
मालूम (होना)	maaluum honaa	to know
दूर	duur	far
रास्ता	raastaa	way
यहाँ से	yahaañ se	from here
पैदल	paidal	on foot
कितने	kitne	how many
का	kaa	of
पंद्रह	pandrah	fifteen
लगभग	lagbhag	about, approximately
मिनट	*minute*	minutes (time)
सीधे	siidhe	straight
बायें	baayeñ	left/on the left

दायें	daayeñ	right/on the right
मुड़ना	muRnaa	to turn
मुड़िये	muRiye	please turn
और	aur	else
X तक	X tak	up to X, until X, till you reach X
ठीक है	Thiik hai	OK, fine
उसके बाद	uske baad	after that
एक	ek	one, a
X के सामने ही	X ke saamne hii	just opposite X
के लिये	ke liye	for
बहुत बहुत	bahut bahut	too much, very, really
कोई बात नहीं	koii baat nahiiñ	never mind, there is nothing (to thank)
X कहाँ है?	X kahaañ hai?	Where is X?
दूरी क्या है?	Duurii kyaa hai?	How far is it?/What's the distance?
क्या वहाँ बस जाती है?	Kyaa vahaañ *bus* jaatii hai?	Does any bus go there?

Inside a local train

Supplementary Vocabulary
Useful Phrases for Getting Around

क्या...(name of the place) की कोई गाड़ी है?	**Kyaa...kii koii gaaRii hai?**	Is there any train/bus for... (name of the place)?
...(name of the place) की गाड़ी कब आएगी?	**...kii gaaRii kab aaegii?**	When will the train/bus for (name of place) be coming?
कितनी देर में	**kitnii der men**	In how much time (in how many minutes)
... (name of the place) की गाड़ी कितने नंबर प्लेटफ़ॉर्म पर आएगी?	**...kii gaaRii kitne *number platform* par aaegii?**	What (Which) platform will the train for ... be arriving at?
टिकट कितने का है?	***Ticket* kitne kaa hai?**	How much is the ticket?
क्या गाड़ी में ए सी है?	**Kyaa gaaRii men *AC* hai?**	Is there any air-conditioning in the train/bus?
क्या रास्ते में गाड़ी रुकेगी?	**Kyaa raaste men gaaRii rukegii?**	Will the train/bus stop?
क्या गाड़ी में बाथरूम है?	**Kyaa gaaRii men *bathroom* hai?**	Is there any restroom in the train/bus?
क्या गाड़ी में खाना मिलेगा?	**Kyaa gaaRii men khaanaa milegaa?**	Will there be food in the train/bus?
क्या कोई ए सी टिकट है?	**Kyaa koii *AC ticket* hai?**	Is there a ticket for the air-conditioned bus/train?
रिज़र्वेशन फ़ार्म कहाँ है?	***Reservation form* kahaañ hai?**	Where is the reservation form?
क्या प्लेटफ़ॉर्म टिकट ज़रूरी है?	**Kyaa *platform ticket* zaruurii hai?**	Do I need a platform ticket?

दूसरी गाड़ी कब आएगी?	**Duusrii gaaRii kab aaegii?**	When will another/the next train/bus arrive?
आख़िरी गाड़ी कब आएगी?	**Aakhrii gaaRii kab aaegii?**	When will the last train/bus arrive?
पहली गाड़ी कब आएगी?	**Pehlii gaaRii kab aaegii?**	When will the first train/bus arrive?

A train platform in Jaipur

Pattern Practice 1

Match the Hindi phrases below with their English equivalents.

- सुनिये **Suniye**

  I am lost/I forgot the way.

- सुनिये भाई साहब
  Suniye bhaaiisaahab

  Please listen to me.

- मैं रास्ता भूल गयी हूँ
  Maiñ raastaa bhuul gayii huuñ.

  Where do you have to go?

- आपकी मदद चाहिये
  Aapkii madad chaahiye.

  I have to go to the railway station.

- आपको कहाँ जाना है?
  Aap ko kahaañ jaanaa hai?

  Please listen to me, sir.

- मुझको रेल्वे-स्टेशन जाना है।
  Mujh ko *Railway station* jaanaa hai.

  I need your help.

CULTURAL NOTE   Addressing a Male Person using the Polite Word भाईसाहब *Bhaaiisaahab* (03–03)

The term भाईसाहब **bhaaisaahab** is made up of two words: भाई **bhaaii** and साहब **saahab**, literally "brother" and "respected person," "sir." So, **bhaaiisaahab** means "respected brother" or "sir." Indian society is built around strong family ties and relationships. Addressing a man (a stranger or a passerby) as **bhaaiisaahab** is considered polite and helps to create a bond between yourself and the person you are talking to before asking them for anything.

If you need to ask a favor of a woman, you can call them दीदी **didi** "older sister" (if you yourself are female), आंटी जी **auntii-jii** "aunt" or माता जी **maataa ji** "mother," depending on the age of the person.

CULTURAL NOTE   Showing Appreciation

After they have helped you, you can thank them using जी, मदद के लिये बहुत बहुत शुक्रिया। **Jii, madad ke liye bahut bahut shukriyaa** or "Thank you very much for the help." If you wanted to thank someone for something specific, like preparing dinner for you, you can replace the word "help" or मदद **madad** for "dinner" डिनर **dinar** to say "Thank you very much for the dinner."

Other useful phrases you can use to show your appreciation could include यह बहुत सुंदर है। **Yeh bahut sundar hai** "this is very beautiful," बहुत मज़ा आया **Bahut mazaa aayaa** "I had a lot of fun" or बहुत स्वादिष्ट ! **Bahut svaadishT** "Very tasty."

CULTURAL NOTE "I'm Sorry"

Depending on the situation, there are a number of ways you can apologize or say you are sorry that something happened. For example, you could use माफ़ कीजिये। **Maaf kiijiye** "Excuse me" to get through a crowd or to say you're sorry if you did something wrong. You can follow this up with a reason, e.g., "I did not know" or मुझे मालूम नहीं था। **Mujhe maaluum nahiiñ thaa**. If you have learned about something horrible that has happened to a friend or family member of the person you are speaking to, you can say "It is a thing of great sorrow" or बहुत दुख की बात है। **Bahut dukh kii baat hai** or अफ़सोस की बात है। **Afsos kii baat hai** "It is a matter of sadness/regret," the Hindi equivalent of "I'm sorry to hear that."

GRAMMAR NOTE Making Polite Requests (03–04)

In Hindi, "please" is inferred by changing the verb's ending to इये **iye**. "Please come" is आइये **aaiye**, while जाइये **jaaiye** means "please go." Here is how to make polite requests and commands in Hindi:

Step 1: Form the verb root. Take the action word (verb), which has the suffix ना **naa** in its original (infinitive) form and drop the ना **naa** to form the verb root. For example,

आना **aanaa** – ना **naa** = आ **aa**

जाना **jaanaa** – ना **naa** = जा **jaa**

खाना **khaanaa** – ना **naa** = खा **khaa**

Step 2: Add इये **iye** to the verb root to add "please" to its meaning.

आ **aa** + इये **iye** = आइये **aaiye** "please come"

जा **jaa** + इये **iye** = जाइये **jaaiye** "please go"

खा **khaa** + इये **iye** = खाइये **khaaiye** "please eat"

GRAMMAR NOTE ### Forming Polite Requests With Consonant Endings

When forming verbs with a consonant ending, such as बैठना **baiThnaa** "to sit," use the alternative ि ये **iye** to make the verb बैठिये **baiThiye** "please sit." For example,

देखना **dekhnaa** "to see" – ना **naa** + ि ये **iye** = देखिये **dekhiye** "please see"

सोचना **sochnaa** "to think" – ना **naa** + ि ये **iye** = सोचिये **sochiye** "please think"

लिखना **likhnaa** "to write" – ना **naa** + ि ये **iye** = लिखिये **likhiye** "please write"

GRAMMAR NOTE ### Less Formal Requests

The above forms are always used with आप **aap**, the formal "you." Pairing the verbs with the informal तू **tuu** "you" is very easy—just drop ना **naa** from a verb, for e.g., बैठना **baiThnaa** then becomes बैठ **baiTh** or "sit"—which is quite forceful and not very polite. For the informal तुम **tum**, drop ना **naa** and add ओ **o**.

	आप **aap**	तुम **tum**	तू **tuu**
बैठना **baiThnaa** "to sit"	बैठिये **baiThiye**	बैठो **baiTho**	बैठ **baiTh**
आना **aanaa** "to come"	आइये **aaiye**	आओ **aao**	आ **aa**
जाना **jaanaa** "to go"	जाइये **jaaiye**	जाओ **jaao**	जा **jaa**
खाना **khaanaa** "to eat"	खाइये **khaaiye**	खाओ **khaao**	खा **khaa**

In cases where the verb root ends with a consonant, like बैठना **baiThnaa**, use the written alternative form of **o**--ो so the resulting phrase becomes बैठो **baiTho** or "you sit."

Four exceptions to the previous rules are:

	आप **aap**	तुम **tum**	तू **tuu**
लेना **lenaa** (take)	लीजिये **liijiye**	लो **lo**	ले **le**
देना **denaa** (give)	दीजिये **diijiye**	दो **do**	दे **de**
पीना **piinaa** (to drink)	पीजिये **piijiye**	पियो **piyo**	पी **pii**
करना **karnaa** (to do)	कीजिये **kiijiye**	करो **karo**	कर **kar**

Pattern Practice 2

Fill in the chart below, writing the appropriate forms of commands and requests according to the correct form of "you":

Verbs	आप **aap**	तुम **tum**	तू **tuu**
1. बोलना **bolnaa** (to speak)	_____	_____	_____
2. बनाना **banaanaa** (to make)	_____	_____	_____
3. चलना **chalnaa** (to walk)	_____	_____	_____
4. गाना **gaanaa** (to sing)	_____	_____	_____
5. नाचना **naachnaa** (to dance)	_____	_____	_____

Pattern Practice 3

From the dialogue on pages 37–38, practice saying the following phrases in Hindi.

1. The railway station is not far from here.
2. How many minutes on foot?
3. Good/well.
4. Please go straight from here.
5. Please turn left from the traffic light and go to the cinema.
6. OK/fine.
7. After that?
8. After that, please turn right. There is a taxi stand.
9. The railway station is just opposite the taxi stand.
10. Thank you very much for your help.
11. There is nothing to thank (don't mention it).
12. I am lost.
13. Do you know where the…is?
14. Please turn left.
15. Please turn right.

Pattern Practice 4

Fill in the correct forms of the words below.

1. क्या_____ (आप/आपको) मालूम है, रेल्वे-स्टेशन_____ (क्या/कहाँ) है?
    Kyaa_____ (aap/aapko) maaloom hai, *railway-station* _____ (kyaa/kahaañ) hai?

2. पैदल _____(कब/कितने) मिनट का रास्ता है?
    Paidal _____ (kab/kitne) *minute* kaa raastaa hai?

3. यहाँ से सीधे _____ (जाना/जाइये)।
    Yahaañ se siiDhe _____ (jaanaa/jaaiye).

4. उसके बाद दायें _____(मुड़ना/मुड़िये)।
    Uske baad daayeñ_____(muRna/muRiye).

5. मदद_____ (के बाद/के लिये) बहुत बहुत शुक्रिया।
    Madad _____ (ke baad/ke liye) bahut bahut shukriyaa.

EXERCISE 1

Read aloud the Hindi equivalents of the following English words.

1. after that   2. far   3. here
4. to me   5. to forget   6. straight
7. to tell   8. up to X, until X   9. way

EXERCISE 2

Match the Hindi words below to their English meanings.

- जाइये **jaaiye**   for
- पैदल **paidal**   to go
- सुनिये **suniye**   there
- के लिये **ke liye**   needed
- वहाँ **vahaañ**   please listen
- बताइये **bataaiye**   listen to, hear
- सुनना **sunnaa**   on foot

- चाहिये **chaahiye**   please tell
- जाना **jaanaa**   please go

EXERCISE 3

Choose the correct Hindi translation for each English word or phrase.

1. to turn
   a. बताना **bataanaa**   b. मुड़ना **muRnaa**
   c. मुड़िये **muRiye**   d. सुनना **sunanaa**

2. OK, fine
   a. कहिये **kahiye**   b. सीधे **siidhe**
   c. ठीक है **Thiik hai**   d. भूलना **bhuulnaa**

3. please say
   a. जाइये **jaaiye**   b. सुनिये **suniye**
   c. कहिये **kahiye**   d. चाहिये **chaahiye**

4. from here
   a. यहाँ **yahaaañ**   b. बताइये **bataaiye**
   c. वहाँ **vahaañ**   d. यहाँ से **yahaañ se**

5. just opposite X
   a. के लिये **ke liye**   b. X के सामने ही **X ke saamne hii**
   c. कोई बात नहीं **koii baat nahiiñ**   d. यहाँ से **yahaañ se**

6. fifteen
   a. पंद्रह **pandrah**   b. बताना **bataanaa**
   c. रास्ता **raastaa**   d. पैदल **paidal**

7. please turn
   a. मुड़िये **muRiye**   b. मुड़ना **muRnaa**
   c. सुनिये **suniye**   d. के लिये **ke liye**

8. (on) right
   a. बायें **baayeñ**   b. वहाँ **vahaañ**
   c. जाइये **jaaiye**   d. दायें **daayeñ**

9. help
   a. X तक **X tak**   b. पैदल **paidal**
   c. दूर **duur**   d. मदद **madad**

EXERCISE 4

Read each statement carefully and then circle the correct answer.

1. कहना **kehnaa** = to say		True	False
2. कहाँ **kahaañ** = where		True	False
3. कोई बात नहीं **koii baat nahiiñ** = never mind, there is nothing (to thank)		True	False
4. मुझको मदद चाहिये **mujhko aap kii madad chaahiye** = I need help		True	False
5. भूल गयी **bhuul gayee** = I forgot (for man)		True	False
6. भूल गया **bhuul gayaa** = I forgot (for woman)		True	False
7. लगभग **lagbhag** = about, approximately		True	False
8. बायें **baayeñ** = (on) left		True	False
9. मालूम (होना) **maaluum honaa** = to know		True	False

Shopping in a busy street market in Sarojini Nagar, Delhi

EXERCISE 5

Translate the following sentences into Hindi (spoken exercise).

1. I am lost.
2. I need help!
3. How do I get to the railway station?
4. Please turn left.
5. Go straight.

CHECKLIST

Can you do the following things in Hindi now?

- **Tell someone that you are lost**
- **Ask someone for directions**
- **Give directions using simple words**
- **Thank someone for their help**

A crowded street in the Chandni Chowk market vicinity in Delhi

The Hawa Mahal palace in Jaipur

LESSON 4
Going Shopping

In this lesson, Maya is going to buy few things for herself at the shopping center. You will learn how to express what you need/want and also to bargain for these goods. After this lesson you will be able to do these functions:

- **Shop in India**
- **Explain what you need**
- **Bargain at the store**

 **DIALOGUE** **BUYING THINGS AND BARGAINING**
(04–01)

Maya needs to buy a few things so she heads to a shopping center. She first buys a bottle of water from a store.

Maya:	Hello brother!
	Namaste bhaaiisahab!
	नमस्ते भाई साहब !
Shopkeeper:	Hello. Come, please say, what do you need?
	Namaste jii. Aaiye, kahiye, kyaa chaahiye?
	नमस्ते, जी ! आइये, कहिये, क्या चाहिये?
Maya:	I need a bottle of water.
	Jii, mujh ko ek paanii kii botal chaahiye.
	जी, मुझको एक पानी की बोतल चाहिये।
Shopkeeper:	Please take this.
	Yah liijiye.
	यह लीजिये।
Maya:	Thank you!
	Shukriyaa!
	शुक्रिया !

Maya continues shopping in a different store.

Shopkeeper:	Hello! Come, come, what do you need?
	Namaste jii, aaiye, aaiye, kyaa chaahiye?
	नमस्ते जी, आइये आइये, क्या चाहिये?

Jii, kis rang meñ chaahiye?
Which color would you like?

Gehraa bhuuraa, niilaa yaa kaalaa bhii chalegaa.
Dark brown. Blue or black will work too.

Ye dekhiye, yah kaalaa waalaa bahut sundar hai.
Look, this black one is very beautiful.

Haañ, yah bahut sundar hai.
Yes, it is very beautiful.

Daam kyaa hai?
How much does it cost?

Sirf aaTh sau rupaye.
Just 800 rupees.

AaTh sau rupaye suutii shalwaar kurte ke liye bahut zyaadaa hai.
800 rupees is too much for a cotton *shalvaar kurta.*

Achchhaa saaRhe saat sau diijiye.
750 rupees then, is that okay?

Nahiiñ, nahiiñ saat sau Thiik haiñ.
No, 700 rupees will be okay.

Thiik hai, saat sau diijiye.
Okay, 700 rupees then.

Ye aap ke rupaye liijiye.
Here is the money.

Phir aaiyegaa, aapkii hii dukaan hai.
Please come to this store again.

Jii shukriyaa!
Thank you!

Namaste!
Goodbye!

Namaste!
Goodbye!

Maya:	Hello! I need to buy some clothes.
	Namaste jii! Mujhe ek shalwaar kurtaa chaahiye.
	नमस्ते जी ! मुझे एक सूती शलवार कुर्ता चाहिये।
Shopkeeper:	Are you buying (the clothes) for yourself?
	Aap ke liye, hai naa?
	आपके लिये, है ना?
Maya:	Yes, yes, for myself.
	Haañ haañ mere liye.
	हाँ हाँ मेरे लिये।
Shopkeeper:	Which color would you like?
	Jii, kis rang meñ chaahiye?
	जी, किस रंग में चाहिये?
Maya:	Dark brown. Blue or black will work too.
	Gehraa bhuuraa, niilaa yaa kaalaa bhii chalegaa.
	गहरा भूरा, नीला या काला भी चलेगा।
Shopkeeper:	Look, this black one's very beautiful.
	Ye dekhiye, yah kaalaa waalaa bahut sundar hai.
	ये देखिये, यह काला वाला बहुत सुंदर है।
Maya:	Yes, it's very beautiful. How much does it cost?
	Haañ, yah bahut sundar hai. Daam kyaa hai?
	हाँ, यह बहुत सुंदर है। दाम क्या है?
Shopkeeper:	Not much, just 800 rupees.
	Zyaadaa nahiiñ hai, sirf aaTh sau rupaye.
	ज़्यादा नहीं है, सिर्फ़ आठ सौ रुपये।
Maya:	800 rupees is too much for a cotton *shalvaar kurta.* Please reconsider (lit., "see").
	AaTh sau rupaye suutii shalwaar kurte ke liye bahut zyaadaa hai. Kuchh kam kiijiye.
	आठ सौ रुपये सूती शलवार कुर्ते के लिये बहुत ज़्यादा है। कुछ कम कीजिये।
Shopkeeper:	750 rupees then, is that okay?
	Achchhaa saaRhe saat sau diijiye.
	अच्छा साढे सात सौ दीजिये।
Maya:	No, 700 rupees will be okay.
	Nahiiñ, nahiiñ saat sau Thiik haiñ.
	नहीं नहीं, सात सौ ठीक हैं।

Shopkeeper:	Okay, 700 rupees then. What else do you need?
	Thiik hai, saat sau diijiye. Aur kyaa chaahiye?
	ठीक है, सात सौ दीजिये। और क्या चाहिये?
Maya:	Could you show me a silk scarf?
	Ek silk vaalaa dupaTTAa dikhaaiye.
	एक सिल्क वाला दुपट्टा दिखाइये।
Shopkeeper:	See here. These are all silk.
	Ye dekhiye. Ye sab silk ke haiñ.
	ये देखिये। ये सब सिल्क के हैं।
Maya:	Please show me that yellow one and that red one.
	Vah piilaa vaalaa aur laal vaalaa dikhaaiye.
	वह पीला वाला और लाल वाला दिखाइये।
Shopkeeper:	Here they are.
	Ye liijiye.
	ये लीजिये।
Maya:	How much is the red one?
	Yah laal vaalaa kitne kaa hai?
	यह लाल वाला कितने का है?
Shopkeeper:	400 rupees, just for you.
	Yah chaar sau kaa hai, sirf aap ke liye.
	यह चार सौ का है, सिर्फ़ आपके लिये।
Maya:	350 rupees would be okay.
	SaaRhe tiin sau Thiik haiñ.
	साढ़े तीन सौ ठीक हैं।
Shopkeeper:	Okay, good. 350 rupees only please.
	Achchha Thiik hai, laaiye saaRhe tiin sau hii diijiye.
	अच्छा ठीक है, लाइये साढ़े तीन सौ ही दीजिये।
Maya:	Here is the money.
	Ye aap ke rupaye liijiye.
	ये आपके रुपये लीजिये।
Shopkeeper:	Please come to this store again (lit., "this is your store!"). Goodbye!
	Phir aaiyegaa, aapkii hii dukaan hai. Namaste!
	फिर आइयेगा, आपकी ही दुकान है। नमस्ते !
Maya:	Thank you! Goodbye!
	Jii shukriyaa! Namaste!
	जी शुक्रिया ! नमस्ते !

Vocabulary List (04–02)

भाई साहब	**bhaaiisaahab**	brother (respected)
आइये	**aaiye**	please come
कहिये	**kahiye**	please say
क्या चाहिये?	**Kyaa chaahiye?**	What do you need?
मुझको/मुझे	**mujhko/mujhe**	to me
लीजिये	**liijiye**	please take
शलवार (m)-कुर्ता (m)	**shalwaar-kurtaa**	a common Indian outfit consisting of trousers and a long loose shirt, worn primarily by women
है ना?	**Hai naa?**	Isn't it?
आपके लिये	**aap ke liye**	for you
मेरे लिये	**mere liye**	for me
रंग (m)	**rañg**	color
गहरा	**gehraa**	deep/dark/dense
भूरा	**bhuuraa**	brown
नीला	**niilaa**	blue
काला	**kaalaa**	black
सुंदर	**sundar**	beautiful
बहुत	**bahut**	very
दाम (m)	**daam**	price
ज़्यादा	**zyaadaa**	much
सिर्फ़	**sirf**	only
रुपये (m)	**rupaye**	money (rupees)
आठ सौ	**aaTh sau**	800
साढे सात सौ	**saaRhe saat sau**	750
दुपट्टा (m)	**dupaTTaa**	scarf
पीला	**piilaa**	yellow
कितने का है?	**Kitne kaa hai?**	How much?
साढे तीन सौ	**saaRhe tiin sau**	350

लाइये	**laaiye**	please bring/give
फिर आइयेगा	**phir aaiyegaa**	please come again
दुकान (f)	**dukaan**	shop/store
न यह चाहिये न वह चाहिये।	**Na yah chaahiye na vah chaahiye.**	do not need this nor that (neither...nor)
यह वाला ठीक है।	**Yah vaalaa Thiik hai.**	This one is okay.
पानी की बोतल	**ek paanii kii botal**	bottle of water
या	**yaa**	or
चलेगा	**chalegaa**	(it) will work/do

Supplementary Vocabulary
Useful Phrases

यह कितने का है?	**Yah kitne kaa hai?**	How much does it cost? (for a masculine gender noun/item)
यह कितने की है?	**Yah kitne kii hai?**	How much does it cost? (for a feminine gender noun/item)
दाम क्या है?	**Daam kyaa hai?**	What is the cost?

Daam kyaa hai?
How much does it cost?

वह वाला दिखाइये।	**Vah vaalaa dikhaaiye.**	Show me that one.
यह ठीक है।	**Yah thiik hai.**	This one is ok.
यह ठीक नहीं है।	**Yah thiik nahiiñ hai.**	This (one) is not ok.
यह ठीक-ठाक है।	**Yah thiik-thaak hai.**	This is not that great.
इससे बेहतर दिखाइये।	**Is se behtar dikhaaiye.**	Show me (something) better than this.
यह तो बहुत महँगा है।	**Yah to bahut meheñgaa hai.**	This is very expensive.
कुछ कम कीजिये।	**Kuchh kam kiijiye.**	Please lower the price.
क्या ... (an amount) ठीक है?	**Kyaa… thiik hai?**	Is this amount okay?
... (an amount) ठीक है।	**… thiik hai.**	This amount is OK.
फिर कभी	**phir kabhii**	anytime else
मेरे पास इतने रुपये नहीं हैं।	**Mere paas itne rupaye nahiiñ haiñ.**	I do not (have) this much money.
क्या आप कार्ड लेते हैं।	**Na yah chaahiye na vah chaahiye.**	Do you take credit cards?
क्या आसपास कोई ए टी एम मशीन है?	**Kyaa aas-paas koii *ATM machine* hai?**	Is there any ATM machine nearby?
क्या रिटर्न पॉलिसी है?	**Kyaa *return policy* hai?**	Is there any return policy?

रिटर्न पॉलिसी क्या है?	*Return policy* kyaa hai?	What is the return policy (like)?
क्या कोई छूट है?	Kyaa koii chhuuT hai?	Is there any discount?
कितनी छूट है?	Kitnii chhuuT hai?	How much is (the) discount?
क्या गारंटी है?	Kyaa *guarantee* hai?	What is the guarantee?
कितने दिन की गारंटी है?	Kitne din kii *guarantee* hai?	How long is the guarantee (for this product)?

Hindi Numbers (04–03)

1	एक	ek	31	इकतीस	iktiis
2	दो	do	32	बत्तीस	battiis
3	तीन	tiin	33	तैंतीस	taiñtiis
4	चार	chaar	34	चौंतीस	chauñtiis
5	पाँच	paañch	35	पैंतीस	paiñtiis
6	छह	chhah	36	छत्तीस	chhattiis
7	सात	saat	37	सैंतीस	saiñtiis
8	आठ	aaTh	38	अड़तीस	aRtiis
9	नौ	nau	39	उनतालीस	untaaliis
10	दस	das	40	चालीस	chhaliis
11	ग्यारह	gyaarah	41	इकतालीस	iktaaliis
12	बारह	baarah	42	बियालीस	biyaaliis
13	तेरह	terah	43	तियालीस	tiyaaliis
14	चौदह	chaudah	44	चवालीस	chavaaliis
15	पंद्रह	pandrah	45	पैंतालीस	paiñtaaliis
16	सोलह	solah	46	छियालीस	chhiyaaliis
17	सत्रह	satrah	47	सैंतालीस	saiñtaaliis
18	अट्ठारह	aTThharah	48	अड़तालीस	aRtaaliis
19	उन्नीस	unniis	49	उनचास	unchaas
20	बीस	biis	50	पचास	pachaas
21	इक्कीस	ikkiis	51	इक्यावन	ikyaavan
22	बाईस	baaiis	52	बावन	baavan
23	तेईस	teiis	53	तिरेपन	tirpan
24	चौबीस	chaubiis	54	चौपन	chaupan
25	पच्चीस	pachchiis	55	पचपन	pachpan
26	छब्बीस	chhabiis	56	छप्पन	chhappan
27	सत्ताईस	sattaaiis	57	सत्तावन	sattaavan
28	अट्ठाईस	atthaaiis	58	अट्ठावन	aTThaavan
29	उनतीस	untiis	59	उनसठ	unsaTh
30	तीस	tiis	60	साठ	saaTh

61	इकसठ	iksaTh	81	इक्यासी	ikyaasii
62	बासठ	baasaTh	82	बयासी	bayaasii
63	तिरेसठ	tirasaTh	83	तिरासी	tiraasii
64	चौसठ	chausaTh	84	चौरासी	chaurasii
65	पैंसठ	paiñsaTh	85	पचासी	pachaasii
66	छियासठ	chhiyaasaTh	86	छियासी	chhiyaasii
67	सड़सठ	saRsaTh	87	सत्तासी	sattaasii
68	अड़सठ	aRsaTh	88	अट्ठासी	atThasii
69	उनहत्तर	unhattar	89	नवासी	navasii
70	सत्तर	sattar	90	नब्बे	nabbe
71	इकहत्तर	ikhattar	91	इक्यानवे	ikyaanave
72	बहत्तर	bahattar	92	बानवे	baanave
73	तिहत्तर	tihattar	93	तिरानवे	tiraanave
74	चौहत्तर	chauhattar	94	चौरानवे	chauranave
75	पचहत्तर	pachhattar	95	पचानवे	pachaanave
76	छिहत्तर	chhihattar	96	छियानवे	chhiyaanave
77	सतहत्तर	satahattar	97	सत्तानवे	sattanave
78	अठहत्तर	aTThahattar	98	अट्ठानवे	aTThaanave
79	उन्यासी	unyaasii	99	निन्यानवे	ninyaanave
80	अस्सी	assii	100	१०० सौ	sau

Numbers (04-03b)

101	१०१ एक सौ एक	ek sau ek
200	२०० दो सौ	do sau
201	२०१ दो सौ एक	do sau ek
500	५०० पाँच सौ	paañch sau
1000	१००० हज़ार	hazaar
2000	२००० दो हज़ार	do hazaar
100,000	१००,००० लाख	laakh
10,000,000 (100,00,000)	१००,००,००० करोड़	karoR (crore)
100,000,000 (10,00,00,000)	१०,००,००,००० अरब	arab
1.5	१.५ डेढ़	DeRh
2.5	२.५ ढाई	Dhaaii

Colors (04–04)

रंग	**Rañg**	colors
हरा	**haraa**	green
लाल	**laal**	red
काला	**kaalaa**	black
सफ़ेद	**safed**	white
नीला	**niilaa**	blue
गुलाबी	**gulaabii**	pink

Pattern Practice 1

After reading the dialogue, answer the following questions.

1. माया को शलवार-कुर्ता किसके लिये चाहिये?
   Maya ko shalwaar-kurtaa kiske chaahiye?
2. माया को शलवार-कुर्ता किस रंग में चाहिये?
   Maya ko shalwaar-kurtaa kis rang meñ chaahiye?
3. शलवार-कुर्ता के अलावा (besides) उसको और क्या चाहिये?
   Shalwaar-kurtaa ke alaavaa usko aur kyaa chaahiye?
4. शलवार-कुर्ते का दाम क्या है?
   Shalwaar-kurtaa kaa daam kyaa hai?
5. क्या शलवार-कुर्ते का दाम आपके हिसाब से (according to you) ज़्यादा है?
   Kyaa shalwaar-kurtaa kaa daam aapke hisaab se zyaadaa hai?

CULTURAL NOTE Clothing in India (04–05)

Clothing in India varies and is based on the regional climate, ethnicity, social hierarchy, and cultural traditions. Women generally wear saris, **ghaghra-choli**, **shalwaar-qamiiz** (*shalwar-kameez*) or western clothes, while men generally wear *kurta*-pajamas, Nehru jackets, or western clothes. Travelers should be mindful to keep their shoulders and legs covered. Bring clothes in lightweight fabrics, as the weather can be quite warm, and a scarf or shawl to cover your head or shoulders, especially when visiting religious places.

If you're buying "Western" clothing in a shop, use their English names to differentiate them from their indigenous equivalents. **Ghaaghraa** and **leheñga**, for instance, are traditional skirts, but a Western-style skirt is likely to be called "skirt." पतलून **patluun** "trousers/pants" might be the one somewhat common exception to this.

GRAMMAR NOTE **Expressing Needs and Requests** (04–06a)

The word चाहिये **chaahiye** ("What do you need?") is used to express a need or request in Hindi. The logical subject (one who needs something) is followed by the word को **ko** ("to"). The use of को denotes that "something is needed to" the logical subject rather than "subject needs something." This indirect way of expressing that you need something makes the sentence more polite, especially if you are asking for something using the first person pronoun (I or we).

Sentence construction with चाहिये (**chaahiye**):

Logical subject + को + logical object (the thing needed) + चाहिये।

e.g.: माया को चाय चाहिये। **Maya ko chaay chaahiye**. Maya would like tea.

When pronouns are followed by को **ko**, some of them change their original forms. This applies also for words like पर **par** ("on"), e.g., मुझपर **mujh par** "on me," but do not have a second contracted form like मुझे **mujhe**.

Pronoun	को ko	Final form
मैं **maiñ**	को ko	मुझको/मुझे **mujh mko/mujhe** "to me"
हम **ham**	को ko	हमको/हमें **ham ko** "to us"
यह **yah**	को ko	इसको/इसे **is ko/isse** "to him/her"
ये **ye**	को ko	इनको इन्हें **in ko** "to them/these/those"
वह **vah**	को ko	उसको/उसे **us ko** "to him/her"
वे **ve**	को ko	उनको/उन्हें **un ko** "to them/these/those"
आप **aap** (formal)	को ko	आपको **aap ko** "to you"
तुम **tum** (informal)	को ko	तुमको/तुम्हें **tum ko** "to you"
तू **tuu** (informal)	को ko	तुझको/तुझे **tujh ko/tujhe** "to you"

CULTURAL NOTE Bargaining with मोल-तोल करना *Mol–tol karnaa*

Bargaining/haggling (मोल-तोल **mol-tol**) is very common in India and generally expected in markets and more traditional shops, as well as many cases with rickshaw and auto-rickshaw drivers, though not in modern Western-style shops. The price quoted at the beginning of bargaining will often be outrageously high, with the assumption that a mutually agreeable price will eventually be reached. Haggling can get quite animated and all sorts of emotional appeals are often made by both sides. This is completely normal, though, and neither side should be upset about it afterwards. One should be friendly but firm when bargaining—and be at peace with the fact that one will not likely get the best deal until after a fair bit of practice.

Bargaining is a necessity in an Indian market

Pattern Practice 2

Match the Hindi words and phrases to their English meanings below.

- आइये। **Aaiye.**
- कहिये। **Kahiye.**
- क्या चाहिये? **Kyaa chaahiye?**
- एक बोतल पानी चाहिये।
  Ek botal paanii chaahiye.
- कौनसी वाली? **Kaunsii vaalii?**
- शुक्रिया ! **Shukriyaa.**

Which one?

Thank you.

Please say/tell.

What do you need?

I need a bottle of water.

Please come.

Pattern Practice 3

You are at a grocery store and you would like to buy some items. Practice making the following statements in Hindi.

1. I'd like to buy some milk.
2. I'd like to buy some eggs.
3. How much for that toothbrush?
4. Can I buy bread?
5. Can you help me get the ice cream?

GRAMMAR NOTE Using वाला/वाले/वाली *Vaalaa/Vaale/Vaalii—* "The...One" (04–06b)

वाला/वाले/वाली (**vaalaa/vaale/vaalii**) is a suffix meaning "the one," "the one who/which is," "one who/which is characterized by..." etc. used with nouns, adjectives and question words.

वाला (**vaalaa**) also has three different forms; वाला (**vaalaa**) is for the masculine singular, वाली (**vaalii**) for the feminine singular and plural, and वाले (**vaale**) for the masculine plural, masculine singular but formal, and a mixed group of male and female. Examples of these include:

दूध + वाला = दूधवाला   milk + the...one = milkman
duudh + **vaalaa** = **duudhvaala**

लाल + वाला = लालवाला **laal** + **vaalaa** = **laalvaalaa**   the red one

कहाँ + वाला = कहाँवाला **kahaañ** + **vaalaa** = **kahaañvaalaa**
(lit., "a thing or person from where" or "where is this thing or person from?")

We can see that adding वाला (**vaalaa**) has modified the noun to become the person in charge of the noun—in this case the milkman who delivers the milk.

In the instance of adding वाला (**vaalaa**) to लाल (**laal**), the phrase now indicates which item the speaker is referring to, i.e., the red one out of all the other items. Finally, in adding वाला (**vaalaa**) to the question word कहाँ (**kahaañ**), the phrase now identifies the thing or person the speaker is talking about.

Pattern Practice 4

Fill in the blanks (choose the appropriate form of वाला/वाला/वाली **vaalaa/ vaale/vaalii** according to the number and gender of the nouns) and then translate the sentences into English):

1. हिंदी_____(वाला/वाले/वाली) किताब चाहिये।
   Hindi _____ (vaalaa/vaale/vaalii) kitaab chaahiye.
   Translation:

2. लकड़ी (wooden) _____(वाला/वाले/वाली) कुर्सी पर बैठिये।
   LakRii _____ (vaalaa/vaale/vaalii) kursii par baiThiye.
   Translation:

3. क्या आपको दूध (milk)_____(वाला/वाले/वाली) चाय चाहिये?
   Kyaa aap ko duudh _____ (vaalaa/vaale/vaalii) chaay chaahiye?
   Translation:

4. सिल्क _____(वाला/वाले/वाली) साड़ी दिखाइये।
   Silk _____ (vaalaa/vaale/vaalii) saaDii dikhaaiye.
   Translation:

5. हिंदी _____(वाला/वाले/वाली) विद्यार्थी यहाँ आइये।
   Hindi _____(vaalaa/vaale/vaalii) vidyaarthii yahaañ aaiye.
   Translation:

Pattern Practice 5

Referring to the vocabulary on pages 59–60, fill in the blanks with the correct Hindi words.

1. आइये, आइये_____? (what do you need)
   Aaiye, aaiye_____?

2. मुझे एक कुर्ता _____। (I need a *kurta*)
   Mujhe ek kurtaa _____.

3. लालवाले कुर्ते का _____ है? (what is the price)

   Laalvaale kurte kaa _____ hai.

4. _____ आठ सौ रुपये है। (only for you)

   _____**aaTh sau rupaye hai.**

5. यह तो _____ है। (too much)

   Yah to_____ hai.

6. दाम कुछ _____ । (lower the price)

   Daam kuchh _____.

7. ठीक है, _____ । (please give 700 rupees)

   Thiik hai_____.

8. यह _____ आपके रुपये। (please take)

   Yah _____ aapke rupaye.

EXERCISE 1

Match the Hindi words below to the English meanings.

• दुपट्टा (m) **dupaTTaa**	please come again
• लाइये **laaiye**	rupees
• लीजिये **liijiye**	blue
• गहरा **gehraa**	scarf
• फिर आइयेगा **phir aaiyegaa**	please give
• रंग (m) **rañg**	please take
• नीला **niilaa**	How much?
• रुपये (m) **rupaye**	color
• साढ़े तीन सौ **saaRhe tiin sau**	350
• कितने का है? **kitne kaa hai?**	deep/dark/dense

EXERCISE 2

Choose the right translation from the options below.

1. beautiful
   a. भूरा **bhuuraa**
   b. लाइये **laaiye**
   c. पीला **piilaa**
   d. सुंदर **sundar**
2. to me
   a. मेरे लिये **mere liye**
   b. दुपट्टा (m) **dupaTTaa**
   c. आपके लिये **aap ke liye**
   d. मुझको (मुझे) **mujhko/mujhe**
3. black
   a. गहरा **gehraa**
   b. नीला **niilaa**
   c. काला **kaalaa**
   d. पीला **piilaa**
4. for you
   a. मेरे लिये **mere liye**
   b. कहिये **kahiye**
   c. लीजिये **liijiye**
   d. आपके लिये **aap ke liye**
5. very
   a. नीला **niilaa**
   b. बहुत **bahut**
   c. काला **kaalaa**
   d. गहरा **gehraa**

6. price
   a. रंग (m) **rang**
   b. दुकान (m) **dukaan**
   c. दाम (m) **daam**
   d. काला **kaalaa**
7. only
   a. सिर्फ़ **sirf**
   b. सुंदर **sundar**
   c. गहरा **gehraa**
   d. कहिये **kahiye**
8. 800
   a. आइये **aaiye**
   b. आठ सौ **aaTh sau**
   c. काला **kaalaa**
   d. गहरा **gehraa**
9. brown
   a. भूरा **bhuuraa**
   b. पीला **piilaa**
   c. गहरा **gehraa**
   d. नीला **niilaa**

A local textile shop offering traditional sari in Jaipur

Mother and daughter shopping for clothes in a shopping mall

EXERCISE 3

Circle the correct answer for the statements below.

1. कहिये **kahiye** = please say	True	False
2. भाईसाहब **bhaiisahab** = brother (respected)	True	False
3. साढ़े सात सौ **saaRhe saat sau** = 350	True	False
4. आइये **aaiye** = please come	True	False
5. क्या चाहिये? **Kyaa chaahiye?** = What do you need?	True	False
6. दुकान (m) **dukaan** = money	True	False
7. पीला **piilaa** = yellow	True	False
8. मेरे लिये **mere liye** = for you	True	False
9. ज़्यादा **zyaadaa** = brother (respected)	True	False
10. है ना **Hai naa?** = Isn't it?	True	False

CHECKLIST

Can you do the following things in Hindi now?

- **Shop in India**
- **Explain what you need**
- **Bargain at the store**

LESSON 5
Talking About Your Family

At a party, Kabir and Maya talk about their families and different occupations
After this lesson you should be able to do these functions in Hindi:

- **Talk about your family**
- **List their occupations**

🎧  **FAMILY** (05–01)

Kabir and Maya are talking about their families.

Kabir:	Maya, where is your family (now)?
	Maya, aapkaa parivaar kahaañ hai?
	माया, आपका परिवार कहाँ है?
Maya:	My family is in America. What about your family?
	Meraa parivaar *Amerika* meñ hai. Aur aap kaa parivaar?
	मेरा परिवार अमेरिका में है? और आपका परिवार।
Kabir:	My family is in Jaipur.
	Meraa parivaar Jaipur meñ hai.
	मेरा परिवार जयपुर में है।
Maya:	Who are your family members (lit., "in your family")?
	Aap ke parivaar meñ kaun kaun hain?
	आपके परिवार में कौन-कौन हैं?
Kabir:	(In) my family (there) is my father, mother, a brother, a sister, my wife and our two daughters.
	Mere parivaar meñ pitaa jii haiñ, maataa jii haiñ, ek behen hai, merii patnii hai, aur do beTiyaañ haiñ.
	मेरे परिवार में पिताजी हैं, माता जी हैं, एक भाई है, एक बहन है, मेरी पत्नी है, और दो बेटियाँ हैं।
Maya:	Wow! What a big family!
	Vah! Bahut baRaa parivaar hai.
	वाह, बहुत बड़ा परिवार है।
Kabir:	Yes. Who is in your family?
	Jii haañ. Aap ke parivaar meñ kaun kaun haiñ?
	जी हाँ। आपके परिवार में कौन कौन हैं?

Aap kii behen aap se baRii hai yaa chhoTii?
Is your sister older or younger than you?

Behen sab se baRii hai. Us ke baad main huuñ.
My sister is the oldest, then me.

Meraa bhaaii mujh se chhoTaa hai.
My brother is the youngest.

Aap ke maataa-pitaa kyaa karte haiñ?
What do your parents do?

Mere pitaa jii sarkaarii daftar meñ kaam karte hai. Aur merii maataa jii darjii haiñ.
My father works in the government and my mother is a tailor.

Achchhaa.
I see.

Aap ke maataa-pitaa kyaa karte haiñ?
What do your parents do?

Mere pitaa jii retired haiñ aur merii maataa jii adhyaapikaa haiñ.
My father is retired and my mother is a teacher.

Achchhaa! Ek baat hai. Kal meraa janamdin hai.
I see! One more thing. Tomorrow is my birthday.

Mubaarak ho!
Congratulations!

Maya: My father, my mother, my sister and my brother.

Mere parivaar meñ pitaa jii haiñ, maataa jii haiñ, ek behen hai, aur ek bhaaii hai.

मेरे परिवार में पिता जी हैं, माता जी हैं, एक बहन है, और एक भाई है।

Kabir: Is your sister older or younger than you?

Aap kii behen aap se baRii hai yaa chhoTii?

आप की बहन आप से बड़ी है या छोटी?

Maya: My sister is the oldest, then me. My brother is the youngest.

Behen sab se baRii hai. Us ke baad main huuñ. Meraa bhaaii mujh se chhoTaa hai.

बहन सब से बड़ी है। उसके बाद मैं हूँ। मेरा भाई मुझ से छोटा है।

Are your sister and brother married?

Kyaa aapke bhaaii-behen shaadi-shudaa haiñ?

क्या आपके भाई-बहन शादी-शुदा हैं?

Kabir: My brother is married but my sister is not.

Meraa bhaaii shaadii-shudaa hai aur behen shaadii-shudaa nahiiñ hai.

मेरा भाई शादी-शुदा है और बहन शादी-शुदा नहीं है।

Maya: Is your sister younger than you?

Kyaa aapkii behen aap se chhoTii hai?

क्या आपकी बहन आप से छोटी है?

Kabir: Yes, my sister is younger. Are your siblings married?

Jii haañ, behen sab se chhoTii hai. kyaa aapke bhaii-behen shaadii-shudaa hai?

जी हाँ बहन सब से छोटी है। क्या आपके भाई-बहन शादी-शुदा हैं?

Maya: My sister is divorced. My brother is not married.

Merii behen talaaq-shudaa hai aur bhaaii shaadi-shudaa nahiiñ hai.

मेरी बहन तलाक-शुदा है और भाई शादी-शुदा नहीं है।

Kabir: What do your parents do?

Aap ke maataa-pitaa kyaa karte haiñ?

आपके माता-पिता क्या करते हैं?

Maya: My father works in the government and my mother is a tailor.

Mere pitaa jii sarkaarii daftar meñ kaam karte hai. Aur merii maataa jii darjii haiñ.

मेरे पिता जी सरकारी दफ़्तर में काम करते हैं। और मेरी माता जी दर्जी हैं।

Kabir:	I see.
	Achchhaa.
	अच्छा।
Maya:	What do your parents do?
	Aap ke maataa-pitaa kyaa karte haiñ?
	आपके माता- पिता क्या करते हैं?
Kabir:	My father is retired and my mother is a teacher.
	Mere pitaa jii *retired* haiñ aur merii maataa jii adhyaapikaa haiñ.
	मेरे पिताजी रिटायर्ड हैं और मेरी माता जी अध्यापिका हैं।
Maya:	I see. And your siblings?
	Achchhaa. Aur bhaaii-behen?
	अच्छा। और भाई-बहन?
Kabir:	My sister is a bank manager and my brother is a student.
	Behen *bank-manager* hai aur bhaaii vidyaarthii hai.
	बहन बैंक मैनेजर है और भाई विद्यार्थी है।
Maya:	I see! One more thing. Tomorrow is my birthday.
	Achchhaa! Ek baat hai. Kal meraa janamdin hai.
	अच्छा ! एक बात है। कल मेरा जनमदिन है।
Kabir:	Congratulations!
	Mubaarak ho!
	मुबारक हो !
Maya:	You and your wife, please come to my party.
	Aap aur aap kii patnii merii party meñ aaiye.
	आप और आपकी पत्नी मेरी पार्टी में आइये।
Kabir:	Okay, thanks.
	Thiik hai. Shukriyaa.
	ठीक है। शुक्रिया।

Vocabulary List (05–02)

अमेरिकन	*American*	American
हिंदुस्तानी	**Hindustaanii**	Indian
परिवार	**parivaar**	family
मेरा, मेरी, मेरे	**meraa, merii, mere**	my, mine
लोग	**log**	people
माता	**maataa**	mother

पिता	**pitaa**	father
बच्चे	**bachche**	children
लड़का	**laRkaa**	boy
लड़के	**laRke**	boys
लड़की	**laRkii**	girl
लड़कियाँ	**laRkiyaañ**	girls
नाम (m)	**naam**	name
भाई	**bhaaii**	brother
बहन	**behen**	sister
पत्नी	**patnii**	wife
पति	**pati**	husband
बड़ा, बड़ी, बड़े	**baRaa, baRii, baRe**	big, old
छोटा, छोटी, छोटे	**chhoTaa, chhoTii, chhoTe**	small, short, young
सब से बड़ा	**sab se baRaa**	oldest
सब से छोटा	**sab se chhoTaa**	youngest
मुझ से	**mujh se**	than me
आप से	**aap se**	than you
लंबा, लंबी, लंबे	**lambaa, lambii, lambe**	tall
शहर (m)	**sheher**	city
सुंदर	**sundar**	beautiful
जानवर	**jaanvar**	animal
रसोई (f)	**rasoii**	kitchen
शौचालय, बाथरूम	**shauchaalaya, _bathroom_**	bathroom, toilet
मेज़ (f)	**mez**	table
कुर्सी (f)	**kursii**	chair
सस्ता/सस्ती/सस्ते	**sastaa, sastii, saste**	cheap
कौन-कौन	**kaun-kaun**	who all
उस के बाद	**uske baad**	after that
शादी (f)	**shaadii**	marriage

शादी-शुदा	shaadii-shudaa	married
तलाक़ (m)	talaaq	divorce
तलाक़-शुदा	talaaq-shudaa	divorced
सरकारी	sarkaarii	government
दफ़्तर (m)	daftar	office
अध्यापिका	adhyaapikaa	teacher (woman)
अध्यापक	adhyaapak	teacher (man)
विद्यार्थी	vidyaarthii	student
जनमदिन (m)	janamdin	birthday
मुबारक़ हो !	Mubaarak ho!	Congratulations! (usually said for celebrations and occasions like birthdays.)
मेरा एक भाई है।	Meraa ek bhaai hai.	I have a brother.
मेरी कोई बहन नहीं है।	Merii koii behen nahiiñ hai.	I don't have a sister.
मैं इकलौता (m)/ इकलौती (f) हूँ।	Main iklautaa/iklautii huuñ.	I am the only child.
तलाक़ हो गया है।	talaaq ho gayaa hai.	My parents are divorced.

CULTURAL NOTE Kinship Terms (05-03)

In India people are likely to give you details about their entire family. Note that Kabir does not say he has just a wife and two children (nuclear family), but he also mentions his brother, sister and parents. Some might even include their extended family (grandparents, aunts, uncles) in the list.

As in many Asian countries, kinship terms in Hindi are extensive, with terms for your paternal, younger uncle चाचा **chaachaa** or maternal uncle's wife मामी **maamii** rather than the terms "uncle" and "aunt." Here is a list of some of the most common kinship terms in Hindi.

माता/माँ	mātā/mañ	mother
पिता/बाप	pitā/bāp	father
पति	pati	husband
पत्नी	patnii	wife
बेटा	beTa	son
बेटी	beTii	daughter

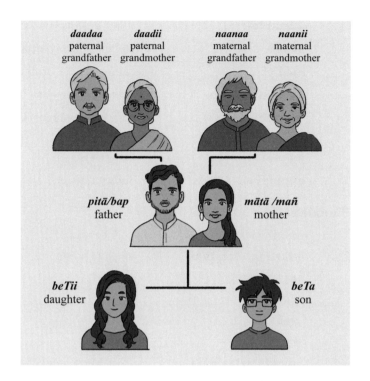

नानी	**naanii**	maternal grandmother, mother's mother
दादी	**daadii**	paternal grandmother, father's mother
नाना	**naanaa**	maternal grandfather, mother's father
दादा	**daadaa**	paternal grandfather, father's father
बड़ी बहन/दीदी	**baRii behen/dīdī**	elder sister
छोटी बहन	**chhotii behen**	younger sister
भैया/दादा	**bhaiyaa/daadaa**	elder brother
छोटा भाई	**chhoTaa bhaaii**	younger brother
मामा	**maamaa**	mother's elder brother/ mother's younger brother
मामी	**maamii**	mother's brother's wife
मौसी	**mausii**	mother's sister
मौसा	**mausaa**	mother's sister's husband

भाभी	bhaabhii	elder brother's wife
ताऊ	taauu	father's elder brother
ताई	taaii	father's elder brother's wife
चाचा	chaachaa	father's (younger) brother
चाची	chaachii	father's (younger) brother's wife
बुआ	buaa	father's sister
फूफा	phuuphaa	father's sister's husband

Common Occupations (05-04)

वेब डेवलपर	veb Devalapar	web developer
बिक्री प्रबंधक	bikrii prabandhak	sales manager
इंजीनियर	injiiniyar	engineer
वकील	vakiil	lawyer
डाक्टर	DaakTar	doctor
नर्स	nars	nurse
निवेशकर्ता बैंकर	niveshkartaa baiñkar	investment banker
मुनीम	muniim	chartered accountant
अभिनेता	abhinetaa	actor
पत्रकार	patrakaar	journalist

Pattern Practice 1

Match the Hindi phrases below with their English meanings.

- मेरा नाम माया है।
  Meraa naam Maya hai.

  There are five people in my family.

- मैं अमेरिकन हूँ।
  Maiñ *American* huuñ.

  My name is Maya.

- मेरा परिवार अमेरिका में है।
  Meraa parivaar *Amerika* meñ hai.

  I am American.

- मेरे परिवार में पाँच लोग हैं।
  Mere parivaar meñ paañch log haiñ.

  I have a mother and father, and two siblings.

- परिवार में माता-पिता हैं, और हम तीन बच्चे हैं।
  Parivaar meñ maataa-pitaa haiñ, aur ham tiin bachche haiñ.

  My family is in America.

Pattern Practice 2

Complete the following sentences about your family.

1. मेरा नाम _____ है। **Meraa naam…hai.**

2. मैं _____ हूँ (nationality)। **Main…huuñ.**

3. मेरे परिवार में _____ लोग हैं। **Mere parivaar meñ… log haiñ.**

4. मेरा परिवार_____ में है। **Meraa parivaar…meñ hai.**

5. मेरे परिवार में _____ (माता-पिता, माता जी, पिता जी, पत्नी, पति, भाई, बहन) हैं। **Mere parivaar meñ…(maataa-pitaa, maataa jii, pitaa jii, patnii, pati, bhaaii, behen) haiñ.**

GRAMMAR NOTE Comparing Two Things

Comparisons are made in this manner: Subject A + Subject B (to be compared against Subject A) + से **se** + adjective + "to be." When used in this manner से **se** means "than." When comparing two people or things, use this structure: Subject A + Subject B + से **se** "than" + adjective (tall, short, old, etc.) + है **hai** "is."

For example:

a. कबीर माया से लंबा है। **Kabir Maya se lambaa hai.**
   Kabir is taller than Maya (lit., Kabir Maya than taller is)

b. माया कबीर से छोटी है। **Maya Kabir se chhoTii hai.**
   Maya is younger (lit,. smaller) than Kabir. (lit. Maya Kabir than younger is)

Maya Kabir se chhoTii hai.
Maya is younger than Kabir.

| Useful Tip | You may have to ask for further clarification on this statement, as **chhoTii** can also mean "shorter" or "smaller." |

c. मुम्बई जयपुर से बड़ा शहर है | **Mumbai Jaipur se baRaa sheher hai.**
Mumbai is a bigger city than Jaipur. (lit., Mumbai Jaipur than bigger city is)

GRAMMAR NOTE Using सब *sab* to mean "most of all"

When comparing something to all other items to form a superlative ("the X-est," "the most X"), the structure will look like this: X + सब **sab** "all" + से **se** "than" + adjective + है **hai** "is."

For example:

a. जयपुर सब से सुंदर शहर है।
Jaipur sab se sundar sheher hai.
Jaipur is the most beautiful city of all. (lit., Jaipur all than beautiful city is)

b. क्लास में, माया सबसे लंबी लड़की है।
Class **meñ Maya sab se lambii laRkii hai.**
Maya is the tallest girl in class. (lit., In class, Maya all than tall girl is)

c. जिराफ़ सबसे लंबा जानवर है।
Jiraf sab se lambaa jaanvar hai.
The giraffe is the tallest animal. (lit., Giraffe all than tall animal is)

GRAMMAR NOTE Negative Statements and Questions in Hindi

The word "no" in Hindi is **nahiiñ** नहीं and is also the word used to negate a sentence in Hindi, by putting "no" before the verb "is/am/are." If you wanted to say you are short in this structure, phrase it as "I am not tall" or मैं लंबा नहीं हूँ। **Main lambaa nahiiñ huuñ**, which literally means "I tall not am."

You can also use this to make negative questions in Hindi, such as "Aren't you tall?" आप लंबे नहीं हैं? **Aap lambaa nahiiñ haiñ?** or literally "You tall not are?"

Pattern Practice 3

How would you say the following statements in Hindi?

1. The kitchen is bigger than the bathroom.
2. The table is cheaper than the chair.
3. Leela is the youngest of all (her siblings).

Pattern Practice 4

Read through the dialogue again and answer these questions in Hindi.

1. माया का परिवार कहाँ है?
   Maya kaa parivaar kahaañ hai?

2. कबीर का परिवार कहाँ है?
   Kabir ka parivaar kahaañ hai?

3. माया के परिवार में कौन-कौन हैं?
   Maya ke parivaar meñ kaun-kaun haiñ?

4. कबीर के परिवार में कौन-कौन हैं?
   Kabir ke parivaar meñ kaun-kaun haiñ?

5. क्या माया की बहन, माया से छोटी है?
   Kyaa Maya kii behen Maya se chhoTii hai?

6. क्या माया का भाई, माया से छोटा है?
   Kyaa Maya ka bhaaii Maya se chhoTaa hai?

7. माया के परिवार में कौन शादी-शुदा है?
   Maya ke parivaar meiñ kaun shaadii-shudaa hai?

8. क्या माया की बहन तलाक-शुदा है?
   Kyaa Maya kii behen talaaq-shudaa hai?

9. कबीर के परिवार में कौन शादी-शुदा है?
   Kabir ke parivaar meñ kaun shaadii-shudaa hai?

10. माया के माता-पिता क्या करते हैं?
    Maya ke maataa-pitaa kyaa karte haiñ?

11. कबीर के माता-पिता क्या करते हैं?
    Kabir ke maataa-pitaa kyaa karte haiñ?

12. माया का जनमदिन कब है?
    Maya kaa janmdin kab hai?

Pattern Practice 5

Translate the following negative statements and questions into Hindi.

1. She is not tall.
2. Leela is not the oldest of all (her siblings).
3. Are you not going to the office?
4. Are you not married?
5. The post office (डाक घर (f) **Daak ghar**) is not over there.
6. He is not going to Germany (जर्मनी **Jarmanii**).

GRAMMAR NOTE The Present Tense

We have learned how to create simple sentences in Hindi, using the verb (to be), e.g., "I am" and "you are." Now we will learn how to use other active verbs to construct sentences like "He works in an office." This sentence becomes वह दफ़्तर में काम करता है। **Voh daftar meñ kaam kartaa hai**.

In Hindi, when we want to say "X does something" we put the words in this order: Subject + Object + Verb-stem (verb without ना-**naa**) + ता **taa**/ते **te**/ती **tii** (as a suffix to the verb stem) + "to be" है **hai**/हूँ **huuñ**/हो **ho**/हैं **haiñ**. For example,

```
He    office  in      works                 is = He works in an office.
वह    दफ़्तर   में      काम करना (-ना) + ता     है = वह दफ़्तर में काम करता है
Voh   daftar  meñ     kaam karanaa (-naa) + taa  hai
= Voh daftar meñ kaam kartaa hai.
```

```
She   (a) book   reads              is   = She reads a book.
यह    किताब      पढ़ना (-ना) + ती      है   = यह किताब पढ़ती है
Yah   kitaab     paRhnaa (-naa) + tii  hai = Yah kitaab paRhtii hai.
```

```
They pool  in   swim                is    = They swim in a pool.
ये    पूल    में   तैरना   (-ना) + ते      हैं   = ये पूल मे तैरते      हैं
Ye    pool  men  tairnaa (-naa) + te   haiñ  = Ye pool men tairte haiñ.
```

GRAMMAR NOTE Verb, Number and Gender Agreement

In Hindi, the verb always agrees with the number and gender of the subject. Whether the suffix added to the verb stem is ता **taa**, ते **te** or ती **tii** depends on the subject that precedes it. Thus if the the subject is singular and masculine, i.e., "he" or "the man," we use खाता **khaata**. If the subject is feminine, whether singular or plural, we use खाती **khaatii**. Finally, if the subject is plural and masculine—"the men," or a single highly respected man, or a group of women and men, we would use खाते **khaate**.

Male sing. Subject	+ Object	+ Verb stem	+ "to be" =	Final Sentence
मैं **Maiñ** I	चावल **chaaval** rice	खाता **khaataa** eat	हूँ **huuñ** am	मैं चावल खाता हूँ। **Maiñ chaaval khaataa huuñ.** I eat rice.
यह **Yah/** वह **Vah** (pronounced yeh/voh) He	चावल **chaaval** rice	खाता **khaataa** eat	है **hai** is	यह/वह चावल खाता है। **Yeh/vah chaaval khaataa hai.** He eats rice.
तू **Tuu** You	चावल **chaaval** rice	खाता **khaataa** eat	है **hai** is	तू चावल खाता है। **Tuu chaaval khaataa hai.** You eat rice.

Male pl. Subject	+ Object	+ Verb stem	+ "to be" =	Final Sentence
हम **Ham** We	चावल **chaaval** rice	खाते **khaate** eat	हैं **haiñ** are	हम चावल खाते हैं। **Ham chaaval khaate haiñ.** We eat rice.
ये **Ye /**वे **Ve** (pronounced yeh/voh) They	चावल **chaaval** rice	खाते **khaate** eat	हैं **haiñ** are	ये/वे चावल खाते हैं। **Ye/ve chaaval khaate haiñ.** They eat rice.
आप **Aap** You	चावल **chaaval** rice	खाते **khaate** eat	हैं **haiñ** are	आप चावल खाते हैं। **Aap chaaval khaate haiñ.** You eat rice.
तुम **Tum** You [less formal]	चावल **chaaval** rice	खाते **khaate** eat	हो **ho** be	तुम चावल खाते हो। **Tum chaaval khaate ho.** You eat rice.

Fem. sing. Subject	+ Object	+ Verb Stem	+ "to be" =	Final Sentence
मैं **Maiñ** I	चावल **chaaval** rice	खाती **khaatii** eat	हूँ **huuñ** am	मैं चावल खाती हूँ। **Main chaaval khaatii huuñ.** I eat rice.

Fem., sing. + Subject	Object	+ Verb Stem	+ "to be" =	Final Sentence
यह **Yah** / वह **Vah** She	चावल chaaval rice	खाती khaatii eat	है hai is	यह/वह चावल खाती है। **Yah/vah chaaval khaatii hai.** She eats rice.
तू **Tuu** You	चावल chaaval rice	खाती khaatii eat	है hai is	तू चावल खाती है। **Tuu chaaval khaatii hai.** You eat rice.

Fem., pl. + Subject	Object	+ Verb stem	+ "to be" =	Final Sentence
हम **Ham** We	चावल chaaval rice	खाती khaatii eat	हैं haiñ are	हम चावल खाती हैं। **Ham chaaval khaatii haiñ.** We eat rice.
ये **ye**/ वे **ve** They	चावल chaaval rice	खाती khaatii eat	हैं haiñ are	ये/वे चावल खाती हैं। **Ye/ve chaaval khaatii haiñ.** They eat rice.
आप **Aap** You	चावल chaaval rice	खाती khaatii eat	हैं haiñ are	आप चावल खाती हैं। **Aap chaaval khaatii haiñ.** You eat rice.
तुम **Tum** You [less formal]	चावल chaaval rice	खाती khaatii eat	हो ho be	तुम चावल खाती हो। **Tum chaaval khaatii ho.** You eat rice.

Here are some other examples:

मैं (I, masc.) हिंदी सीखता हूँ।
Maiñ Hindii siikhtaa huuñ. (सीखना **siikhnaa** "to study, learn")
I study Hindi.

मैं (I, fem.) हिंदी सीखती हूँ। **Maiñ Hindi siikhtii huuñ.**
I study Hindi.

माता जी खाना बनाती हैं।
Maataa jii khaanaa banaatii haiñ.   (खाना बनाना **khaanaa banaanaa**
Mother cooks.   "to make food, to cook")

लड़के (boys) फ़ुटबाल खेलते हैं।
LaRke *football* **khelte haiñ.** (खेलना **khelnaa** "to play")
The boys play football.

लड़कियाँ (girls) हँसती हैं।
LaRkiyaañ hañstii haiñ. (हँसना **hañsnaa** "to laugh")
The girls laugh.

Pattern Practice 6

How would you say the following statements in Hindi?

1. I (m) play football.
2. You (f) work in an office.
3. They (f) cook.
4. We (m) study Hindi.
5. Do you (f) study Hindi?

Pattern Practice 7

Practice saying the following statements about your family in Hindi.

1. There are five people in my family.
2. They live in America.
3. My mother is a teacher, my father works in the government, my sister is a student and my brother is a bank manager.
4. My sister is married, but my brother is not.

EXERCISE 1

Practice reading out the following in Hindi:

1. father	2. boys
3. beautiful	4. divorce
5. marriage	6. eight
7. teacher (man)	8. after that
9. teacher (woman)	10. nine
11. husband	12. brother
13. three	14. American

EXERCISE 2

Match the Hindi words below to their English meanings:

- पाँच **paañch**
- कुर्सी **kursii**
- बहन **behen**
- छह **chhah**
- सब से बड़ा **sab se baRaa**
- शहर **sheher**
- लोग **log**
- जनमदिन **janmdin**
- दफ़्तर **daftar**
- बड़ा **baRaa**
- बच्चे **bachche**
- परिवार **parivaar**
- सब से छोटा **sab se chhoTaa**
- लंबा **lambaa**

tall

oldest

people

chair

family

five

children

sister

office

six

city

youngest

big, old

birthday

EXERCISE 3

Circle the correct Hindi word for each English term.

1. government
   a. सरकारी **sarkaarii**
   b. परिवार **parivaar**
   c. पत्नी **patnii**
   d. लड़की **laRkii**

2. than me
   a. आप से **aap se**
   b. लड़के **laRke**
   c. मुझ से **mujh se**
   d. सुंदर **sundar**

3. congratulations
   a. अध्यापिका **adhyaapikaa**
   b. सरकारी **sarkaarii**
   c. मुबारक हो ! **Mubaarak ho!**
   d. विद्यार्थी **vidyaarthii**

4. table
   a. नाम (m) **naam**
   b. माता **maataa**
   c. रसोई (f) **rasoii**
   d. मेज़ (f) **mez**

5. wife
   a. बच्चे **bachche**
   b. पत्नी **patnii**
   c. पति **pati**
   d. लड़की **laRkii**
7. girls
   a. लड़का **laRkaa**
   b. परिवार **parivaar**
   c. लड़के **laRke**
   d. लड़कियाँ **laRkiyaañ**
9. name
   a. नाम (m) **naam**
   b. सात **saat**

   c. शहर (m) **sheher**

   d. चार **chaar**
11. Indian
   a. हिंदुस्तानी
      Hindustaanii
   b. तलाक़-शुदा
      Talaaq-shudaa
   c. शादी-शुदा
      Shaadii-shudaa
   d. लड़कियाँ **LaRkiyaañ**
13. boy
   a. लड़की **laRkii**
   b. लड़का **laRkaa**
   c. माता **maataa**
   d. लड़के **laRke**

6. than you
   a. बच्चे **bachche**
   b. लड़के **laRke**
   c. आप से **aap se**
   d. मुझ से **mujh se**
8. bathroom, toilet
   a. अध्यापिका **adhyaapikaa**
   b. शौचालय **shauchaalaya**
   c. विद्यार्थी **vidyaarthii**
   d. मुबारक हो ! **Mubaarak ho!**
10. cheap
   a. बड़ा, बड़ी, बड़े **baRaa, baRii, baRe**
   b. सस्ता/सस्ती/सस्ते **sastaa, sastii, saste**
   c. लंबा, लंबी, लंबे **lambaa, lambii, lambe**
   d. मेरा, मेरी, मेरे **meraa, merii, mere**
12. who all
   a. सुंदर **sundar**

   b. लड़का **laRkaa**

   c. कौन-कौन **kaun-kaun**

   d. लड़की **laRkii**
14. seven
   a. पति **pati**
   b. बहन **behen**
   c. भाई **bhaaii**
   d. सात **saat**

Gadi Sagar Lake in Jaisalmer, well-known for its architecture and ruins

EXERCISE 4
Circle the correct answer for the statements below.

1. मेरा, मेरी, मेरे **meraa, merii, mere** = my, mine   True   False
2. दस **das** = ten   True   False
3. जानवर **jaanvar** = beautiful   True   False
4. छोटा, छोटी, छोटे **chhoTaa, chhoTii, chhoTe** = tall   True   False
5. विद्यार्थी **vidyaarthii** = teacher (woman)   True   False
6. रसोई (f) **rasoii** = wife   True   False
7. माता **maataa** = mother   True   False
8. दो **do** = ten   True   False
9. चार **chaar** = four   True   False
10. लड़की **laRkii** = girl   True   False
11. एक **ek** = ten   True   False
12. शादी-शुदा **shaadii-shudaa** = married   True   False
13. तलाक़-शुदा **talaaq-shudaa** = divorced   True   False

CHECKLIST
Can you do the following things in Hindi now?

- **Talk about your family and family members**
- **List your family's occupations**

Namaste! Maya, janmdin mubarak ho!
Hello! Happy birthday Maya!

Jii, shukriyaa!
Thank you!

Bahut baRii party hai. Bahut log haiñ.
It's a big party. There are many people.

Achchhaa!
I see!

Jii haañ, mujhe janmdin par dostoñ se milnaa pasand hai.
Yes, I like to meet friends on my birthday.

Aap janmdin par kyaa-kyaa karte haiñ?
What do you do on your birthday?

Maya yah aap ke janmdin kaa tohfaa hai.
Maya, this is your birthday present.

Iskii kyaa zaruurat thii. Tohfe ke liye bahut bahut shukriyaa!
You shouldn't have. Thank you very much for the gift!

Maiñ parivaar ke saath mandir jaataa huuñ. Maataa-pitaa ke paañv chhuutaa huuñ. MiThaaii khaataa huuñ. Aur Parivaar ke saath Hindi filmeñ dekhtaa huuñ.
I go with my family to the temple, I touch my parents' feet (to show them respect), eat desserts and watch Hindi films with my family.

LESSON 6
Celebrating Birthdays

In this lesson we will see how Maya celebrates her birthday and how it differs from the Indian customs. After this lesson you will be able to do these functions in Hindi:

- **Describe how you celebrate birthdays or festivals in your country**
- **Compare two events**
- **Likes and dislikes**

 **BIRTHDAYS AND FESTIVALS IN INDIA**
(06-01)

Kabir and his wife are at Maya's birthday party. Kabir and Maya are discussing how they celebrate their birthdays and special occasions like Diwali.

Kabir:	Hello! Happy birthday Maya!
	Namaste! Maya, janmdin mubarak ho!
	नमस्ते ! माया, जन्मदिन मुबारक हो !
Maya:	Thank you!
	Jii, shukriyaa!
	जी, शुक्रिया !
Kabir:	Maya, this is your birthday present.
	Maya yah aap ke janmdin kaa tohfaa hai.
	माया यह आपके जन्मदिन का तोहफ़ा है।
Maya:	You shouldn't have. Thank you very much for the gift!
	Iskii kyaa zaruurat thii. Tohfe ke liye bahut bahut shukriyaa!
	इसकी क्या ज़रूरत थी। तोहफ़े के लिये बहुत बहुत शुक्रिया !
Kabir:	It's a big party. There are many people.
	Bahut baRii *party* hai. Bahut log haiñ.
	बहुत बड़ी पार्टी है। बहुत लोग हैं।
Maya:	Yes, I like to meet friends on my birthday.
	Jii haañ, mujhe janmdin par dostoñ se milnaa pasand hai.
	जी हाँ, मुझे जन्मदिन पर दोस्तों से मिलना पसंद है।
Kabir:	I see!
	Achchhaa!
	अच्छा !

Maya: Do you like having a party on your birthday?

            Aap ko janmdin par kyaa karnaa pasand hai?

            आपको जन्मदिन पर क्या करना पसंद है?

Kabir: I don't like to party and I don't like to cut a cake.

            Mujhe *party* karnaa aur *cake* kaaTnaa pasand nahiiñ hai.

            मुझे पार्टी करना और केक काटना पसंद नहीं है।

Maya: So, you don't celebrate your birthday?

            To, kyaa aap janmdin nahiiñ manaate haiñ?

            तो, क्या आप जन्मदिन नहीं मनाते हैं?

Kabir: No, no, I do celebrate my birthday.

            Nahiiñ, nahiiñ, maiñ janmdin manaataa huuñ.

            नहीं, नहीं, मैं जन्मदिन मनाता हूँ।

Maya: What do you do on your birthday?

            Aap janmdin par kyaa-kyaa karte haiñ?

            आप जन्मदिन पर क्या-क्या करते हैं?

Kabir: I go with my family to the temple, I touch my parents' feet (to
            show them respect), eat desserts and watch Hindi films with my
            family.

            **Maiñ parivaar ke saath mandir jaataa huuñ. Maataa-pitaa ke
            paañv chhuutaa huuñ. MiThaaii khaataa huuñ. Aur Parivaar
            ke saath Hindi filmeñ dekhtaa huuñ.**

            मैं परिवार के साथ मंदिर जाता हूँ। माता-पिता के पाँव छूता हूँ। मिठाई
            खाता हूँ। और परिवार के साथ हिंदी फ़िल्में देखता हूँ।

Maya: Is this the Indian way of celebrating birthdays?

            Kyaa yah janmdin manaane kaa Hindustaanii tariikaa hai?

            क्या यह जन्मदिन मनाने का हिंदुस्तानी तरीका है?

Kabir: Yes, many Indian people do this. Some people also cut cake.

            **Jii haañ, bahut Hindu log aisaa karte haiñ, kuchh log *cake* bhii
            kaaTte haiñ.**

            जी हाँ, बहुत हिंदू लोग ऐसा करते हैं , कुछ लोग केक भी काटते हैं।

Maya: Kabir, how do people in India celebrate Diwali?

            Kabir ji, Bhaarat meñ log Diwaalii kaise manaate haiñ?

            कबीर जी, भारत में लोग दिवाली कैसे मनाते हैं?

Kabir: Indian people celebrate Diwali with a lot of pomp and show.

            Hindu log Diwaalii bahut dhuum-dhaam se manate haiñ.

            हिंदू लोग दिवाली बहुत धूम-धाम से मनाते हैं।

Maya:	What do people do?

Log kyaa-kyaa karte haiñ?
लोग क्या-क्या करते हैं?

Kabir:	People decorate their homes, make sweets and worship (the deities in the temple).

Log ghar sajaate haiñ, miThaaii banaate haiñ, puujaa karte haiñ.
लोग घर सजाते हैं, मिठाई बनाते हैं, पूजा करते हैं।

Maya:	And?

Aur?
और?

Kabir:	They also wear new clothes and set off fireworks.

Naye kapRe pehente haiñ, aatishbaazii karte haiñ.
नये कपड़े पहनते हैं, आतिशबाज़ी करते हैं।

Maya:	How many days do people celebrate Diwali?

Log kitne din Diwaalii manaate haiñ?
लोग कितने दिन दिवाली मनाते हैं?

Kabir:	The festival is about five days. People celebrate Diwali on all these five days.

Yah lag-bhag paañch din kaa tyohaar hotaa hai. Log paañch din Diwaalii manaate haiñ.
यह लगभग पाँच दिन का त्योहार होता है। लोग पाँच दिन दिवाली मनाते हैं।

Maya:	Thanks for the information!

Jaankaarii ke liye shukriyaa!
जानकारी के लिये शुक्रिया!

Kabir:	There's nothing to thank (me for).

Koii baat nahiiñ.
कोई बात नहीं।

Vocabulary List (06–02)

आज	aaj	today
उमर (f)	umar/umra	age
पर	par	at, one, to, on
काटना	kaaTnaa	to cut
करना	karnaa	to do
पार्टी करना *party*	PaarTii karnaa	to have a party

मिलना	**milnaa**	to meet
दोस्त	**dost**	friend
दोस्तों से मिलना	**dostoñ se milnaa**	to meet friends
तोहफ़ा (m)	**tohfaa**	gift
इसकी क्या ज़रूरत थी।	**Is kii kyaa zaruurat thii.**	There was no need of it./You shouldn't have
मनाना	**manaanaa**	to celebrate
मंदिर (m)	**mandir**	temple
पाँव (m)	**paanv**	feet
छूना	**chhuunaa**	to touch
देखना	**dekhnaa**	to see
मिठाई	**miThaaii**	sweets, desserts
हिंदुस्तानी तरीका	**Hindustaanii tariikaa**	Indian way
ऐसा	**aisaa**	such
पसंद	**pasand**	liked, pleasing, agreeable (by/to someone)
चलाना	**chalaanaa**	to drive, ride
खेलना	**khelnaa**	to play
आजकल	**aajkal**	these days
कभी-कभी	**kabhii-kabhii**	sometimes
खबरें (f)	**khabreñ**	news
दिवाली	**Diwali**	a Hindu festival (festival of lamps)
धूम-धाम से	**dhuum-dhaam se**	with pomp and show
सजाना	**sajaanaa**	to decorate
घर	**ghar**	home, house
घर-घर	**ghar-ghar**	each single house
पूजा करना	**puujaa karnaa**	to worship
और	**aur**	and
नया/नयी/नये	**nayaa/nayii/naye**	new
कपड़ा (m)	**kapRaa**	cloth
आतिशबाज़ी (f)	**aatishbaazii**	fireworks
त्योहार (m)	**tyohaar**	festival
जानकारी (f)	**jaankaarii**	information

Celebrating Diwali as a family

Supplementary Vocabulary

बचपन में	bachpan meñ	in childhood
मज़ा आ गया।	Mazaa aa gayaa.	I had fun.
जनमदिन की बधाइयाँ !	Janmdin kii badhaaiyaañ!	Best wishes on (your) birthday!
आशीर्वाद दीजिये !	Aashiirvaad diijiye!	Bless me.
खुश रहो !	__Khush raho!__	Be happy!

CULTURAL NOTE Touching Elders' Feet

This practice, common in much of North India, is called a चरणस्पर्श **charanasparsha** and is one of the most common **pranamas** (respectful forms of greeting/bowing) in (northern) India, to demonstrate subservience to an elder person in a higher position of authority, like a parent, community elder or teacher. While the person is performing the **charanasparsha**, the elder should touch the person's head and bless them (usually with long life, fortune and wisdom). In practice, the one being shown respect often stops the person bowing and pulls him or her back up in a gesture of blessing and affection.

Touching an elder's feet is a respectful show of greeting/bowing

Pattern Practice 1

Answer these questions in Hindi.

1. What do Indian people do to celebrate Diwali?
2. What does Kabir do on his birthday?
3. Why does Maya have such a big party on her birthday?
4. How does an Indian person show respect to their parents?
5. How many days do Indian people celebrate Diwali?

GRAMMAR NOTE   The Past Tense

The verb "to be" also has the past tense forms. Depending on the number and gender of the person(s) you are talking about, there are two different forms for "was" and two for "were." For example, if you are describing something a woman did in the past you say "she was" थी **thii**. If this person is male, you use the masculine form, which is था **thaa**. For groups of men, you use the masculine form "were," which is थे **the** for males, and थीं **thiiñ** for females.

In the same way if we want to say "X used to do" we use the same forms with verbs added. In such sentences verbs also agree in number and gender with the subject or person we are talking about. Refer to the table.

Male sing. +	Present Tense +	Past Tense	= Sentence
मैं **Main** I	हूँ **huuñ** am	था **thaa** was	मैं चावल खाता था **Maiñ chaaval khaataa thaa.** I used to eat rice.
यह **Yah**/ वह **Vah** He	है **hai** is	था **thaa** was	यह/वह चावल खाता था **Yah/vah chaaval khaataa thaa.** He used to eat rice.
तू **Tuu** You	है **hai** is	था **thaa** was	यह/वह चावल खाता था **Tuu chaaval khaataa thaa.** You used to eat rice.
Fem., sing. +	Present Tense +	Past Tense	= Sentence
मैं **Maiñ** I	हूँ **huuñ** am	थी **thii** was	मैं चावल खाती थी **Maiñ chaaval khaatii thii.** I used to eat rice.
यह **Yah**/ वह **Vah** she	है **hai** is	थी **thii** was	यह/वह चावल खाती थी **Yah/vah chaaval khaatii thii.** She used to eat rice.

Fem., sing.+	Present Tense+	Past Tense	=	Sentence
तू **Tuu** You	है **hai** is	थी **thii** was		यह/वह चावल खाती थी **Tuu chaaval khaatii thii.** You used to eat rice.

Male pl. +	Present Tense+	Past Tense	=	Sentence
हम **Ham** We	हैं **haiñ** are	थे **the** were		हम चावल खाते थे **Ham chaaval khaate the.** We used to eat rice.
आप **Aap** You	हैं **haiñ** are	थे **the** were		आप चावल खाते थे **Ham chaaval khaate the.** You used to eat rice.
ये **Ye/** वे **Ve** He	हैं **haiñ** are	थे **the** were		ये/वे चावल खाते थे **Ye/Ve chaaval khaate the.** They used to eat rice.
तुम **Tum** You	हो **ho** be	थे **the** were		तुम चावल खाते थे **Tum chaaval khaate the.** You used to eat rice.

Fem., pl. +	Present Tense+	Past Tense	=	Sentence
हम **Ham** We	हैं **haiñ** are	थी **thiiñ** were		हम चावल खाती थीं **Ham chaaval khaatii thiiñ.** We used to eat rice.
आप **Aap** You	हैं **haiñ** are	थीं **thiiñ** were		आप चावल खाती थीं **Aap chaaval khaatii thiiñ.** You used to eat rice.
ये **Ye/**वे **Ve** They	हैं **haiñ** are	थीं **thiiñ** were		ये/वे चावल खाती थीं **Ye/Ve chaaval khaatii thiiñ.** They used to eat rice.
तुम **Tum** You	हो **ho** be	थीं **thiiñ** were		तुम चावल खाती थीं **Tum chaaval khaatii thiiñ.** You used to eat rice.

Pattern Practice 2

Practice forming these sentences in Hindi.

1. He used to throw a party for his birthday.
2. They used to go to the temple with their family.
3. The Indian people used to celebrate Diwali with a lot of pomp and show.
4. I used to meet my friends on my birthday.
5. She used to watch Hindi movies.

GRAMMAR NOTE — Passive Constructions—Expressing Likes and Dislikes in Hindi

माया को मिठाई पसंद है। **Maya ko miThaaii pasand hai**. The translation of this sentence is "Maya likes sweets." This statement is an example of the unique way of expressing likes and dislikes in Hindi.

In order to understand this, let's translate this sentence word-by-word. माया **Maya** को **ko** "to," मिठाई **miThaaii** "sweets," पसंद **pasand** "liking," है **hai** "is," that is, "Maya to sweets liking is" or essentially "the sweets are liked by Maya." This is rather grammatically awkward in English, but it is the culturally appropriate and most common way of expressing what you like in Hindi.

The verb usually agrees with the number and gender in Hindi sentences, such as तुम चावल खाती थीं **Tum chaaval khaatii thiiñ** "you (plural) used to eat rice" unless passive voice markers are inserted into the sentence. In this case, the verb becomes है **hai** "is" or था **thaa** or थी **the** "was" because it will agree with the logical object of the sentence—the thing being liked, for instance—or, if there is no object, it will go to the "default" masculine singular.

Remember that some pronouns change their suffix when followed by को **ko** "to." See page 67 for the chart.

Pattern Practice 3

Using the vocabulary and the grammar taught in this lesson, translate these statements to English.

1. माया को जन्मदिन पर क्या-क्या करना पसंद है?
   Maya ko janmdin par kyaa-kyaa karnaa pasand hai?
2. मुझको केक पसंद है।
   Mujh ko *cake* pasand hai.
3. कबीर को जन्मदिन पर क्या करना पसंद नहीं है?
   Kabir ko janmdin par kyaa karnaa pasand nahiñ hai?
4. कबीर जन्मदिन पर क्या-क्या करता है?
   Kabir janmdin par kyaa-kyaa kartaa hai?

Pattern Practice 4

Translate the following statements to English.

1. बचपन में, मैं सायकल चलाता था, लेकिन आजकल कार चलाता हूँ।
   Bachpan meñ, maiñ *cycle* chalaataa thaa, lekin aajkal *car* chalaataa huuñ.
2. बचपन में, हर दिन (every day) फुटबाल खेलता था/खेलती थी, लेकिन आजकल कभी-कभी खेलता/खेलती हूँ।
   Bachpan meñ, har din footbaal kheltaa thaa/kheltii thii, lekin aajkal kabhii-kabhii kheltaa/kheltii huuñ.
3. बचपन में, बहुत कार्टून देखता था/देखती थी, लेकिन आजकल बहुत खबरें (news) देखता/देखती हूँ।
   Bachpan meñ, bahut *cartoon* dekhtaa thaa/dekhtii thii, lekin aajkal bahut khabreñ dekhtaa huuñ/dekhtii huuñ.

EXERCISE 1

Write the Hindi translations of these words.

1. Indian way
2. and
3. to eat
4. liking
5. in childhood
6. sometimes
7. information
8. to do
9. friend
10. at, on

EXERCISE 2

Match the Hindi words below to their English meanings.

• धूम-धाम से **dhuum-dhaam se**	to decorate
• देखना **dekhnaa**	these days
• मंदिर **mandir**	to celebrate
• सजाना **sajaanaa**	to cut
• मनाना **manaanaa**	with pomp and show
• काटना **kaaTnaa**	to meet
• पूजा करना **puujaa karnaa**	temple
• आजकल **aajkal**	to worship
• मिलना **milnaa**	to see

EXERCISE 3

Select the right Hindi answer from the four options below.

1. to play
   - a. मिलना **milnaa**
   - b. खेलना **khelnaa**
   - c. खाना **khaanaa**
   - d. देखना **dekhnaa**
2. festival
   - a. तोहफ़ा (m) **tohfaa**
   - b. मंदिर (m) **mandir**
   - c. जानकारी (f) **jaankaarii**
   - d. त्योहार (m) **tyohaar**
3. to meet friends
   - a. पूजा करना **puujaa karnaa**
   - b. दोस्तों से मिलना **dostoñ se milnaa**
   - c. हिंदुस्तानी तरीका **hindustaanii tariikaa**
   - d. पार्टी करना *party* **karnaa**
4. Hindu Festival (festival of lamps)
   - a. सजाना **sajaanaa**
   - b. मिलना **milnaa**
   - c. बनाना **banaanaa**
   - d. दिवाली **divaalii**
5. fireworks
   - a. जानकारी (f) **jaankaarii**
   - b. दिवाली **divaalii**
   - c. आतिशबाज़ी (f) **aatishbaazii**
   - d. त्योहार (m) **tyohaar**
6. today
   - a. ऐसा **aisaa**
   - b. पर **par**
   - c. आज **aaj**
   - d. और **aur**
7. rice
   - a. खाना **khaanaa**
   - b. उमर (f) **umar**
   - c. आजकल **aajkal**
   - d. चावल (m) **chaaval**
8. There was no need of it/You shouldn't have.
   - a. X को ... पसंद है। **X ko... pasand hai.**
   - b. दोस्तों से मिलना **dostoñ se milnaa**
   - c. हिंदुस्तानी तरीका **hindustaanii tariikaa**
   - d. इसकी क्या ज़रूरत थी। **Is kii kyaa zaruurat thii.**
9. to touch
   - a. खेलना **khelnaa**
   - b. छूना **chhuunaa**
   - c. खाना **khaanaa**
   - d. करना **karnaa**
10. age
   - a. ऐसा **aisaa**
   - b. और **aur**
   - c. पर **par**
   - d. उमर (f) **umar**

EXERCISE 4
Circle the correct answer for the statements below.

1. तोहफ़ा (m) **tohfaa** = gift   True   False
2. ख़बरें (f) **khabreñ** = news   True   False
3. चलाना **chalaanaa** = to drive, ride   True   False
4. ऐसा **aisaa** = and   True   False
5. पार्टी करना **party karnaa** = to have a party, give a party   True   False
6. बनाना **banaanaa** = to celebrate   True   False
7. पाँव (m) **paanv** = feet   True   False
8. मुबारक हो ! **Mubaarak ho!** = with pomp and show   True   False
9. कपड़ा **kapRaa** = to cut   True   False
10. नया/नयी/नये **nayaa/nayii/naye** = new   True   False

CHECKLIST
Check the things you can do in Hindi:

- **Ask and describe how birthdays or festivals are celebrated**
- **Compare two events**
- **Talk about likes and dislikes**

A birthday celebration is a joyous occasion

LESSON 7
Being Invited to an Indian Wedding

Maya receives an invitation to a friend's sibling's wedding. You will learn about common practices in Hindu weddings, and wedding related terms. After this lesson you will be able to do the following:

- **Give and receive invitations**
- **Name the days in Hindi**

🎧 ┆DIALOGUE┆ **THE WEDDING INVITATION** (07-01)

Maya meets a friend from her university, Leela, who invites Maya to her brother's wedding.

Leela:	Hello Maya!
	Namaste Maya!
	नमस्ते माया !
Maya:	Hello Leela. How are you?
	Namaste Leela. Aao, tum kaisii ho?
	नमस्ते लीला। आओ, तुम कैसी हो?
Leela:	I'm fine. And you?
	Maiñ Thiik huuñ. Aur tum?
	मैं ठीक हूँ। और तुम?
Maya:	I'm fine too. Are you very busy nowadays?
	Maiñ bhii Thiik huuñ. Tum sunaao, kyaa aajkal bahut vyast ho?
	मैं भी ठीक हूँ। तुम सुनाओ, क्या आजकल बहुत व्यस्त हो?
Leela:	Yes Maya, I've been very busy. My older brother is getting married.
	Haañ Maya, bahut vyast huuñ. Mere baRe bhaaii kii shaadii hai.
	हाँ माया, बहुत व्यस्त हूँ। मेरे बड़े भाई की शादी है।
Maya:	Wow! That's great news! Congratulations!
	Vah! Yah to bahut <u>kh</u>ushii kii baat hai. Mubaarak ho!
	वाह! यह तो बहुत ख़ुशी की बात है। मुबारक हो !
Leela:	Thank you! You must come to my brother's wedding
	Shukriyaa! Tum ko mere bhaii kii shaadii meñ zaruur aanaa hai.
	शुक्रिया ! तुमको मेरे भाई की शादी में ज़रूर आना है।
Maya:	Sure, sure, why not? Which day is the wedding?
	Haañ, haañ, kyoñ nahiiñ. Shaadii kab hai?
	हाँ, हाँ क्यों नहीं। शादी कब है? कौन सा दिन है?

Leela: Next month, on 20th March. It's on a Friday.
            Ek mahiine baad, biis *March* ko. Us din Shukrvaar hai.
            एक महीने बाद, बीस मार्च को। उस दिन शुक्रवार है।
Maya: I see.
            Achchhaa.
            अच्छा।
Leela: Here's the invitation card. Be sure to come, don't forget!
            **Yah hai tumhaaraa nimantraN *card*. Zaruur aanaa, bhuulnaa
            nahiiñ.**
            यह है तुम्हारा निमंत्रण कार्ड। ज़रूर आना, भूलना नहीं !
Maya: Thanks for the invitation!
            NimantraN ke liye shukriyaa!
            निमंत्रण के लिये शुक्रिया !

Vocabulary List (07–02)

सुनाना	**sunaanaa**	to narrate
सुनना	**sunnaa**	to listen, hear
बहुत	**bahut**	very
व्यस्त	**vyast**	busy
शादी (f)	**shaadii**	wedding, marriage
ख़ुशी (f)	**khushii**	happiness
शुक्रिया	**shukriyaa**	thank you
ख़ुशी की बात	**khushii kii baat**	a thing of happiness; a happy event, great news
ज़रूर	**zaruur**	sure
क्यों नहीं	**kyoñ nahiiñ**	why not
मुबारक हो	**mubaarak ho**	congratulations
कब	**kab**	when
महीना (m)	**mahiinaa**	month
बीस	**biis**	twenty
शुक्रवार	**Shukrvaar**	Friday
निमंत्रण	**nimantraN**	invitation (adj.)

| भूलना | **bhoolanaa** | to forget |
| शादी में ज़रूर पधारें ! | **Shaadii meñ zaruur padhaareñ!** | You must come to the wedding! |

Supplementary Vocabulary

Days of the Week

सोमवार	**Somvaar**	Monday
मंगलवार	**Mangalvaar**	Tuesday
बुधवार	**Budhvaar**	Wednesday
गुरूवार	**Guruuvaar**	Thursday
शुक्रवार	**Shukrvaar**	Friday
शनिवार	**Shanivaar**	Saturday
रविवार	**Ravivaar**	Sunday

Useful Time Words

दिन	**din**	day
हफ़्ता	**haftaa**	week
महीना	**mahiinaa**	month
साल	**saal**	year
हफ़्ते की छुट्टी	**hafte kii chhuttii**	weekend
शाम को	**shaam ko**	in the evening
रात को	**raat ko**	in the night
सुबह	**subah**	morning
दोपहर में	**dopahar meñ**	in the afternoon
आधी रात को	**aadhii raat ko**	at midnight
सुबह-सुबह	**subah-subah**	early in the morning
हमेशा	**hameshaa**	always
कभी-कभी	**kabhii-kabhii**	sometimes
कभी नहीं	**kabhii nahiñ**	never
आम तौर से	**aam-taur se**	usually

CULTURAL NOTE ### Congratulating Someone at Their Wedding (07–03)

In the conversation above, Maya congratulates Leela with **Mubaarak ho!** which is also used to congratulate people on their birthdays (as we saw in Lesson 6). Other phrases she can use include शादी मुबारक हो! **Shaadii mubaarak ho!** "Congratulations on getting married!," शादी की बहुत बहुत शुभकामनाएँ! **Shaadii kii bahut bahut shubhkaamnaaeñ!** "Best wishes on (your) wedding!" or even आपकी जोड़ी सलामत रहे ! **Aap kii joRii salaamat rahe!** "May you (couple) be safe!"

If she wanted to say that the couple is beautiful (that is, good-looking or very suitable for each other), she can say आपकी जोड़ी बहुत सुंदर है। **Aap kii joRii bahut sundar hai**.

CULTURAL NOTE ### Indian Wedding Invitations

In India, the wedding guest list may not be restricted to just the couple's friends and relatives, but you'll notice that even the parents' and siblings' friends will attend. It's quite common for the number of people at an Indian wedding to number in the thousands, many of whom the bride and groom may not even know.

Indian weddings are lavish affairs that always include music and dancing

Pattern Practice 1

Write the following sentences out in Hindi in the blanks provided.

1. This is your invitation card.

_____

2. Don't forget. Make sure you come.

_____

3. Thanks for inviting me.

_____

Pattern Practice 2

Read out the Hindi equivalent of these words.

1. whose
2. to look happy
3. bride
4. Thank you for your help
5. yesterday, tomorrow
6. twenty one
7. red

GRAMMAR NOTE The Present Continuous Tense

The Hindi sentence for "I am eating food" is मैं खाना खा रहा/रही हूँ। **Meñ khaanaa khaa rahaa/rahii huuñ**, expressing a continuing action. The last three words खा रहा/रही हूँ **khaa rahii huuñ** are translated as "am eating." This is made up of the verb root खा **khaa**, रहा/रही **rahii/rahaa** (the equivalent of the English suffix "-ing") and followed by the verb "to be" हूँ **huuñ** "am." The added words रहा/रही **rahii/rahaa** and the verb "to be" agree with the number and gender of the subject. This means the verb root does not change—only the suffix "-ing" and the copula "to be" change to correspond with the subject.

Here are some examples of how to construct such a sentence using the structure: Subject + Verb + Verb root + "ing" + "to be."

1. **Singular Male Subject**

   यह खाना खा रहा है   or वह खाना खा रहा है।
   Yah khaanaa khaa rahaa hai or **Vah khaanaa khaa rahaa hai.**
   He is eating.

   तू खाना खा रहा है। **Tuu khaanaa khaa rahaa hai.** You are eating.

2. **Singular Female Subject**

यह खाना खा रही है   or वह खाना रही है।
Yah khaanaa khaa rahii hai or **Vah khaanaa khaa rahii rai.**
She is eating.

तू खाना खा रही है। **Tuu khaanaa khaa rahii hai.** You are eating.

3. **First Person Singular Subject**

(m) मैं खाना खा रहा हूँ। **Maiñ khaanaa khaa rahaa huuñ.** I am eating.

(f) मैं खाना खा रही हूँ। **Maiñ khaanaa khaa rahii huuñ.** I am eating.

4. **Plural Subjects for "We, You, They" (male)**

हम खाना खा रहे हैं। **Ham khaanaa khaa rahe haiñ.** We are eating.

आप खाना खा रहे हैं। **Aap khaanaa khaa rahe haiñ.**
You (formal) are eating.

ये खाना खा रहे हैं   or वे खाना खा रहे हैं।
Ye khaanaa khaa rahe haiñ or **Ve khaanaa khaa rahe haiñ.**
They are eating.

तुम खाना खा रहे हो। **Tum khaanaa khaa rahe ho.**
You (informal) are eating.

The bridegroom receiving blessings from his mother on his wedding day

5. **Plural Subjects for "We, You, They" (female)**

हम खाना खा रही हैं। **Ham khaanaa khaa rahii haiñ.** We are eating.

आप खाना खा रही हैं। **Aap khaanaa khaa rahii haiñ.**
You (formal) are eating.

ये खाना खा रही हैं   or वे खाना खा रही हैं।
Ye khaanaa khaa rahe haiñ or **Ve khaanaa khaa rahee haiñ.**
They are eating.

तुम खाना खा रही हो। **Tum khaanaa khaa rahii ho.**
You (informal) are eating.

Pattern Practice 3

Select the correct form of the verb below.

1. मैं (m) एक हिंदी फ़िल्म देख _____ (रहा / रहे / रही) हूँ।

   Maiñ ek Hindi film dekh_____ **(rahaa/rahe/rahii) huuñ.**

2. आप आज क्या _____(करना / कर) रही हैं?

   Aap aaj kyaa _____ **(karnaa/kar) rahii haiñ?**

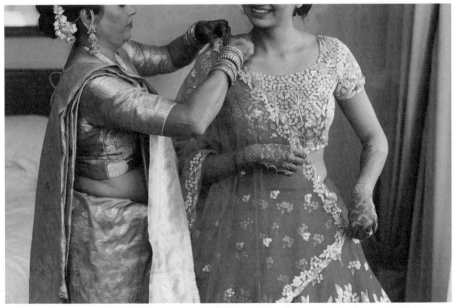

An Indian bride preparing for her big day

3. वे लोग भारत जा _____ (रहा / रहे / रही) हैं।

   Ve log bhaarat jaa _____ **(rahaa/rahe/rahii) haiñ.**

4. माया ख़ुश लग _____ (रहा / रहे / रही) है।

   Maya khush lag _____ **(rahaa/rahe/rahii) hai.**

5. मैं हिंदी _____ (सीखना / सीख "to learn") रहा हूँ।

   Maiñ Hindi _____ **(siikhnaa/siikh) rahaa huuñ.**

EXERCISE 1

Write the Hindi translations of these words.

1. to listen, hear _____ 2. why not _____

3. congratulations _____ 4. wedding, marriage _____

5. Friday _____ 6. to narrate _____

Family and friends with the bridal couple

EXERCISE 2

Circle the correct translation of the words given below.

1. invitation (adj.)
   a. व्यस्त **vyast**
   b. शुक्रिया **shukriyaa**
   c. निमंत्रण **nimantraN**
   d. सुनाना **sunaanaa**
2. when
   a. बीस **biis**
   b. बहुत **bahut**
   c. ज़रूर **zaruur**
   d. कब **kab**
3. a thing of happiness
   a. ख़ुशी **khushii** (f)
   b. शुक्रवार **shukrvaar**
   c. ख़ुशी की बात **khushii kii baat**
   d. शुक्रिया **shukriyaa**
4. happiness
   a. ख़ुशी **khushii** (f)
   b. बीस **biis**
   c. शादी **shaadii** (f)
   d. सुनना **sunnaa**
5. very
   a. कब **kab**
   b. बीस **biis**
   c. ज़रूर **zaruur**
   d. बहुत **bahut**
6. thank you
   a. शुक्रवार **shukrvaar**
   b. शुक्रिया **shukriyaa**
   c. सुनना **sunnaa**
   d. सुनाना **sunaanaa**

EXERCISE 3

Circle the correct answer for the statements below.

1. बीस **biis** = very	True	False
2. व्यस्त **vyast** = busy	True	False
3. महीना **mahiinaa** (m) = to listen, hear	True	False
4. भूलना **bhuulnaa** = to forget	True	False
5. ज़रूर **zaruur** = sure	True	False
6. उपहार **upahaar** (m) = question	True	False

CHECKLIST

Can you do the following things in Hindi now?

- **Invite someone to a party, wedding, etc.**
- **Name the days in Hindi**

Maya, kyaa baat hai?
What's up, Maya?

Maiñ ek shaadii meñ jaa rahii huuñ.
I'm going to a wedding tomorrow.

Vah! Yah to bahut achchhi baat hai.
Wow! That's a very happy event.

To aap shaadii meñ kyaa pehen rahii haiñ?
What will you be wearing to the wedding?

Maiñ gulaabii saaRii pehen rahii huuñ.
I am wearing a pink sari.

Aur kuchh phuul le jaa rahii huuñ.
I'm also taking some flowers.

Haañ saaRii Thiik hai.
Yes, the sari will be fine.

Shaadii ke liye kaunsaa uphaar achchhaa hai?
What is a good wedding gift?

Kuchh bhii Thiik hai. Lekin shaadii meñ shagun ke rupaye denaa hai.
Anything is fine, but it would be good to give them an auspicious sum of money.

LESSON 8
Indian Wedding Customs

Maya is excited to attend Leela's brother's wedding. A day before the wedding, she has some questions. She asks Kabir for help. After this lesson, you should be able to:

- **Count from 1–100 in Hindi**
- **Identify some of the unique customs in a wedding**
- **Identify auspicious numbers in Hindi**

🎧 ┆ DIALOGUE ┆ **BEING A WEDDNG GUEST** (08–01)

Kabir:	What's up Maya? You look like you're very happy today.
	Maya, kyaa baat hai? Aaj aap bahut <u>kh</u>ush lag rahii haiñ?
	माया, क्या बात है? आज आप बहुत खुश लग रही हैं?
Maya:	Yes, I'm going to a wedding tomorrow.
	Jii haañ. Maiñ ek shaadii meñ jaa rahii huuñ.
	जी हाँ। मैं एक शादी में जा रही हूँ।
Kabir:	Wow! That's a very happy event. Whose wedding is it?
	Vah! Yah to bahut achchhi baat hai. Kis kii shaadii hai?
	वाह ! यह तो बहुत खुशी की बात है। किसकी शादी है?
Maya:	It's Leela's brother's wedding.
	Leelaa ke bhaaii kii shaadii hai.
	लीला के भाई की शादी है।
Kabir:	I see! What will you be wearing to the wedding?
	Achchhaa! To aap shaadii meñ kyaa pehen rahii haiñ?
	अच्छा ! तो आप शादी में क्या पहन रही हैं?
Maya:	I am wearing a pink sari. I'm also taking some flowers.
	Maiñ gulaabii saaRii pehen rahii huuñ. Aur kuchh phuul le jaa rahii huuñ.
	मैं गुलाबी साड़ी पहन रही हूँ। और कुछ फूल ले जा रही हूँ।
Kabir:	Yes, the sari will be fine.
	Haañ saaRii Thiik hai.
	हाँ, साड़ी ठीक है।

Maya: I have a question. What is a good wedding gift?

Ek sawaal hai. Shaadii ke liye kaunsaa uphaar achchhaa hai?

एक सवाल है. शादी के लिये कौनसा उपहार अच्छा है?

Kabir: Anything is fine. But it would be good to give them an auspicious sum of money.

Kuchh bhii Thiik hai. Lekin shaadii meñ shagun ke rupaye denaa hai.

कुछ भी ठीक है। लेकिन शादी में शगुन के रुपये देना अच्छा है।

Maya: What is "**shagun ke rupaye?**"

Shagun ke rupaye kyaa hai?

शगुन के रुपये क्या है?

Kabir: Put the money in an envelope to pass to the bride and groom.

Log kuchh rupaye ek lifaafe meñ duulhaa-dulhan ko dete haiñ.

लोग कुछ रुपये एक लिफ़ाफ़े में दूल्हा-दुल्हन को देते हैं।

Maya: How much would be good?

Kitne rupaye achchhe haiñ?

कितने रुपये अच्छे हैं?

Kabir: It's up to you. The auspicious numbers are 11, 21, 51, 101 and 501.

Jitnii aap kii marzii. Gyaarah, ikkiis, ikyaawan, ek sau ek, paañch sau ek, achchhaa shagun haiñ.

जितनी आपकी मर्ज़ी ग्यारह, इक्कीस, इक्यावन, एक सौ एक, पाँच सौ एक ठीक हैं।

Maya: Thank you for your help.

Madad ke liye shukriya.

मदद के लिये शुक्रिया।

Maya: What are the customs in a Hindu wedding?

Ek aam shaadii mein kyaa riiti-rivaaz hote haiñ?

एक आम शादी में क्या रीति-रिवाज़ होते हैं?

Kabir: Usually there are three special customs in Hindu weddings.

Aamtaur se Hindu shaadii meñ tiin khaas riiti-rivaaz hote haiñ.

आमतौर से हिंदू शादी में तीन ख़ास रीति-रिवाज़ होते हैं?

Maya: What are these?

Kaun-kaun se?

कौन-कौन से?

Ek aam shaadii mein kyaa riiti-rivaaj hote haiñ?
What are the customs in a Hindu wedding?

Aamtaur se Hindu shaadii meñ tiin <u>kh</u>aas riiti-rivaaz hote haiñ.
Usually there are three special customs in Hindu weddings.

Kaun-kaun se?
What are these?

Mehandii, mahilaa sangiit, aur phere.
Henna, a bridal shower, and walking around the holy fire.

Mehandii meñ duulhaa-dulhan ke paarivaar ke logoñ ko mehandii lagaate haiñ.
At the henna party, henna is drawn on the palms of the female family members of the bride and groom.

Mahilaa sangiit meiñ aurateñ naachtii-gaatii haiñ.
Women play music, sing and dance at the bridal shower.

Aur phere meñ duulhaa-dulhan aag ke chaaroñ aur saat chakkar lagaate haiñ.
And, the bride and groom will have to walk in circles around the holy fire seven times.

Madad ke liye shukriyaa!
Thanks for your help!

Koii baat nahiiñ.
There's nothing to thank (me for).

Kabir:　　　Henna, a bridal shower, and walking around the holy fire.

Mehandii, mahilaa sangiit, aur phere.

मेंहदी, महिला संगीत, और फेरे।

At the henna party, henna is drawn on the palms of the female family members of the bride and groom.

Mehandii meñ duulhaa-dulhan ke parivaar ke logoñ ko mehandii lagaate haiñ.

मेंहदी में लोग दूल्हा-दुल्हन के परिवार के लोगों को मेंहदी लगाते हैं।

Women play music, sing and dance at the bridal shower.

Mahilaa sangiit meiñ aurateñ naachtii-gaatii haiñ.

महिला-संगीत में औरतें नाचती-गाती हैं।

And, the bride and groom will have to walk in circles around the holy fire seven times.

Aur phere meñ duulhaa-dulhan aag ke chaaroñ aur saat chakkar lagaate haiñ.

और, फेरे में दूल्हा-दुल्हन आग के चारों ओर सात चक्कर लगाते हैं।

Maya:　　　Thanks for your help!

Madad ke liye shukriyaa!

मदद के लिये शुक्रिया !

Kabir:　　　There's nothing to thank (me for).

Koii baat nahiiñ.

कोई बात नहीं।

Henna decoration on the palms of the bridal couple's female family members

Vocabulary List (08–02)

शगुन (m)	**shagun**	auspicious time; wedding gift consisting of an auspicious amount of money
रुपये (m)	**rupaye**	Indian currency, money
लिफ़ाफ़ा (m)	**lifaafaa**	envelope
दूल्हा	**duulhaa**	groom
दुल्हन	**dulhan**	bride
जितनी आपकी मर्ज़ी	**jitnii aapkii marzii**	however much you like; up to you
मदद (f)	**madad**	help
मदद के लिये शुक्रिया	**Madad ke liye shukriyaa.**	Thank you for (your) help.
कोई बात नहीं	**koii baat nahiiñ**	never mind
रीति (f)	**riiti**	customs/norms
रिवाज़ (m)	**rivaaz**	customs, traditions
रीति-रिवाज़	**riiti-rivaaz**	ceremonies, customs
ख़ास	<u>**kh**</u>**aas**	special, important
मेंहदी (f)	**mehandii**	henna
मेंहदी लगाना	**mehandii lagaanaa**	to apply henna
महिला/औरत	**mahilaa/aurat**	woman
संगीत (m)	**sangiit**	music
महिला संगीत	**mahilaa sangiit**	the Hindu equivalent of a bridal shower, where women play music and sing songs (usually poking fun at the groom)
फेरे (m)	**phere**	the custom of walking in circles around a holy fire to recite their wedding vows to the God of Fire, Agnideva, who witnesses and blesses the couple's union
नाचना	**naachnaa**	to dance
गाना	**gaanaa**	to sing
आग (f)	**aag**	fire

चक्कर लगाना	**chakkar/lagaanaa**	to go around something in circles
चारों ओर	**chaaroñ aur**	around (all four directions)
किसका/किसकी/ किसके	**kisaa/kiskii/kiske**	whose
पहनना	**pehenanaa**	to wear
लाल	**laal**	red
साड़ी (f)	**saarii**	sari
सवाल (m)	**sawaal**	question
कौनसा/कौनसी/ कौनसे	**kaunsaa/kaunsii/ kaunse**	which (one)
उपहार (m)	**upahaar**	gift
कुछ भी	**kuchh bhii**	anything

Supplementary Vocabulary

Auspicious Numbers

ग्यारह	**gyaarah**	eleven
इक्कीस	**ikkiis**	twenty one
इक्यावन	**ikyaawan**	fifty one
एक सौ पाँच	**ek sau ek**	one hundred and one
पाँच सौ एक	**paañch sau ek**	five hundred and one

Indian currency—notes and coins

CULTURAL NOTE *Shagun* "An Auspicious Time or Gift"

शगुन **Shagun** (m) is a Sanskrit word that means "an auspicious time." In India, Hindus use their calendar to arrange for important events to start at an auspicious time. **Shagun** can also mean an auspicious gift given at the time of an event like a wedding. At such events, people often prefer to give money rather than gifts. In Indian culture, figures ending in a one (that is, 101, 501) are considered to be auspicious. Also, your Indian friends will likely open your gift when you are not around.

CULTURAL NOTE Walking Around the Fire

During a Hindu wedding, the "Seven Steps" occur when the bride is led by the groom in seven rounds (each considered to be a "step") around the fire. The priest will chant seven blessings or vows to bless them with a strong marriage. By walking around the fire, they are assenting to these vows. As they walk they also often throw puffed rice into the fire, a sign of prosperity in their new life together. This part of the ceremony is considered to seal the bond between the couple forever.

The bride is led by the groom to go around the fire seven times

Pattern Practice 1

Translate these sentences into Hindi.

1. They apply henna on their hands.
2. They are walking around the fire.
3. They sing and dance.
4. They go to a wedding.
5. There are special customs in Hindu weddings.

Pattern Practice 2

Answer these questions in Hindi.

1. What are the special customs at an Indian wedding?
2. What are the auspicious numbers in Indian culture?
3. What do people do at the bridal shower?
4. What type of wedding gifts should one give?

Pattern Practice 3

Using the vocabulary and the grammar taught in this lesson, translate these statements into English.

1. माया लीला के भाई की शादी में जा रही है।
   Maya Leela ke bhaaii kii shaadii meiñ jaa rahii hai.
2. हिंदू शादी में तीन ख़ास रीति-रिवाज होते हैं।
   Hinduu shaadii meñ tiin khaas riiti-rivaaj hote haiñ.
3. माया गुलाबी साड़ी पहन रही है।
   Maya gulaabii saaRii pehen rahii hai.
4. माया शादी के लिये फूल ले जा रही है।
   Maya shaadii ke liye phuul le jaa rahii hai.

Pattern Practice 4

Translate the following from Hindi into English.

1. आज मैं सायकल चला रहा हूँ, लेकिन आम तौर पर मैं कार चलाता हूँ।
   Aaj maiñ *cycle* chala rahaa huuñ, lekin aam taur par *car* chalaataa huuñ.
2. हमारे बच्चे फुटबाल खेल रहे हैं। **Hamaare bachche *football* khel rahe haiñ.**
3. मेरी बहनें अभी ख़बरें (news) देख रही हैं।
   Merii beheneñ abhii khabreñ dekh rahii haiñ.

4. महिला-संगीत में औरतें क्या करती हैं?
   Mahila sangiit meñ aurateñ kyaa kartii haiñ?

5. फेरे में क्या होता है?
   Phere meñ kyaa hotaa hai?

EXERCISE 1

Read the dialogue again and answer these questions in Hindi.

1. माया क्यों ख़ुश लग रही है?
   Maya kyoñ <u>kh</u>ush lag rahii hai?

2. शादी में माया क्या पहन रही है?
   Shaadii meiñ Maya kyaa pehen rahii hai?

3. शगुन के कितने रुपये ठीक हैं?
   Shagun ke kitne rupaye Thiik haiñ?

4. आजकल लीला क्यों व्यस्त है?
   Aajkal Leela kyoñ vyast hai?

5. किसकी शादी है?
   Kiskii shadii hai?

Indian women preparing boron dala *(assortment of goodies) for the wedding ceremony*

6. शादी कब है?
   Shaadii kab hai?

7. आमतौर में एक हिंदू शादी में कौनसे खास रीति-रिवाज होते हैं?
   Aamtaur se ek Hindu shaadii meñ kaunse khaas riiti-rivaaj hote haiñ?

8. मेंहदी में लोग क्या करते हैं?
   Mehendii meñ log kyaa karte haiñ?

EXERCISE 2

Write the Hindi equivalents of these words:

1. music _____

2. to dance _____

3. henna _____

4. ceremonies, customs _____

5. around (all four directions) _____

EXERCISE 3

Circle the correct Hindi translation for the following English words.

1. Indian currency, money
   a. उपहार **Upahaar** (m)   b. साड़ी **SaaRii** (f)
   c. सवाल **Savaal** (m)   d. रुपये **Rupaye** (m)
2. question
   a. शगुन **shagun** (m)   b. मदद **madad** (f)
   c. उपहार **upahaar** (m)   d. सवाल **savaal** (m)
3. auspicious time
   a. सवाल **savaal** (m)   b. मदद **madad** (f)
   c. शगुन **shagun** (m)   d. साड़ी **saaRii** (f)
4. one hundred and one
   a. लिफ़ाफ़ा **lifaafaa** (m)   b. इक्यावन **ikyaawan**
   c. एक सौ पाँच **ek sau paañch**   d. खुश लगना <u>khush laganaa</u>
5. eleven
   a. ग्यारह **gyaarah**   b. इक्यावन **ikyaawan**
   c. दूल्हा **duulhaa**   d. दुल्हन **dulhan**

6. What is the matter?

    a. ग्यारह **Gyaarah**

    b. क्या बात है? **Kyaa baat hai?**

    c. लिफ़ाफ़ा **Lifaafaa** (m)

    d. कौन-कौन से? **Kaun-kaun se?**

7. to go around something in circles

    a. फेरे लगाना **phere lagaanaa**

    b. मेंहदी लगाना **mehandii lagaanaa**

    c. महिला संगीत **mahilaa sangiit**

    d. चक्कर लगाना **chakkar lagaanaa**

8. customs/norms

    a. रीति **riiti** (f)

    b. संगीत **sangiit** (m)

    c. फेरे **phere** (m)

    d. महिला संगीत **mahilaa sangiit**

9. women

    a. नाचना **naachnaa**

    b. औरत **aurat**

    c. गाना **gaanaa**

    d. महिला **mahilaa**

10. to go around the holy fire in circles

    a. चक्कर लगाना **chakkar lagaanaa**

    b. फेरे लगाना **phere lagaanaa**

    c. गाना **gaanaa**

    d. मेंहदी लगाना **mehandii lagaanaa**

A stunning Indian bride dressed in traditional wedding clothes embroidered with gold

EXERCISE 4

Read the words and phrases below and circle the correct answer.

1. मदद **madad** (f) = red	True	False
2. ख़ुश **<u>kh</u>ush** = happy	True	False
3. कुछ भी **kuchh bhii** = anything	True	False
4. पाँच सौ एक **paañch sau ek** = five hundred and one	True	False
5. कोई बात नहीं **koii baat nahiiñ** = What is the matter?	True	False
6. महिला संगीत **mahilaa sangiit** = the Hindu version of a bachelorette party	True	False
7. रिवाज़ **rivaaz** (m) = customs/norms	True	False
8. आग **aag** (f) = special, important	True	False
9. ख़ास **khaas** = to sing	True	False

EXERCISE 5

Match the Hindi words below to their English meanings.

- कौनसा **kaunsaa**   envelope
- लिफ़ाफ़ा **lifaafaa** (m)   however much you like

Bridal couple putting garland flowers in a ritual ceremony

• दूल्हा **duulhaa**	to wear
• साड़ी **saaRii** (f)	which (one)
• जितनी आपकी मर्ज़ी **jitnii aapkii marzii**	fifty one
• इक्यावन **ikyaawan**	groom
• पहनना **pehennaa**	sari
• फेरे **phere** (m)	woman
• गाना **gaanaa**	to sing
• औरत **aurat**	to apply henna
• मेंहदी लगाना **mehandii lagaanaa**	circles (around holy fire)

CHECKLIST

Are you able to do the following things in Hindi now?

- **Count from 1–100 in Hindi**
- **Identify some of the unique customs in a wedding**
- **Identify auspicious numbers in Hindi**

Bridal couple in traditional dress

Gopura (tall pyramid-like gateway) in the Kapaleeshwarar Temple in Chennai

LESSON 9
Planning a Trip

Maya's school will be closed for a week for their vacation. Maya is planning a trip to South India. After this lesson you will be able to do these functions:

- **Discuss planning a trip**
- **Talk about where you want to go**
- **Reserve a hotel room**
- **Negotiate the price**

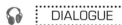 **BOOKING A HOTEL ROOM** (09–01)

Kabir asks Maya about her plans during the one-week vacation.

Kabir:	Maya, what are you doing on your vacation?
	Maya, aap chhuTTiyoñ meñ kyaa kar rahii haiñ?
	माया, आप छुट्टियों में क्या कर रही हैं?
Maya:	I'm thinking of going to the south of India.
	Maiñ dakShiN bhaarat jaane ke baare meñ soch rahii huuñ.
	मैं दक्षिण भारत जाने के बारे में सोच रही हूँ।
Kabir:	That's a good idea. South India has many sights worth seeing.
	Achchha vichaar hai. dakShiN bhaarat meñ dekhne laayak bahut jagaheñ haiñ.
	अच्छा विचार है। दक्षिण भारत में देखने लायक बहुत जगहें हैं।
Maya:	Yes.
	Jii, haañ.
	जी हाँ।
Kabir:	Where will you be going?
	Aap kahaañ-kahaañ jaaeñgii?
	आप कहाँ-कहाँ जाएँगी?
Maya:	I will go to Kerala, Chennai and Mysore.
	Maiñ Kerala, Chennai, aur Mysore jaauuñgii.
	मैं केरल, चैन्नई, और मैसूर जाऊँगी।
Kabir:	When will you be booking a hotel?
	Aap _hotel_ kab _book_ kareñgii?
	आप होटल कब बुक करेंगी?

Maya:	This evening. Thanks for the reminder!

Aaj shaam ko. Yaad dilaane ke liye bahut bahut shukriyaa!
आज शाम को। याद दिलाने के लिये शुक्रिया !

That evening, Maya calls the hotel she wants to stay in.

Maya: Hello! Is this the Maharani Hotel?
Namaste! Kyaa yah Mahaaraanii hotel hai?
नमस्ते ! क्या यह महारानी होटल है?

Receptionist: Hi, yes this is the Empress hotel. How can I be of service?
Namaste! Jii haañ, yah Mahaaraanii hotel hai. Kahiye kyaa sevaa karuuñ?
नमस्ते ! जी हाँ, यह महारानी होटल है। कहिये क्या सेवा करूँ?

Maya: Yes, I need a room for three days.
Jii, mujhe tiin din ke liye ek kamraa chaahiye.
जी, मुझे तीन दिन के लिये एक कमरा चाहिये।

Receptionist: From what date to what date?
Kis taariikh se kis taariikh tak?
किस तारीख़ से किस तारीख़ तक?

Maya: 10th to 12th December.
Das Disambar se baarah Disambar tak.
दस दिसंबर से बारह दिसंबर तक।

Receptionist: That's fine. We have a room.
Thiik hai. Hamaare paas ek kamaraa hai.
ठीक है। हमारे पास कमरा है।

Maya: How much will it cost?
Kiraayaa kitnaa hai?
किराया कितना है?

Receptionist: 800 rupees a day. Tax not included.
AaTh sau rupaye pratidin. Tax alag se lagegaa.
आठ सौ रुपये प्रतिदिन। टैक्स अलग से लगेगा।

Maya: It is too expensive. I am a student, could you lower the price please?
Yah to bahut zyaadaa hai. Maiñ vidyaarthii huuñ, kuchh kam kiijye.
यह तो बहुत ज़्यादा है। मैं विद्यार्थी हूँ, कुछ कम कीजिये।

Receptionist: 700 rupees for you. Is that okay? This will be the lowest price.

Aap ke liye saat sau rupaye. Thiik hai? Is se kam nahiiñ hogaa.

आपके लिये सात सौ रुपये। ठीक है? इस से कम नहीं होगा।

Maya: Okay. Is breakfast included in the price?

Thiik hai. Kyaa kiraaye meñ subah kaa naashtaa shaamil hai?

ठीक है। क्या किराये में सुबह का नाश्ता शामिल है?

Receptionist: Yes. Also, our hotel has free Internet, a swimming pool and gym too.

Jii haañ. Aur, hamaare *hotel* meñ muft *Internet*, *swimming pool*, aur *gym* bhii hai.

जी हाँ। और हमारे होटल में मुफ़्त इंटरनेट, स्वीमिंग पूल, और जिम भी है।

Maya: Okay. Please book the hotel room then.

Jii Thiik hai. To kamraa *book* kiijiye.

जी ठीक है। तो कमरा बुक कीजिये।

Receptionist: Okay.

Thiik hai.

ठीक है।

Vocabulary List (09–02)

छुट्टी (f)	**chhuTTii**	day off, vacation
छुट्टियों में	**chhuTTiyoñ meñ**	on vacation
दक्षिण भारत	**dakShiN bhaarat**	South India
विचार (m)	**vichaar**	thought, idea
के बारे में	**ke baare meñ**	about
सोचना	**sochnaa**	to think
देखने लायक	**dekhne laayak**	worth seeing
जगह (f)	**jagah**	place
जगहें (f)	**jagaheñ**	places
बुक करना	***book* karnaa**	to book, reserve
शाम को	**shaam ko**	in the evening
याद दिलाना	**yaad dilaanaa**	to remind

याद दिलाने के लिये	yaad dilaane ke liye	for reminding
सेवा (f)	sevaa	service
सेवा करना	sevaa karnaa	to serve
कहिये	kahiye	please say
क्या सेवा करूँ?	Kyaa sevaa karuuñ?	How can I be of service?
के लिये	ke liye	for
मुझे कमरा चाहिये	Mujhe kamraa chaahiye.	I need a room.
तारीख़ (f)	taariikh	date
किस तारीख़ से किस तारीख़ तक	kis taariikh se kis taariikh tak	from what date to what date
X के पास	X ke paas	X has
हमारे पास	hamaare paas	we have
किराया (m)	kiraayaa	rent/cost
सौ	sau	100
कितना	kitnaa	how much
प्रतिदिन	pratidin	per day
लगना	lagnaa	to be applied, to attach
अलग से	alag se	separately
अलग से लगेगा	alag se lagegaa	will be applied separately
तो	to	indeed, definitely
कुछ	kuchh	some, little
ज़्यादा	zyaadaa	more, much
बहुत ज़्यादा	bahut zyaadaa	a lot, too much
विद्यार्थी	vidyaarthii	student
कम	kam	less, low
कुछ कम कीजिये	kuchh kam kiijiye	please lower (the price) a little
आप के लिये	aap ke liye	for you
इस से कम	is se kam	less than this
सुबह	subah	morning

नाश्ता	naashtaa	breakfast, snack
शामिल	shaamil	included
मुफ़्त	muft	free of charge
आपकी यात्रा सुरक्षित रहे !	Aap kii yaatra surakshit rahe!	Have a safe trip!
यात्रा का मज़ा लीजिये !	Yaatraa kaa mazaa kiijiye!	Have a fun trip!
आपके होटल में क्या-सुविधाएँ हैं?	Aap ke *hotel* meñ kyaa kyaa suvidhaaeñ haiñ?	What facilities does your hotel have?
क्या गरम पानी की सुविधा है?	Kyaa garam paanii kii suvidhaa hai?	Does your hotel have hot water?

Supplementary Vocabulary
Useful Phrases

क्या यहाँ कोई कमरा/अपार्टमेंट ख़ाली है?	Kyaa yahaan koii kamraa/*apartment* khaalii hai?	Is there any vacant room/apartment?
कमरे/अपार्टमेंट का किराया क्या है?	Kamre/*apartment* kaa kiraayaa kyaa hai?	What is the rent for (the) room/apartment?
कमरे में क्या-क्या होगा?	Kamre meñ kyaa-kyaa hogaa?	What furnishings does the room have?
पंखा, फ़्रिज, कूलर, वग़ैरह	pankhaa, *fridge*, kooler, vagairah	fan, refrigerator, cooler etc.
क्या गुसलख़ाना/बाथरूम कमरे/अपार्टमेंट में है?	Kyaa ghusalkhaanaa/*bathroom* kamre/*apartment* meñ hai?	Is there an attached bathroom in the room/apartment?
क्या यहाँ पर मुफ़्त वाई-फ़ाई है?	Kyaa yahaañ par muft *Wifi* hai?	Do you have free Wi-Fi?
वाई-फ़ाई का पासवार्ड क्या है?	*Wifi* kaa *password* kyaa hai?	What's the Wi-Fi password?

CULTURAL NOTE Social Media Phrases (09-03)

Most social media applications are pronounced as you would in English. Here are some useful phrases:

Please add me on Facebook. **Mujhe *Facebook* par joRiye/*add* kiijiye.**
मुझे फ़ेसबुक पर जोड़िये/ऐड कीजिये।

Please follow me on Instagram/Twitter.
Mujhe *Instagram/Twitter* par *follow* kiijiye.
मुझे इंस्टाग्राम/ट्विटर पर फ़ॉलो कीजिये।

Let's take a selfie. **Aaeñ *selfie* khiiñcheñ.** आएँ सेल्फ़ी खींचें।

Pattern Practice 1

Read the text and answer the questions provided.

1. माया छुट्टियों में क्या कर रही है?
   Maya chhuTTiyoñ meñ kyaa kar rahii hai?
2. क्या दक्षिण भारत में देखने लायक बहुत जगहें हैं?
   Kyaa dakShiN bhaarat meñ dekhne laayak bahut jagaheñ haiñ?
3. माया कहाँ-कहाँ जा रही है?
   Maya kahaañ-kahaañ jaa rahii hai?
4. माया होटल कब बुक करेगी?
   Maya *hotel* kab *book* karegii?
5. माया कहाँ रुकेगी?
   Maya kahaañ rukegii?
6. वह कितने दिन रुकेगी? कब से कब तक?
   Vah kitne din rukegii? Kab se kab tak?
7. होटल का किराया क्या है?
   Hotel kaa kiraayaa kyaa hai?
8. माया के लिये होटल का किराया क्या है?
   Maya ke liye *hotel* kaa kiraayaa kyaa hai?
9. होटल किराये में क्या-क्या शामिल है?
   Hotel kiraaye meñ kyaa-kyaa shaamil hai?

Pattern Practice 2

Write the Hindi translation of these English words.

1. about
2. worth seeing
3. South India
4. on vacation

Pattern Practice 3

Match the Hindi words below to their English meanings.

- जगह **jagah** (f)   to remind
- याद दिलाना **yaad dilaanaa**   place
- शाम को **shaam ko**   in the evening
- छुट्टी **chhuTTii** (f)   to think
- मुफ़्त **muft**   included
- शामिल **shaamil**   day off, vacation
- सोचना **sochnaa**   free of charge

Pattern Practice 4

Select the correct answer.

1. to book, reserve
   a. सोचना **sochnaa**
   c. बुक करना *book* **karnaa**
   b. याद दिलाना **yaad dilaanaa**
   d. शाम को **shaam ko**
2. places
   a. छुट्टी **chhuTTii** (f)
   c. जगहें **jagaheñ** (f)
   b. विचार **vichaar** (m)
   d. जगह **jagah** (f)
3. to think
   a. सोचना **sochnaa**
   c. शाम को **shaam ko**
   b. विचार **vichaar** (m)
   d. बुक करना *book* **karnaa**

Pattern Practice 5

After reading the statements below, select the correct answer.

1. याद दिलाने के लिये **yaad dilaane ke liye** = to remind   True   False
2. विचार **vichaar** (m) = places   True   False
3. छुट्टी **chhuTTii** (f) = places   True   False

GRAMMAR NOTE The Future Tense Using Suffixes गा *gaa*, गे *ge* or गी *gii*

If the verb in a sentence in Hindi ends with गा **gaa**, गे **ge**, or गी **gii**, the sentence refers to a future event. You construct a sentence using the tense like this: Subject + Object + [Verb Stem + Future Tense ending]. For the example "I will go to London," the Hindi equivalent is मैं **maiñ** (Subject) + लंदन **Landan** (Object) + जाऊँगा **jaauuñgaa** (verb root + future tense).

Here's how to form sentences using different pronouns with their corresponding future tense endings.

Masc. sing. + Object Subject	+ Future Tense Verb (Verb Root + Future Tense) e.g., "go"	= Sentence
मैं **maiñ**	लंदन **Landan**	जा **jaa** + ऊँगा **uuñgaa** = जाऊँगा **jaauuñgaa**	मैं लंदन जाऊँगा। **Maiñ Landan jaauuñgaa.** I will go to London.

Masc. sing. Subject	+ Object	+ Future Tense Verb"	= Sentence
यह yah/ वह vah	लंदन Landan	जा jaa + एगा egaa = जाएगा jaaegaa	यह/वह लंदन जाएगा। **Yah/Vah Landan jaaegaa.** He will go to London.
तू tuu	लंदन Landan	जा jaa + एगा egaa = जाएगा jaaegaa	तू लंदन जाएगा। **Tuu Landan jaaegaa.** You will go to London.
तुम tum	लंदन Landan	जा jaa + ओगे oge = जाओगे jaaoge	तुम लंदन जाओगे। **Tum Landan jaaoge.** You will go to London.

Masc., pl. Subject	+ Object	+ Future Tense Verb	= Sentence
हम ham	लंदन Landan	जा jaa + एँगे eñge = जाएँगे jaaeñge	हम लंदन जाएँगे। **Ham Landan jaaeñge.** We will go to London.
आप aap	लंदन Landan	जा jaa + एँगे eñge = जाएँगे jaaeñge	आप लंदन जाएँगे। **Aap Landan jaaeñge.** You will go to London.
ये ye/ वे ve	लंदन Landan	जा jaa + एँगे eñge = जाएँगे jaaeñge	ये/वे लंदन जाएँगे। **Ye/Ve Landan jaaeñge.** They will go to London.

Fem., sing. Subject	+ Object	+ Future Tense Verb	= Sentence
मैं maiñ	लंदन Landan	जा jaa + ऊँगी uuñgi = जाऊँगी jaauuñgi	मैं लंदन जाऊँगी। **Maiñ Landan jaauuñgi.** I will go to London.
यह yah/ वह vah	लंदन Landan	जा jaa + एगी egii = जाएगी jaaegii	यह/वह लंदन जाएगी। **Yah/Vah Landan jaaegii.** She will go to London.
तू tuu	लंदन Landan	जा jaa + एगी egii = जाएगी jaaegii	तू लंदन जाएगी। **Tuu Landan jaaegii.** You will go to London.
तुम tum	लंदन Landan	जा jaa+ ओगी ogii = जाओगी jaaogii	तुम लंदन जाओगी। **Tum Landan jaaegii.** You will go to London.

Fem., pl. Subject	+ Object	+ Future Tense Verb	= Sentence
हम **ham**	लंदन **Landan**	जा **jaa** + एँगी **eñgii** = जाएँगी **jaaeñgii**	हम लंदन जाएँगी। **Ham Landan jaaeñgii.** We will go to London.
आप **aap**	लंदन **Landan**	जा **jaa** + एँगी **eñgii** = जाएँगी **jaaeñgii**	आप लंदन जाएँगी। **Aap Landan jaaeñgii.** You will go to London.
ये **ye**/ वे **ve**	लंदन **Landan**	जा **jaa** + एँगी **eñgii** = जाएँगी **jaaeñgii**	ये/वे लंदन जाएँगी। **Ye/Ve Landan jaaeñgii.** They will go to London.

Pattern Practice 6

Choose the correct future form of the verb from the parentheses.

1. माया छुट्टियों में दक्षिण भारत _____। (जाएगी/जाएगा)

   Maya chhuTTiyoñ meñ dakShiN Bhaarat_____. (jaaegii/ jaaegaa)

2. मैं (m) शाम को हिंदी फ़िल्म _____। (देखेगा/देखूँगा)

   Maiñ sham ko Hindii film_____(dekhegaa/dekhuuñgaa)

3. आप (f) कल क्या _____? (करेंगे/करेंगी)

   Aap kal kyaa _____? (kaareñge/kareñgii)

4. वह (f) भी भारत में हिंदी _____। (सीखेगी/सीखूँगी)

   Vah bhii Bhaarat mein Hindii_____. (siikhegii/siikhuuñgii)

5. तुम (m) अब क्या _____? (करोगे/करोगी)

   Tum ab kyaa_____? (karoge/karogii)

Pattern Practice 7

How do you say the following in Hindi?

1. I will be going to London.
2. I will be going to Madame Tussauds and the Tower of London. (You can say these locations in English).
3. I will dine at restaurants. ("to have dinner" रात का खाना खाना **raat ka khaana khaana**)
4. I will stay in a hotel. ("to stay" ठहरना **thehernaa**)

Pattern Practice 8

Practice making the following statements in Hindi.

1. I would like to book a room for three nights.
2. From the 10th to 12th December.
3. How much is a room at your hotel?
4. Can you lower (the price) a bit please?
5. Is breakfast included in the price?

EXERCISE 1

Write the Hindi translations of these English words and phrases.

1. 100
2. service
3. please lower (the price) a little
4. we have
5. How can I help you?
6. for X
7. rent
8. for you

EXERCISE 2

Match the Hindi words below to the correct English meanings.

• तारीख़ **taariikh** (f)   some, little

• कम **kam**   morning

• कहिये **kahiye**   date

• सुबह **subah**   breakfast

• ज़्यादा **zyaadaa**   less, low

• कुछ **kuchh**   more, much

• नाश्ता **naashtaa**   please say

EXERCISE 3

Select the correct Hindi translation for the English words.

1. a little more
   a. कुछ ज़्यादा **kuchh zyaadaa**   b. ज़्यादा **zyaadaa**
   c. सेवा करना **sevaa karnaa**   d. कुछ कम कीजिये **kuchh kam kiijiye**
2. included
   a. सुबह **subah**   b. कितना **kitnaa**
   c. कहिये **kahiye**   d. शामिल **shaamil**

3. per day

a. प्रतिदिन **pratidin**   b. शामिल **shaamil**

c. ज़्यादा **zyaadaa**   d. मुफ़्त **muft**

4. separately

a. लगना **lagnaa**   b. अलग से **alag se**

c. शामिल **shaamil**   d. कहिये **kahiye**

5. indeed, definitely

a. कुछ **kuchh**   b. तो **to**

c. सौ **sau**   d. कम **kam**

6. How much?

a. शामिल **Shaamil**   b. कहिये **Kahiye**

c. कितना **Kitnaa**   d. लगना **Lagnaa**

7. free of charge

a. मुफ़्त **muft**   b. सुबह **subah**

c. कहिये **kahiye**   d. सेवा **sevaa** (f)

EXERCISE 4

Read the statements below and then circle the right answer.

1. सेवा करना **sevaa karnaa** = to serve	True	False
2. विद्यार्थी **vidyaarthii** = more, much	True	False
3. अलग से लगेगा **alag se lagegaa** = will be applied separately	True	False
4. के पास **ke paas** = for	True	False
5. लगना **lagnaa** = how much	True	False
6. इस से कम **is se kam** = less than this	True	False
7. मुझे कमरा चाहिये **mujhe kamraa chaahiye** = please lower (the price) a little	True	False

CHECKLIST

Can you do the following things in Hindi now?

- **Discuss a trip**
- **List the places you will visit**
- **Reserve a hotel room**

Border guards in traditional clothes during the Desert festival in Jaisalmer

The Makar Sankranti (festival of the Sun and Harvest) on the banks of the Ganga

Suniye bhaaiisaahab.
Excuse me, sir.

Jii, kahiye.
Please say.

Kyaa aap mujhe ek menuu de sakte haiñ?
Can I have a menu, please?

Jii haañ, yah lijiye.
Yes, here it is.

MENUU

Aap kyaa-kyaa chiizeñ pasand karte haiñ?
What dishes do you recommend?

Paalak paniir aur daal makkhanii.
The *paneer pasanda* and *daal makhani*.

Agar aap ve donoñ chiizeñ leñ, to bahut achchh hoñge jiiraa chaaval ke saath.
If you have those two, they will be very good with cumin rice.

Thiik hai, zaraayah laaiye.
Okay, bring me that.

Kyaa yahaañ kaa khaanaa bahut masaaledaar hai?
Is the food very spicy?

Bahut nahiiñ.
Not very (spicy).

Piine ke liye kuchh chaahiye?
Something to drink?

Ek aam kii lassii laaiye.
Please bring me a mango lassi.

LESSON 10
Indian Cuisine

In this lesson, Maya will learn how to order some Indian dishes and drinks and follow instructions. After this lesson, you should be able to:

- Order food in a resturant
- Talk about the different indian dishes
- Use the subjunctive tense to express what you might do

 **DIALOGUE : ORDERING FOOD** (10-01)

Maya is at an Indian restaurant and wants to order some food.

Maya:	Excuse me, sir.
	Suniye bhaaiisaahab.
	सुनिये भाईसाहब।
Waiter:	Please say.
	Jii, kahiye.
	जी, कहिये।
Maya:	Can I have a menu, please?
	Kyaa aap mujhe ek menuu de sakte haiñ?
	क्या आप मुझे एक मेनू दे सकते है?
Waiter:	Yes, here it is.
	Jii haañ, yah lijiye.
	जी हाँ, यहाँ है।
Maya:	What dishes do you recommend (lit., "like")?
	Aap kyaa-kyaa chiizeñ pasand karte haiñ?
	आप क्या-क्या चीज़ें पसंद करते हैं?
Waiter:	The *palak paneer* and *daal makhani*. If you have those two, they will be very good with cumin rice.
	Paalak paniir aur daal makkhanii. Agar aap ve donoñ chiizeñ leñ, to bahut achchh hoñge jiiraa chaaval ke saath.
	पालक पनीर और दाल मक्खनी। अगर आप वे दोनों चीजें लें तो बहुत अच्छी होंगी जीरा चावल के साथ।

Maya: Okay, bring me that.
             Thiik hai, zaraa yah laaiye.
             ठीक है, ज़रा यह लाइये।
             Is the food very spicy here?
             Kyaa yahaañ kaa khaanaa bahut masaaledaar hai?
             क्या यहाँ का खाना बहुत मसालेदार है?
Waiter: Not very (spicy).
             Bahut nahiiñ.
             बहुत नहीं।
             Something to drink?
             Piine ke liye kuchh chaahiye?
             पीने के लिये कुछ चाहिये?
Maya: Please bring me a mango lassi.
             Ek aam kii lassii laaiye.
             एक आम की लस्सी लाइये।

The waiter returns to clear Maya's plates.

Waiter: How is the food?
             Khaanaa kaisaa hai?
             खाना कैसा है?
Maya: It is very tasty!
             Bahut laziiz hai!
             बहुत लज़ीज़ है!
Waiter: Thank you for your praise. Would you like anything else?
             Taariif ke liye shukriyaa. Kuchh aur chaahiye?
             तारीफ़ के लिये शुक्रिया। कुछ और चाहिये?
Maya: No, thank you. I have already eaten so much! Please bring me the
             bill.
             Nahiiñ, shukriyaa. Maiñ bahut khaa chukii huuñ! Zaraa *bill* laiye.
             नहीं शुक्रिया। मैं बहुत खा चुकी हूँ! ज़रा बिल लाइये।
Waiter: Okay, here is the bill.
             Achchhaa, yah *bill* hai.
             अच्छा, यह बिल है।
Maya: Can I pay by credit card?
             Kyaa maiñ kreDit kaarb kaa istemaal kar saktii huuñ?
             क्या मैं क्रेडिट कार्ड का इस्तेमाल कर सकती हूँ?

Waiter: Sorry, cash only please.
Maaf kiijiye, kaish.
माफ़ कीजिये, सिर्फ़ कैश।

Vocabulary List (10–02)

मेनू	**menuu**	menu
पसंद करना	**pasand karanaa**	like, prefer
पालक पनीर	**paalak paniir**	*palak paneer* [see p. 157]
दाल मक्खनी	**daal makkhanii**	*daal makhani* (lentils stewed with butter)
जीरा	**jiiraa**	cumin
मसालेदार	**masaaledaar**	spicy
कुछ	**kuchh**	some
आम की लस्सी	**aam kii lassii**	mango lassi (a yoghurt drink that can be served sweet or salty and flavored with things like rose water or mango)
भरा	**bharaa**	full, although it is uncommon to say "I am full" in Hindi
बिल	**bil**	bill
क्रेडिट कार्ड	**kreDiT kaarD**	credit card
नक़द, कैश	**naqd, kaish**	cash

Supplementary Vocabulary

Useful Phrases and Words

क्या आप के पास .... (name of a thing) है?	**Kyaa aap ke paas ... hai?**	Do you have …?
आपको क्या चाहिये?	**Aap ko kyaa chaahiye?**	What do you need/want?
चाय	**chaai**	tea
कॉफ़ी	*coffee*	coffee
पानी	**paanii**	water
गरम	**garam**	hot
ठंडा	**ThanDaa**	cold

छुरी-काँटा	chhurii-kaañTaa	cutlery
शाकाहारी खाना	shaakaahaarii khaanaa	vegetarian food
माँसाहारी खाना	maansaahaarii khaanaa	non-vegetarian food
सबसे पहले	sab se pehle	first of all
जैसे मैं कहती (f)/कहता (m) हूँ वैसे कीजिये	Jaise maiñ kehtii/ kehtaa huuñ, vaise kiijiye.	(lit., "as I say, please") Please do it according to what I've said.
यह तैयार है।	Yah taiyaar hai.	It is ready now.
बहुत लज़ीज़ है	Bahut laziiz hai.	It is very tasty.
तारीफ़ के लिये बहुत-बहुत धन्यवाद।	Taariif ke liye bahut bahut dhanyawaad.	Thank you very much for (your) praise.
क्या बात है !	Kyaa baat hai!	What a wonderful thing!
भूखा/भूखी	bhuukhaa/bhuukhii	hungry
चेक	chek	check
ट्रैवेलर्स चेक	traivelars chek	traveler's check
सिक्के	sikke	coins

Multigenerational family eating together

Popular Indian Foods and Drinks

बटर चिकन	**baTar chikan**	Butter chicken (a Punjabi dish of chicken cooked in a buttery tomato gravy)
तंदूरी चिकन	**tanduurii chikan**	Tandoori chicken (Chicken pieces marinated and grilled in a *tanduur* or traditional clay oven)
रोग़न जोश	**ro<u>gh</u>an josh**	*Rogan Josh* (a Kashmiri lamb dish with lots of clarified butter)
मलाई कोफ़्ता	**malaaii koftaa**	*Malai Kofta* (cheese and flour dumplings in a cream-based gravy)
छोले	**chole**	chickpeas
पालक पनीर	**paalak paniir**	*Palak Paneer* (cheese cubes in a spinach gravy)
काली दाल	**kaalii daal**	*Kaali Daal* (black lentils)
चाट	**chaaT**	*Chaat* (various assorted (savory) snacks/street food)

Every Indian meal features a number of different dishes

नान	**naan**	*Naan* (a fluffy bread baked in the *tanduur* from the northwest of the subcontinent)
मसाला चाय	**masaalaa chaay**	*Masala Chai* (milk tea with spices)
ठंडाई	**Thandaaii**	cold drink
संतरे का रस/ ओरेंज जूस	**santre kaa ras/ oranj jus**	orange juice
दूधवाली चाय	**duudhvaalii caay**	tea with milk
दूध और चीनीवाली काफ़ी	**duudh aur chiiniivaalii kaafii**	coffee with sugar and milk
अंडे	**anDe**	eggs

Tastes

मीठा	**miiThaa**	sweet
नमकीन	**namkiin**	salty
खट्टा	**khaTTaa**	sour
गर्म	**garm**	hot (temperature)
ठंडा	**ThanDaa**	cold (temperature)
कड़वा	**kaRvaa**	bitter

A streetside snack stall in Mumbai

GRAMMAR NOTE The Subjunctive Mood Tense "I may..."

You have learnt how to make the future tense in Hindi, e.g., "I will read a book" (said by a female speaker) मैं किताब पढ़ूँगी **Maiñ kitaab parhuuñgii.** To change this sentence into "I may read a book" (thus, from the future tense to the subjunctive tense), simply drop the last syllable गा/गे/गी (**gaa/ge/gii**) so your sentence becomes मैं किताब पढ़ूँ **maiñ kitaab parhuuñ** or "I may read a book." Raise your intonation and this sentence then means "May I read a book?"; this is how polite requests for permission or approval are commonly made in Hindi.

The subjunctive tense is used to showcase possibilities "I may read a book (or I could do something else)" or propose and suggest something such as "You may have some tea" (a polite request). Compare these two sentences:

मैं भारत जाऊँगा/जाऊँगी **Maiñ bhaarat jaauuñgaa/jaauuñgii.**
"I will go to India."

मैं भारत जाऊँ **Maiñ bhaarat jaauuñ**. "I may go to India."

The first sentence is more definite than the second, which seems to be merely considering the possibility of going to India. Here are some other ways of using the subjunctive tense in Hindi:

1. हो सकता है कि (**ho saktaa hai ki...**): it is possible
   हो सकता है कि मैं भारत जाऊँ। **Ho saktaa hai ki maiñ bhaarat jaauuñ.**
   It is possible that I may go to India.

Dining at the famous Leopold Cafe in Colaba, Mumbai

2. शायद (**shaayad**): perhaps
   शायद मैं भारत जाऊँ।   **Shaayad maiñ bhaarat jaauuñ.**
   Perhaps I will go to India.

Pattern Practice 1

Change these Hindi sentences into the subjunctive tense.

1. मेरा भाई चाय बनाएगा।
   Meraa bhaaii chaay banaaegaa.
   My brother will make tea.
2. वह भी भारत जाएगी।
   Vah bhii bhaarat jaaegii.
   She will also go to India.
3. मैं हिंदी सीखूँगा।
   Maiñ Hindi siikhuuñgaa.
   I will learn Hindi.

Pattern Practice 2

Change the following sentences to the subjunctive tense, then practice reading the new sentences.

1. हो सकता है कि वह भी इस साल हिंदी .... (सीखना)।
   Ho saktaa hai ki vah bhii is saal Hindi .... (siikhnaa)
   She may learn Hindi this year. (She is likely to learn Hindi this year.)
2. आप आज नहीं कल ... (आना)।
   Aap aaj nahiiñ kal ... (aanaa).
   Please come tomorrow, not today.
3. माफ़ कीजिये, लेकिन शायद मैं आज न आ .... (सकना)।
   Maaf kiijiye, lekin, shaayad maiñ aaj na aa ... (saknaa).
   Please excuse me, but, I may not be able to come today.
4. इसके बाद मैं क्या ... (करना)?
   Iske baad maiñ kyaa ... (karnaa)?
   What shall I do after this?
5. आप यहाँ ... (बैठना)।
   Aap yahaañ ... (baithnaa).
   (You) Please sit here.

GRAMMAR NOTE Cause and Effect "If...then"

Using the subjunctive tense, we can also construct sentences using the अगर... तो **agar...to** or यदि...तो **yadi...to**, the "if...then" structure. e.g., अगर मैं भारत <u>जाऊँ</u> तो ताज महल देखूँगा। **Agar main bhaarat <u>jaauuñ</u> to Taj Mahal dekhuuñgaa** or "If I go to India then I will see the Taj Mahal." You can see the subjunctive tense in the underlined word जाऊँ **jaauuñ**. Other examples:

Yadi aap yah poshaak <u>kh</u>ariideñ to maiñ yah *bag* khariiduuñgii.

यदि आप यह पोशाक ख़रीदें, तो मैं यह बैग ख़रीदूँगी।

If you're buying that dress, then I will buy this bag.

Agar tum mere ghar aao to merii maañ zaruur biryaanii pakaaegii.

अगर तुम मेरे घर आओ तो मेरी माँ ज़रूर बिरयानी पकाएगी।

If you come to my house, my mom will definitely cook Biryani.

> *Yadi aap yah poshaak <u>kh</u>ariideñ to maiñ yah* **bag** *khariiduuñgii.*
> If you're buying that dress, then I will buy this bag.

Pattern Practice 3

Translate the following sentences into Hindi.

1. If you make tea then I will drink it.
2. If I learn Hindi then I will go to India.
3. If you go to the store then I will meet you there.
4. If you go to her house then she will cook for you.
5. If you go to India you will be able to go to the Taj Mahal.

GRAMMAR NOTE Expressing What You Want to Do with चाहना *chaahnaa* "to want"

Use the verb चाहना **chaahnaa** "to want" paired with the infinitive form of the verb one wants to carry out, such as "to run," "to travel," or "to eat." For example, गाना चाहना **gaanaa chaahnaa** "to want to sing," or देखना चाहना **dekhnaa chaahnaa** "to want to see."

The structure of the sentence is Subject + Object + The Action You Want to Do + Want + Is. Thus, "I want to watch a movie" is मैं मूवी देखना चाहता हूँ। **Maiñ muuvii dekhnaa chaahtaa huuñ.**

If you want to say, "I don't want to watch a movie," it is मैं मूवी नहीं देखना चाहता। **Maiñ muuvii nahiiñ dekhnaa chaahtaa.** For greater emphasis, नहीं **nahiiñ** can also sometimes be placed between the infinitive and the conjugated form of चाहना **chaahna** "to want" or even after the latter. Also remember that in negated present tense sentences, "is/are/am" is usually dropped.

School children having their midday meal

GRAMMAR NOTE Expressing Ability with सकना *saknaa* and
पाना *paanaa* "to be able to, can"

Use this structure: Subject + (Adjective, if any) + (Object, if any) + Verb stem
describing action + Conjugated सकना **saknaa**/पाना **paanaa** "to be able to, can"
+ "is/are/am" to express the ability to do something. Here are some examples:

मैं	अच्छी तरह	गा	सकता	हूँ।
Maiñ	**acchii tarah**	**gaa**	**saktaa**	**huuñ.**
I	well	sing	can	am = I can sing well.
		(verb stem)	(conjugated)	

वे	अच्छी तरह	फुटबाल	खेल	सकते	हैं।
Ve	**acchii tarah**	*football*	**khel**	**sakte**	**haiñ.**
They	well	football	play	can	are
			(verb stem)	(conjugated)	

= They play football well.

A vegetarian meal served on a banana leaf

EXERCISE 1

Write the Hindi equivalent of these words:

1. spicy
2. tea
3. cumin
4. drink
5. non-vegetarian
6. tea with sugar
7. credit card
8. cash

EXERCISE 2

Translate the following mini-dialogues into Hindi.

1. A: Can you call me tonight? (फ़ोन करना **phone karnaa** "to call")
   B: Yes, I will call you tonight.
2. A: Can you speak Hindi?
   B: I can speak a little.
3. A: Can you eat this food? It's spicy!
   B: I can't eat this. It's too spicy.

A highway roadside restaurant in Delhi

EXERCISE 3

Translate the following sentences into Hindi.

1. I want to eat Indian food.
2. Do you want to eat Indian food?
3. I want to watch a Hindi movie.
4. I want to go shopping.
5. I want to see the Taj Mahal.

CHECKLIST

Can you do the following in Hindi now?

- **Order food in a restaurant.**
- **Talk about the different Indian dishes**
- **Use the subjunctive tense to express what you might do**

At the Lost and Found office

Namaste ji!
Hello sir!

Namaste ji! Kahiye, kyaa kar saktaa huuñ?
Hello! Please tell (me) what I can do (for you).

Baat yah hai ki kal meraa cell phone havaaii-aDDe meñ kahiiñ gir gayaa.
I dropped my cell phone somewhere in the airport yesterday.

Aapkaa cell phone kis company kaa thaa aur kis rang kaa thaa?
What brand is your cell phone and what color is it?

Voh iPhone hai aur us par kaalaa cover hai.
It is an iPhone and it has a black cover.

Cell phone ke piichhe meraa naam likhaa hai, Hindii meñ.
On the back of the cell phone my name is written in Hindi.

Aur aapkaa naam kyaa hai?
And what is your name?

Jii, Maya.
Maya, sir.

Kyaa yeh aapkaa cell phone hai?
Is this your cell phone?

Haañ-haañ. Yahii hai.
Yes. This is it.

Aap apnaa i-card dikhaaiye ki aap hii Maya haiñ.
Please show me your ID that you are Maya.

Yeh liijiye aapkaa phone.
Please take your phone.

Shukriyaa!
Thank you.

Koii baat nahiiñ.
Don't mention it.

LESSON 11
Reporting a Lost Item

In this lesson, you will learn how to narrate a story or event in the past, and should be able to communicate the following in Hindi:

- **How to report a lost item**
- **Talk about past events**

 **LOST AND FOUND** (11–01)

Maya looks upset. Kabir asks her what is wrong and finds out she has lost her phone.

Kabir: Maya, what's the matter? Is everything fine?
          Maya, kyaa baat hai? Sab Thiik-Thaak hai?
          माया, क्या बात है? क्या सब ठीक है?

Maya: No, I have lost my cell phone.
          Jii, nahiiñ, meraa *cell phone* kho gayaa hai.
          जी नहीं, मेरा सैल-फ़ोन खो गया है।

Kabir: That's very bad (news). How did that happen?
          Yah to bahut buraa huaa. Yah kaise huaa?
          यह तो बहुत बुरा हुआ। यह कैसे हुआ?

Maya: I was in New Delhi yesterday (Monday). My parents came from America to India, so I went to the airport to meet them.
          Kal maiñ nayii-dillii meñ thii. Somvaar ko mere maataa-pitaa Amerika se Bhaarat aaye. Maiñ havaaii-aDDe gayii thii aur apne maataa-pitaa se milii.
          कल मैं नयी-दिल्ली में थी। सोमवार को मेरे माता-पिता अमेरिका से भारत आये। मैं हवाई-अड्डे गयी थी और अपने माता-पिता से मिली।

          It was crowded there. I helped them carry the luggage (and) we came out of the airport.
          Vahaañ bahut bhiiRh thii. Maiñne saamaan uThaane meñ unkii madad kii. Ham havaaii-aDDe se bahar aaye.
          वहाँ बहुत भीड़ थी। मैंने सामान उठने में उनकी मदद की। हम हवाई-अड्डे से बाहर आये।

After coming out of the airport, I found that I did not have my cell phone with me. It seems that I dropped my cell phone somewhere in the airport.

Baahar aakar maiñne dekhaa ki meraa *cell phone* mere paas nahiiñ thaa. Lagtaa hai ki meraa *cell phone* havaaii-aDDe meñ kahiiñ gir gayaa.

बाहर आकर मैंने देखा कि मेरा सैल-फ़ोन मेरे पास नहीं था। लगता है कि मेरा सैल-फ़ोन हवाई-अड्डे में कहीं गिर गया।

Kabir: Have you made (lit., "registered") a report about your lost cell phone?

Kyaa aapne *cell phone* ke khone kii *report* darz kii hai?

क्या आपने सैल-फ़ोन के खोने की रिपोर्ट दर्ज़ की है?

Maya: No.

Nahiiñ.

नहीं।

Kabir: In my opinion, you should report this matter to the airport office.

Mere vichaar se aap ko is baat kii jankaarii havaaii-aDDe ke daftar meñ denii chaahiye.

मेरे विचार से आपको इस बात की जानकारी हवाई-अड्डे के दफ़्तर में देनी चाहिये।

Inside the Indira Gandhi International Airport, the busiest airport in India

Maya: That's (lit., "It's") a very good idea. I will go to the airport right
           now. See you tomorrow.

           **Aapkaa vichaar bahut achchhaa hai. Maiñ abhii havaaii-aDDe
           jaatii huuñ. Kal milenge.**

           आपका विचार बहुत अच्छा है। मैं अभी हवाई-अड्डे जाती हूँ। कल मिलेंगे।

Kabir: OK. See you tomorrow.

           Thiik hai. Kal milenge.

           ठीक है। कल मिलेंगे।

Maya has reached the airport and is at the Lost and Found Office.

Maya: Hello sir!

           Namaste ji!

           नमस्ते जी !

Office Worker (OW): Hello! Please tell (me) what I can do (for you).

           Namaste ji! Kahiye, kyaa kar saktaa huuñ.

           नमस्ते जी ! कहिये, क्या कर सकता हूँ।

Maya: I dropped my cell phone somewhere in the airport yesterday.

           **Baat yah hai ki kal meraa *cell phone* havaaii-aDDe meñ kahiiñ
           gir gayaa.**

           बात यह है कि कल मेरा सैल-फ़ोन हवाई-अड्डे में कहीं गिर गया।

OW: What brand (lit., "company") is your cell phone and what color is it?

           Aapkaa *cell phone* kis *company* kaa thaa aur kis rang kaa thaa?

           आपका सैल-फ़ोन किस कंपनी का था और किस रंग का था?

Maya: It is an iPhone and it has a black cover.

           Voh *iphone* hai aur us par kaalaa *cover* hai.

           वह आई-फ़ोन है और उस पर काला कवर है।

OW: There are several such phones here. Please tell me (if there are)
           any other identifying (lit., "recognition") marks?

           Yahaañ to kaii aise *cell phone* haiñ. Koii aur pehchaan bataaiye.

           यहाँ तो कई ऐसे सैल-फ़ोन हैं। कोई और पहचान बताइये।

Maya: OK, on the back of the cell phone my name is written in Hindi.

           Ji, *cell phone* ke piichhe meraa naam likhaa hai, Hindii meñ.

           जी, सैल-फ़ोन के पीछे मेरा नाम लिखा है, हिंदी में।

OW: And what is your name?

           Aur aapkaa naam kyaa hai?

           और आपका नाम क्या है?

Maya: Maya, sir.

Jii, Maya.

जी, माया।

OW: Yes, there is one such cell phone here. Is this your cell phone?

Haan, aisaa *cell phone* to hai. Kyaa yeh aapkaa *cell phone* hai?

हाँ, ऐसा सैल-फ़ोन है यहाँ। क्या यह आपका सैल-फ़ोन है?

Maya: Yes. This is it.

Haañ-haañ. Yahii hai.

हाँ-हाँ। यही है।

OW: Please show me your ID (to show) that you are Maya.

Aap apnaa *i-card* dikhaaiye ki aap hii Maya haiñ.

आप अपना आई-कार्ड दिखाइये कि आप ही माया हैं।

Maya: Please take it.

Yeh liijiye.

यह लीजिये।

OW: Please take your phone.

Yeh liijiye aapkaa *phone*.

यह लीजिये आपका फ़ोन।

Maya: Thank you.

Shukriyaa!

शुक्रिया !

OW: Don't mention it.

Koii baat nahiiñ.

कोई बात नहीं।

A local police station in Puducherry, India

Vocabulary List (11–02)

आये	**aaye**	came, arrived (verb: आना **aanaa** "to come")
हवाई-अड्डा	**havaaii-aDDaa**	airport
गयी थी	**gayii thii**	had gone (verb: जाना **jaanaa** "to go")
मिली	**milii**	met (verb: मिलना **milanaa** "to meet")
भीड़	**bhiiRh**	crowd
सामान	**saamaan**	luggage, goods
मदद की	**madam kii**	helped (verb: X की मदद करना **X kii madad karnaa**: "to help X")
मैंने	**maiñne**	I (in the past tense with transitive verbs)
देखा	**dekhaa**	saw (देखना **dekhanaa** "to see")
कहीं	**kahiiñ**	somewhere
गिर जाना	**gir jaanaa**	to drop
गिर गया है	**gir gayaa hai**	have dropped

GRAMMAR NOTE Transitive and Intransitive Verbs in Hindi

In this lesson, we learn how to use verbs like "to eat," "to do," "to write" and "to see" in the past tense. In the vocabulary, the verbs with the word ने **ne** are in the past tense, and also indicate the presence of a transitive verb in the past tense. First, let's learn what transitive and intransitive verbs are. Transitive verbs usually have a direct object, i.e., "I ate food," while intransitive verbs do not take any direct object, i.e., "I swam." It's important to know the difference between these verbs to modify the subject when forming sentences.

For transitive verbs, the word ने **ne** will be placed after the subject. If the subject is a pronoun, the ने **ne** attaches to it. Third-person pronouns also change their forms when this happens:

Sing.: यह **yah** + ने **ne** = इसने **isne**   "this" वह **vah** + ने **ne** = उसने **usne** "he"

Pl.: ये **ye** + ने **ne** = इन्होंने **inhoñne**   "they" वे **ve** + ने **ne** = उन्होंने **unhoñne** "they"

The subject is now in the oblique case—the form any noun, pronoun and adjective in Hindi takes when followed by a word such as in मैं **maiñ** + को **ko** = मुझको **mujhko** "me"—and the verb agrees with the number and gender of the object rather than the subject. For intransitive verbs, no word is added and the verb continues to agree with the number and the gender of the subject.

Useful Tip How to Know if a Verb is Transitive or Intransitive

Try asking "What" questions to see if the verb is transitive. Compare "I ate" and "I slept." One can certainly create a question like "What did you eat?" but not "What did you sleep?" Using this, we can differentiate "to see," "to do" and "to read" as transitive verbs; and "to lie down," "to swim" and "to go" as intransitive verbs. लाना (**laanaa** "to bring"), समझना (**samajhnaa** "to understand"), and भूलना (**bhuulnaa** "to forget") sound like they should be transitive verbs but they are actually intransitive verbs in Hindi.

The form of the verb used to form the simple past tense—as well as the present perfect and past perfect (pluperfect) tenses discussed below—is called the past participle.

Pattern Practice 1

Identify the transitive and intransitive verbs from the following options.

1. लेना (**lenaa** "to take")
2. देना (**denaa** "to give")
3. सोचना (**sochanaa** "to think")
4. खाना (**khaanaa** "to eat")
5. आना (**aanaa** "to come")

GRAMMAR NOTE Making Past Participles in Hindi

There are two simple steps to making past participles in Hindi. Simply remove the suffix -ना **naa** from the verb, and add the proper ending: **-aa** (T)/**-yaa** (या), **-ii** (ी)/**-yii** (यी), **-aye** (े)/**-ye** (ये) , or **-iiñ** (ीं)/**-yiiñ** (यीं) respectively. If the verb stem ends in a consonant, choose the participles starting with vowels; if it ends in a vowel, choose the version with "y." Here are some examples:

	-aa (T)/-yaa (या)	-ii (ी)/-yii (यी)	-aye (े)/-ye (ये)	-iiñ (ीं)/-yiiñ (यीं)
लिखना **likhnaa** "to write"	लिखा **likhaa**	लिखी **likhii**	लिखे **likhe**	लिखीं **likhiiñ**
खाना **khaanaa** "to eat"	खाया **khaayaa**	खायी **khaayii**	खाये **khaaye**	खायीं **khaayiiñ**

The correct form of the past participle to use depends on whether it is a transitive or intransitive verb, and the gender and number of the object (in the case of a transitive verb) or subject (in the case of an intransitive verb). For example, you would use लिखा **likhaa** with an object that is masculine and singular, लिखी **likhii** with a feminine singular object, लिखे **likhe** with a plural masculine object, and लिखीं **likhiiñ** when the object is a feminine plural.

GRAMMAR NOTE Irregular Verbs

Here are the six common irregular verbs that do not follow the above rules. Try to memorize their past participle forms.

Transitive IrregularVerbs

1. लेना (**lenaa** "to take"): लिया (**liyaa**), ली (**lii**), लिये (**liye**), लीं (**liiñ**)
2. देना (**denaa** "to give"): दिया (**diyaa**), दी (**dii**), दिये (**diye**), दीं (**diiñ**)
3. करना (**karanaa** "to do"): किया (**kiyaa**), की (**kii**), किये (**kiye**), कीं (**kiiñ**)
4. पीना (**piinaa** "to drink"): पिया (**piyaa**), पी (**pii**), पिये (**piye**), पीं (**piiñ**)

Intransitive Irregular Verbs

1. होना (**honaa** "to be, to become"): हुआ (**huaa**), हुई (**huii**), हुए (**hue**), हुईं (**huiiñ**)
2. जाना (**jaanaa** "to go"): गया (**gayaa**), गयी (**gayii**), गये (**gaye**), गयीं (**gayiiñ**)

Pattern Practice 2

Give the past participle forms of these verbs.

1. सीखना (**siikhnaa** "to learn")
2. बोलना (**bolnaa** "to speak")
3. सोचना (**sochnaa** "to think")
4. सोना (**sonaa** "to sleep")
5. आना (**aanaa** " to come")

EXERCISE 1

Answer the following questions from the dialogue in Hindi.

1. कल माया हवाई-अड्डे क्यों गयी?
   Kal Maya hawaaii-aDDe kyoñ gayii?
2. माया का सैल-फ़ोन कहाँ गिर गया?
   Maya kaa *cell phone* kahaañ gir gayaa?
3. कौन अमेरिका से भारत आये?
   Kaun Amerika se bhaarat aaye?
4. क्या माया ने फ़ोन के खोने की रिपोर्ट दर्ज़ की है?
   Kyaa Maya ne *phone* ke khone kii *report* darz kii hai?
5. सैल-फ़ोन के पीछे क्या लिखा है?
   ***Cell phone* ke piichhe kyaa likhaa hai?**

| GRAMMAR NOTE | Making the Present Perfect (Perfect) Tense |

There are three common ways to express an event in the past tense. For example:

Past: मैंने खाना खाया। **Mainñe khaana khaaya.** "I ate."

Present Perfect (Perfect); when an action has been "made complete" or "completely done" at the time of the conversation:

मैं ने खाना खाया है। **Mainñe khaana khaaya hai.** "I have eaten."

Past Perfect (Pluperfect); when a completed action is compared to another in the past:

मैंने खाना खाया था। **Mainñe khaana khaaya tha.** "I had eaten."

More examples of these include:

यह कैसे हुआ?   मेरे माता-पिता अमेरिका से आये हैं।
Yah kaise hua?   **Mere maata-pitaa Amerika se aaye haiñ.**
"How did it happen?"   "My parents have come from America."

तो क्या आपका सैल-फ़ोन हवाई-अड्डे में गिर गया था?
To kyaa aapkaa *cell phone* **havaaii-aDDe meñ gir gayaa thaa?**
"So, did you drop your cell phone in (the) airport?"

To go from a simple past tense sentence to a present perfect one, first create the past tense of the sentence, e.g., मैंने रात का खाना खाया **Mainñe raat kaa khaanaa khaayaa** or "I ate dinner."

Then identify if the verb is transitive or intransitive, and add the correct form of होना **honaa** "to be," i.e., "is/are" है (or हैं, हूँ, हो) **hai** (or **haiñ**, **huuñ**, or **ho**). In this case, the verb is transitive, so it will agree with the number and gender of the object, which is the masculine singular खाना **khaanaa** "food," thus the sentence becomes मैंने रात का खाना खाया है **Mainñe raat kha khaanaa khaayaa hai** "I have eaten dinner."

Creating Past Perfect Sentences

Create the past tense version of the sentence as above, मैं ने रात का खाना खाया **Mainñe raat kaa khaanaa khaayaa** or "I ate dinner." Identify whether the verb is transitive or intransitive and add था **thaa** (or थे **the**, थी **thii**, थीं **thiiñ**) to the end of the sentence. Thus, this example becomes: मैंने रात का खाना खाया था **Mainñe raat kaa khaanaa khaayaa thaa** or "I had eaten dinner."

Pattern Practice 3

Write the correct form of the verb in the past tense.

1. क्या _____ (होना)?
   Kyaa _____ (honaa)?
   What happened?

2. मेरे माता-पिता भारत _____ (आना)
   Mere maataa-pitaa Bhaarat _____ (aanaa) haiñ.
   My parents have come to India.

3. मैं बाज़ार में _____ (खो जाना) थी।
   Maiñ baazaar meñ _____ (kho jaanaa) thii.
   I had gotten lost in the market.

4. आप वहाँ क्यों _____ (जाना)?
   Aap vahaañ kyoñ _____ (jaanaa)?
   Why did you go there?

5. उसने वह फ़िल्म _____ (देखना) है।
   Usne voh film _____ (dekhnaa) hai.
   She/He has seen that movie.

EXERCISE 2

How would you say the following sentences and questions in Hindi?

1. I have lost my computer.
2. I had watched this movie two months before.
3. It seems to me.
4. Have you registered a report about your lost computer?
5. In my opinion…
6. Your idea (suggestion) is very good.
7. What can I do for you?
8. There are many such books here.
9. Please show me your ID?
10. Thank you.
11. Don't mention it.

EXERCISE 3

Translate these sentences into Hindi:

1. आप पिछले साल कहाँ गये थे?
   Aap pichhle saal kahaañ gaye the?
2. क्या आपने यह फ़िल्म देखी है?
   Kyaa aapne yah film dekhii hai?
3. यह फ़िल्म मैंने बचपन में देखी थी।
   Yah film maiñne bachpan meñ dekhii thii.

EXERCISE 4

Match the Hindi sentences below to their English meanings:

• मेरा सामान खो गया है **Meraa saamaan kho gayaa hai**	Never mind (don't mention it).
• कैसे हुआ? **Kaise huaa?**	In my opinion.
• ऐसा ही लगता है **Aisaa hii lagtaa hai**	See you tomorrow.
• मेरे विचार से **Mere vichaar se**	I have lost my luggage.
• क्या कर सकता हूँ? **Kyaa kar saktaa huuñ?**	What can I do?
• कोई बात नहीं **Koii baat nahiiñ**	How (that) happened?
• कल मिलेंगे **Kal mileñge**	It seems so.

EXERCISE 5

Give the Hindi words for the English terms below.

1. bad
2. worker
3. to inform
4. information
5. luggage, goods

EXERCISE 6

Match the Hindi phrases below with their correct English meanings.

• कहीं **kahiiñ**	any other
• कोई और **koii aur**	to help
• उठाना **uThaanaa**	someone
• हवाई-अड्डा **havaaii-aDDaa**	airport
• मदद करना **madad karnaa**	to carry

EXERCISE 7

Select the correct Hindi translation from the options below.

1. to register

   a. गिर जाना **gir jaanaa**

   b. मदद करना **madad karanaa**

   c. कर्मचारी **kaarmchaarii**

   d. दर्ज करना **darz karanaa**

2. such

   a. लिखा **likhaa**

   b. ऐसा **aisaa**

   c. बुरा **buraa**

   d. ही **hii**

3. to drop, fall

   a. खो जाना **ho jaanaa**

   b. गरि जाना **gir jaanaa**

   c. दर्ज़ करना **darz karanaa**

   d. मदद करना **madad karanaa**

4. identifying mark

   a. पहचान **pehchaan**

   b. उठाना **uthaanaa**

   c. सामान **saamaan**

   d. लखि **likhaa**

5. crowd

   a. ही **hii**

   b. बुरा **buraa**

   c. कहीं **kahiiñ**

   d. भीड़ **bhiiRh**

EXERCISE 8

Check if the statements are true, then circle either True or False.

1. लिखा **likhaa** = written	True	False
2. X से मिलना **X se milnaa** = to lose, to be lost	True	False
3. खो जाना **kho jaanaa** = to lose, to be lost	True	False
4. ही **hii** = somewhere	True	False
5. दफ़्तर **daftar** = luggage, goods	True	False

CHECKLIST

Can you do the following in Hindi now?

- **Report a lost item**
- **Talk about past events**

Cultural Notes at a Glance

Answer Key

LESSON 1

Writing Exercise 1

1. gaa गा 2. bi बि 3. lii ली 4. ku कु 5. puu पू 6. me मे
7. tai तै 8. jo जो 9. mau मौ 10. kri कृ 11. fam फ़म 12. maH माह

Writing Exercise 2

1. pa प	paa पा	pi पि	pii पी	pu पु	puu पू
2. pe पे	pai पै	po पो	pau पौ	pañ पं	
3. paa पा पा	paamaa पामा	pimaa पिमा	piimaa पीमा	puma पुम	puumaa पूमा
4. pemaa पेमा	paimaa पैमा	pomaa पोमा	paumaa पौमा	pañbaa पंबा	
5. lala लल	laalaa लाला	lilaa लिला	liilaa लीला	lulaa लुला	luulaa लूला
6. lelaa लेला	lailaa लैला	lolaa लोला	laulaa लौला	lañbaa लंबा	
7. tata तत	taataa ताता	titaa तिता	tiitaa तीता	tutaa तुता	tootaa तूता
8. tetaa तेता	taitaa तैता	totaa तोता	tautaa तौता	taañbaa तांबा	
9. kiila कील	kilaa किला	maami मामि	maamii मामी	maamu मामु	maamuu मामू
10. maame मामे	maamai मामै	mamo ममो	mamau ममौ	jañbo जंबो	

Exercise 1

मेरा नाम माया है। इसका नाम लीला है।
Meraa naam maayaa hai. Iskaa naam liilaa hai.

Pattern Practice 1

a) क ka	का kaa	कि ki	की kii	कु ku	कू kuu
के ke	कै kai	को ko	कौ kau	कं kañ	कल kal
b) काला kaalaa	किला kilaa	कीला kiilaa	कुल kul	कूल kuul	केला kelaa
कैला kailaa	कोला kolaa	कौला kaulaa	कंज kañj		
c) मन man	माना maanaa	मिना minaa	मीना miinaa	मुन mun	मून muun
मेना menaa	मैना mainaa	मोना monaa	मौना maunaa	मंज mañj	
d) जल jal	जाला jaalaa	जिला jilaa	जीला jiilaa	जुल jul	जूल juul
जेला jelaa	जैना jainaa	जोना jonaa	जौना jaunaa	जंच jañch	

e) सम **sam**   समा **samaa**   समिना   सनीमा   समुल   समूल
  saminaa   saniimaa   samul   samuul

समेल **samel**   समैल **samail**   समोना   समौना   संट **sañT**
  samonaa   samaunaa

LESSON 2

Pattern Practice 1

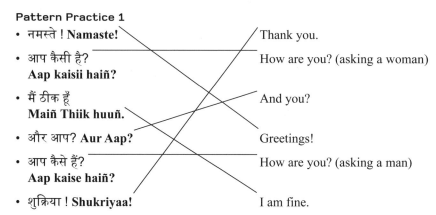

- नमस्ते ! **Namaste!**   Thank you.
- आप कैसी है? **Aap kaisii haiñ?**   How are you? (asking a woman)
- मैं ठीक हूँ **Maiñ Thiik huuñ.**   And you?
- और आप? **Aur Aap?**   Greetings!
- आप कैसे हैं? **Aap kaise haiñ?**   How are you? (asking a man)
- शुक्रिया ! **Shukriyaa!**   I am fine.

Pattern Practice 2

You: नमस्ते ! आप कैसे/कैसी हैं? **Namaste! Aap kaise/ kaisii haiñ?**

Passenger: नमस्ते ! मैं ठीक हूँ , शुक्रिया! और आप? **Namaste! Maiñ Thiik huuñ, shukriyaa! Aur aap?**

You: मैं ठीक हूँ , शुक्रिया ! **Maiñ Thiik huuñ, shukriyaa!**

Pattern Practice 3

1. नाम **naam**
2. आप कैसे/कैसी हैं? **Aap kaise/kaisii haiñ?**
3. शुक्रिया। **Shukriyaa.**
4. आप कहाँ से हैं? **Aap kahaañ se haiñ?**
5. मैं अमेरिका से हूँ। **Maiñ Amerika se huuñ.**
6. आप से मिल कर बड़ी खुशी हुई। **Aap se milkar baRii khushii huii.**
7. मुझे भी। **Mujhe bhii.**

Pattern Practice 4

1. आप कैसी हैं? **Aap kaisii haiñ?**
2. मैं ठीक हूँ। शुक्रिया। **Maiñ Thiik huuñ. Shukriyaa.**
3. मैं अमेरिका से हूँ। **Maiñ Amerika se huuñ.**
4. आप कहाँ से हैं? **Aap kahaañ se haiñ?**
5. आप से मिल कर बड़ी खुशी हुई। **Aap se milkar baRii khushii huii.**
6. मुझे भी। **Mujhe bhii.**

Pattern Practice 5

1. **meraa naam...hai** मेरा नाम ...है
2. **maiñ...se huuñ** मैं से हूँ ...

Pattern Practice 6

Question: Who is this?

Answer: This is Michael Jackson.

Pattern Practice 7

1. मेरा नाम माया है। <u>**Meraa**</u> **naam Maya** <u>**hai.**</u>
2. आपका नाम क्या है? <u>**Aap**</u> **kaa naam kyaa** <u>**hai?**</u>
3. आप कहाँ से हैं? <u>**Aap**</u> **kahaañ se** <u>**haiñ?**</u>
4. आप कैसे हैं? <u>**Aap**</u> **kaise** <u>**haiñ?**</u>
5. मैं अमेरिका से हूँ। <u>**Maiñ**</u> **Amerika se huuñ.**
6. ये हिंदुस्तानी हैं। <u>**Ye**</u> **Hindustaanii** <u>**haiñ.**</u>
7. वे अमेरिकन हैं। <u>**Ve**</u> **American** <u>**haiñ.**</u>
8. तुम कैसी हो? <u>**Tum**</u> **kaisii** <u>**ho?**</u>
9. तू बच्चा है। <u>**Tuu**</u> **bahchhaa** <u>**hai.**</u>
10. हम हिंदी विद्यार्थी हैं। <u>**Ham**</u> **Hindi vidyaarthii** <u>**haiñ.**</u>

Pattern Practice 8

1. यह मेरा भाई (brother) है। **Yah** <u>**meraa**</u> **bhaaii hai.**
2. वह मेरी बहन (sister) है। **Vah** <u>**merii**</u> **behen hai.**
3. यह अच्छी किताब (f) है। **Yah** <u>**achchhii**</u> **kitaab hai.**
4. आपका नाम क्या है? <u>**Aapkaa**</u> **naam kyaa haai?**
5. ये आपके हिंदी अध्यापक हैं। **Ye** <u>**aapke**</u> **Hindi adhyaapak hain.**

Exercise 1

1. मेरा नाम...है। **Meraa naam...hai.**
2. मैं...से हूँ। **Maiñ...se huuñ.**
3. मैं ठीक हूँ। **Maiñ Thiik huuñ.**
4. जी हाँ, मैं अमेरिकन हूँ। / जी नहीं, मैं अमेरिकन नहीं हूँ।
   Jii haañ, main American huuñ. Jii nahiiñ, main American nahiiñ huuñ.

Exercise 2

1. पिता **Pitaa**
4. किताब **kitaab**
2. मैं **Maiñ**
5. जी हाँ **jii haañ**
3. हम **ham**

Exercise 3

1. b. वे **ve**
4. a. और **aur**
2. b. बच्चा **bachchhaa**
5. a. मुझे भी। **mujhe bhii**
3. a. से **se**

Exercise 4

1. T   2. T   3. T   4. T   5. T

Exercise 5

- कैसा/ कैसे/ कैसी **kaisaa/ kaise/ kaisii** — Fine, OK
- विद्यार्थी **vidyaarthii** — Introduction
- ठीक **Thiik** — Mine
- परिचय **parichay** — How
- मेरा/ मेरे/ मेरी **meraa/mere/merii** — Student

LESSON 3

Pattern Practice 1

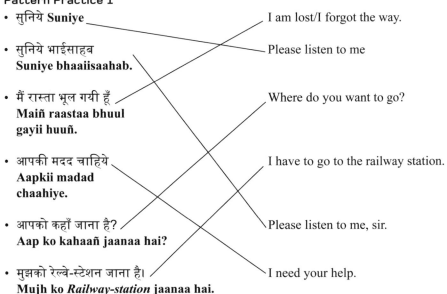

- सुनिये **Suniye** — I am lost/I forgot the way.
- सुनिये भाईसाहब **Suniye bhaaiisaahab.** — Please listen to me
- मैं रास्ता भूल गयी हूँ **Maiñ raastaa bhuul gayii huuñ.** — Where do you want to go?
- आपकी मदद चाहिये **Aapkii madad chaahiye.** — I have to go to the railway station.
- आपको कहाँ जाना है? **Aap ko kahaañ jaanaa hai?** — Please listen to me, sir.
- मुझको रेल्वे-स्टेशन जाना है। **Mujh ko *Railway-station* jaanaa hai.** — I need your help.

Pattern Practice 2

Verb	आप aap	तुम tum	तू tuu
1. बोलना	बोलिये boliye	बोलो bolo	बोल bol
2. बनाना	बनाइये banaaiye	बनाओ banaao	बना banaa
3. चलना	चलिये chaliye	चलो chalo	चल chal
4. गाना	गाइये gaaiye	गाओ gaao	गा gaa
5. नाचना	नाचिये naachiye	नाचो naacho	नाच naach

Pattern Practice 3

1. रेल्वे-स्टेशन यहाँ से दूर नहीं है। *Railway-station* **yahaañ se duur nahiiñ hai.**
2. पैदल कितने मिनट का रास्ता है? **Paidal kitne *minute* kaa raastaa hai?**
3. अच्छा। **Achchha.**
4. आप यहाँ से सीधे जाइये। **Aap yahaañ se siidhe jaaiye.**
5. ट्रैफ़िक लाइट से बायें मुड़िये, और सिनेमा-हाल तक जाइये। *Traffic light* **se baayeñ muRiye, aur *cinema-hall* tak jaaiye.**

6. ठीक। **Thiik.**
7. उसके बाद? **Uske baad?**
8. उसके बाद दायें मुड़िये। वहाँ एक टेक्सी-स्टैंड है। **Uske baad daayeñ muRiye. Vahaañ ek** *taxi-stand* **hai.**
9. टैक्सी-स्टैंड के सामने ही रेल्वे-स्टेशन है। *Taxi-stand* **ke saamne hii** *Railway-station* **hai.**
10. मदद के लिये बहुत बहुत शुक्रिया। **Madad ke liye bahut bahut shukriyaa.**
11. कोई बात नहीं। **Koii baat nahiiñ.**
12. मैं रास्ता भूल गया/गयी हूँ। **Maiñ raastaa bhuul gayaa/gayii huuñ.**
13. क्या आपको मालूम है...कहाँ है? **Kyaa aap ko maaluum hai...kahaañ hai?**
14. बायें मुड़िये। **Baayeñ muRiye.**
15. दायें मुड़िये। **Daayeñ muRiye.**

Pattern Practice 4

1. आपको; कहाँ **aapko; kahaañ**
2. कितने **kitne**
3. जाइये **jaaiye**
4. मुड़िये **muRiye**
5. के लिये **ke liye**

Exercise 1

1. उसके बाद **uske baad**
2. दूर **duur**
3. यहाँ **yahaañ**
4. मुझको/मुझे **mujhko/mujhe**
5. भूलना **bhuulnaa**
6. सीधे **siiDhe**
7. बताना **bataanaa**
8. X तक **X tak**
9. रास्ता **raastaa**

Exercise 2

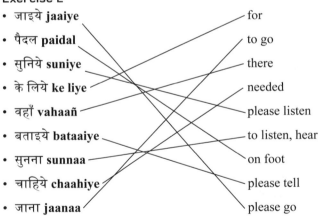

- जाइये **jaaiye**   for
- पैदल **paidal**   to go
- सुनिये **suniye**   there
- के लिये **ke liye**   needed
- वहाँ **vahaañ**   please listen
- बताइये **bataaiye**   to listen, hear
- सुनना **sunnaa**   on foot
- चाहिये **chaahiye**   please tell
- जाना **jaanaa**   please go

Exercise 3

1. b. मुड़ना **muRnaa**
2. c. ठीक है **Thiik hai**
3. c. कहिये **kahiye**
4. d. यहाँ से **yahaañ se**
5. b. X के सामने ही **X ke saamne hii**
6. a. पंद्रह **pandrah**
7. a. मुड़िये **muRiye**
8. d. दायें **daayeñ**
9. d. मदद **madad**

Exercise 4

1. T   2. T   3. T   4. T   5. T
6. T   7. T   8. T   9. T

Exercise 5

1. मैं रास्ता भूल गया/गयी हूँ। **Maiñ raastaa bhuul gayaa/gayii huuñ.**
2. मुझको मदद चाहिये। **Mujhko madad chaahiye.**
3. रेल्वे-स्टेशन कैसे जाती/जाता हूँ? *Railway-station* **kaise jaatii/jaataa huuñ?**
4. बायें मुड़िये। **Baayeñ muRiye.**
5. सीधे जाइये। **Siidhe jaaiye.**

LESSON 4

Pattern Practice 1

1. माया को शलवार-कुर्ता अपने आप के लिये चाहिये। **Maya ko shalvaar-kurtaa apne aap ke liye chaahiye.** Maya wants a *shalvaar-kurtaa* for herself.
2. माया को गहरा भूरा, नीला या काला शलवार-कुर्ता चाहिये। **Maya ko gehraa bhuuraa, niilaa yaa kaalaa shalvaar-kurtaa chaahiye.** Maya wants a deep brown, blue, or black *shalvaar-kurtaa.*
3. शलवार-कुर्ता के अलावा उसको एक सिल्क वाला दुपट्टा चाहिये। **Shalvaar-kurte ke alaavaa usko ek silkvaalaa dupaTTaa chaahiye.** Besides the *shalvaar-kurtaa,* she wants a silk *dupatta.*
4. शलवार-कुर्ते का दाम आठ सौ रुपये है। **Shalvaar-kurtaa kaa daam aaTh sau rupaye hai.** The price of the *shalvaar-kurtaa* is 800 rupees.
5. जी हाँ/जी नहीं, शलवार-कुर्ते का दाम मेरे हिसाब से ज़्यादा है/नहीं है। **Jii haañ/jii nahiiñ, shalvaar-kurtaa kaa daam mere hisaab se zyaadaa hai/nahiiñ hai.** Yes/no, in my opinion the the price of the *shalvaar-kurtaa* is/is not too high.

Pattern Practice 2

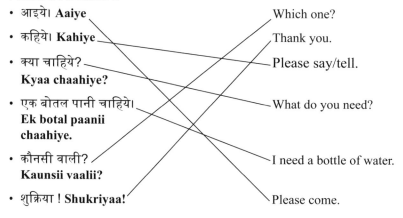

- आइये। **Aaiye**   Which one?
- कहिये। **Kahiye**   Thank you.
- क्या चाहिये?   Please say/tell.
  Kyaa chaahiye?
- एक बोतल पानी चाहिये।   What do you need?
  Ek botal paanii
  chaahiye.
- कौनसी वाली?   I need a bottle of water.
  Kaunsii vaalii?
- शुक्रिया ! **Shukriyaa!**   Please come.

Pattern Practice 3

1. मुझे दूध चाहिये। **Mujhe duudh chaahiye.**
2. मुझे अंडे चाहिये। **Mujhe anDe chaahiye.**
3. उस टूथब्रश का दाम क्या है? **Us** *toothbrush* **kaa daam kyaa hai?**
4. क्या मैं रोटी ख़रीद लूँ? **Kyaa main roTii khariid luuñ?**
5. क्या आप आइसक्रीम लेने में मेरी मदद कर सकते हैं? **Kyaa aap** *ice cream* **lene meñ merii madad kar sakte haiñ?**

Pattern Practice 4

1. वाली **vaalii** (Translation: I need/want a book in Hindi.)
2. वाली **vaalii** (Translation: Sit on the wooden chair.)
3. वाली **vaalii** (Translation: Would you like tea with milk?)
4. वाली **vaalii** (Translation: Please show (me) a silk sari.)
5. वाले **vaale** (Translation: Hindi-speaking students came here.)

Pattern Practice 5

1. क्या चाहिये **kyaa chaahiye**
2. चाहिये **chaahiye**
3. दाम क्या **daam kyaa**
4. सिर्फ़ आप के लिये **Sirf aap ke liye**
5. ज़्यादा है **zyaadaa hai**
6. कम कीजिये **kam kiijiye**
7. सात सौ रुपये दीजिये **saat sau rupaye diijiye**
8. लीजिये **liijiye**

Exercise 1

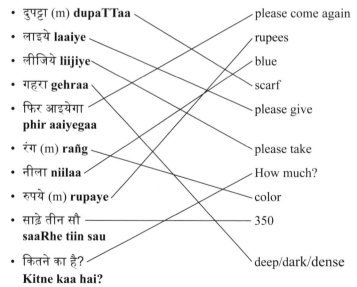

- दुपट्टा (m) **dupaTTaa**　　　　please come again
- लाइये **laaiye**　　　　rupees
- लीजिये **liijiye**　　　　blue
- गहरा **gehraa**　　　　scarf
- फिर आइयेगा **phir aaiyegaa**　　　　please give
- रंग (m) **rañg**　　　　please take
- नीला **niilaa**　　　　How much?
- रुपये (m) **rupaye**　　　　color
- साढ़े तीन सौ **saaRhe tiin sau**　　　　350
- कितने का है? **Kitne kaa hai?**　　　　deep/dark/dense

Exercise 2

1. d. सुंदर **sundar**
2. d. मुझको (मुझे) **mujhko/ mujhe**
3. c. काला **kaalaa**
4. d. आपके लिये **aap ke liye**
5. c. काला **kaalaa**
6. c. दाम (m) **daam**
7. a. सिर्फ़ **sirf**
8. b. आठ सौ **aaTh sau**
9. a. भूरा **bhuuraa**

Exercise 3

1. T
2. T
3. F
4. T
5. T
6. F
7. T
8. F
9. F
10. T

LESSON 5

Pattern Practice 1

- मेरा नाम माया है।
  Meraa naam Maya hai. —————— My name is Maya.

- मैं अमेरिकन हूँ।
  Maiñ Amerikan huuñ. —————— I am American.

- मेरा परिवार अमेरिका में है।
  Meraa parivaar Amerika meñ hai. —— There are five people in my family.

- मेरे परिवार में पाँच लोग हैं।
  Mere parivaar meñ paañch log haiñ. —— I have a mother and father, and two siblings.

- परिवार में माता-पिता हैं, और हम तीन बच्चे हैं।
  Parivaar meñ maataa-pitaa haiñ, aur ham tiin bachche haiñ. —— My family is in America.

Pattern Practice 2

(Open-ended answers.)

Pattern Practice 3

1. रसोई ग़ुसलख़ाने से बड़ी है। **Rasoii ghuslkhaane se baRii hai.**
2. मेज़ कुर्सी से सस्ती है। **Mez kursii se sastii hai.**
3. लीला सबसे छोटी है। **Lila sabse chhoTii hai.**

Pattern Practice 4

1. माया का परिवार अमेरिका में है। **Maya ka parivaar Amerika main hai.**
2. कबीर का परिवार जयपुर में है। **Kabir ka parivaar Jaipur main hai.**
3. माया के परिवार में पिता हैं, माता हैं, एक बहन है, और एक भाई है। **Maya ke parivaar meñ pitaa hai, maataa haiñ, ek bahan haiñ, aur ek bahee hai.**

4. कबीर के परिवार में पिता हैं, माता हैं, एक भाई है, एक बहन है, उसकी पत्नी है, और दो बेटियाँ हैं। **Kabir ke parivaar meñ pitaa jii haiñ, maataa jii haiñ, ek behen hai, merii patnii hai, aur do beTiyaañ hai.**

5. नहीं,बहन सब से बड़ी है। **Nahiiñ, behen sab se baRii hai.**

6. जी हाँ, भाई उससे छोटा है। **Jii haañ, bahee usaase chhoTaa hai.**

7. सिर्फ़ उसके माता-पिता शादी-शुदा हैं। **Sirf baad maataa-pitaa shaadii-shudaa hai.**

8. बहन तलाक-शुदा है। **Behen talaaq-shudaa hai.**

9. भाई शादी-शुदा है। **Bahee shaadii-shudaa hai.**

10. पिता सरकारी दफ़्तर में काम करते हैं और माता दर्जी है। **Pitaa sarkaarii daftar meñ kaam karate hain hai aur maataa darjii hai.**

11. कबीर के माता-पिता क्या करते हैं? **Kabir ke maataa-pitaa kyaa karte haiñ?** पिता रिटायर्ड हैं। और माता अध्यापिका हैं। **Pitaa *retired* hain aur maataa adhyaapikaa hain.**

12. कल जनमदिन है। **Kal janmdin hai.**

Pattern Practice 5

1. वह लंबी नहीं है। **Vah lambii nahiiñ hai.**
2. लीला सब से बड़ी नहीं है। **Liilaa sab se baRii nahiiñ hai.**
3. क्या आप दफ़्तर नहीं जा रहे/रही हैं? **Kyaa aap daftar nahiiñ jaa rahe/rahii haiñ?**
4. क्या आप शादी-शुदा नहीं हैं? **Kyaa aap shaadii-shudaa nahiiñ haiñ?**
5. डाक घर वहाँ नहीं है। **Daak ghar vahaañ nahiiñ hai.**
6. वह जर्मनी नहीं जा रहा है। **Vah Jarmanii nahiiñ jaa rahaa hai.**

Pattern Practice 6

1. मैं फ़ुटबाल खेलता हूँ। **Maiñ fuTbaal kheltaa huuñ.**
2. तुम दफ़्तर में काम करती हो। **Tum daftar meñ kaam kartii ho.**
3. वे खाना बनाती हैं। **Ve khaanaa banaatii haiñ.**
4. हम हिंदी सीखते हैं। **Ham Hindii siikhte haiñ.**
5. क्या आप हिन्दी सीखती हैं? **Kyaa aap Hindii siikhtii haiñ?**

Pattern Practice 7

1. मेरे परिवार में पाँच लोग हैं। **Mere parivaar meñ paañch log haiñ.**
2. वे अमेरिका में रहते हैं। **Ve Amerika meñ rehte haiñ.**
3. मेरी माता जी अध्यपिका हैं, मेरे पिता जी सरकार में काम करते हैं, मेरी बहन विद्यार्थी है और मेरा भाई बैंक मैनेजर है। **Merii maataa jii adhyapikaa haiñ, mere pitaa jii sarkaar meñ kaam karte haiñ, merii behen vidyaarthii hai aur meraa bhaaii baink mainejar hai.**
4. मेरी बहन शादी-शुदा है लेकिन मेरा भाई शादी-शुदा नहीं है। **Merii behen shaadii-shudaa hai lekin meraa bhaaii shaadii-shudaa nahiiñ hai.**

Exercise 1

1. पिता **pitaa**
2. लड़के **laRke**
3. सुंदर **sundar**
4. तलाक़ **talaaq**
5. शादी **shaadii**
6. आठ **aaTh**
7. अध्यापक **adhyaapak**
8. उसके बाद **uske baad**
9. अध्यापिका **adhyaapikaa**
10. नौ **nau**
11. पति **pati**
12. भाई **bhaaii**
13. तीन **tiin**
14. अमेरिकन **amerikan**

Exercise 2

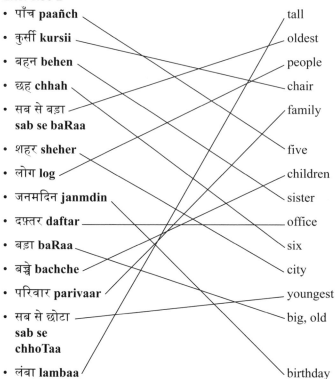

- पाँच **paañch** — tall
- कुर्सी **kursii** — oldest
- बहन **behen** — people
- छह **chhah** — chair
- सब से बड़ा **sab se baRaa** — family
- शहर **sheher** — five
- लोग **log** — children
- जनमदिन **janmdin** — sister
- दफ़्तर **daftar** — office
- बड़ा **baRaa** — six
- बच्चे **bachche** — city
- परिवार **parivaar** — youngest
- सब से छोटा **sab se chhoTaa** — big, old
- लंबा **lambaa** — birthday

Exercise 3

1. a. सरकारी **sarkaarii**
2. c. मुझ से **mujh se**
3. c. मुबारक हो ! **Mubaarak ho!**
4. d. मेज़ (f) **mez**
5. b. पत्नी **patnii**
6. c. आप से **aap se**
7. d. लड़कियाँ **laRkiyaañ**
8. b. शौचालय **shauchaalaya**
9. a. नाम (m) **naam**
10. b. सस्ता/ सस्ती/ सस्ते **sastaa, sastii, saste**
11. a. हिंदुस्तानी **Hindustaanii**
12. c. कौन-कौन **kaun-kaun**
13. b. लड़का **laRkaa**
14. d. सात **saat**

Exercise 4

1. T	2. T	3. F	4. F	5. F
6. F	7. T	8. F	9. T	10. T
11. F	12. T	13. T		

LESSON 6

Pattern Practice 1

1. लोग घर सजाते हैं, मिठाई बनाते हैं, पूजा करते हैं, नये कपड़े पहनते हैं, आतिशबाज़ी करते हैं। **Log ghar sajaate haiñ, miThaaii banaate haiñ, puujaa karte haiñ, naye kapRe pehente haiñ, aatishbaazii karte haiñ.**
2. परिवार के साथ मंदिर जाता है। माता-पिता के पाँव छूता है। मिठाई खाता है। परिवार के साथ हिंदी फ़िल्में देखता है। **Parivaar ke saath mandir jaataa hai. Maataa-pitaa ke paañv chhuutaa hai. MiThaaii khaataa hai. Parivaar ke saath Hindii film eñ dekhtaa hai.**
3. उसे जन्मदिन पर दोस्तों से मिलना पसंद है। **Use janmdin par dostoñ se milnaa pasand hai.**
4. माता-पिता के पाँव छूता है। **Maataa-pitaa ke paañv chhuutaa hai.**
5. लोग पाँच दिन दिवाली मनाते हैं। **Log paanch din divaalii manaate haiñ.**

Pattern Practice 2

1. वह जन्मदिन के लिये पार्टी करता था। **Vah janmdin ke liye paarTii kartaa thaa.**
2. वे परिवार के साथ मंदिर जाते थे। **Ve parivaar ke saath mandir jaate the.**
3. हिंदुस्तानी लोग दिवाली बहुत धूम-धाम से मनाते थे। **Hindustaanii log divaalii bahut dhuum-dhaam se manaate the.**
4. मैं जन्मदिन पर दोस्तों से मिलता था/मिलती थी। **Maiñ janmdin par dostoñ se miltaa thaa/miltii thii.**
5. वह हिंदी फ़िल्में देखती थी। **Vah Hindii filmeñ dekhtii thii.**

Pattern Practice 3

1. What does Maya like to do on her birthday?
2. I like cake.
3. What does Kabir not like to do on his birthday?
4. What does Kabir do on his birthday?

Pattern Practice 4

1. In my childhood, I used to ride a bicycle but these days I drive a car.
2. In my childhood, I used to play football every day but these days I only play occasionally.
3. In my childhood, I watched a lot of cartoons but these days I watch a lot of news.

Exercise 1

1. हिंदुस्तानी तरीक़ा **Hindustaanii tariiqaa**
2. और **aur**
3. खाना **khaanaa**
4. पसंद **pasand**
5. बचपन में **bachpan meñ**
6. कभी कभी **kabhii kabhii**
7. जानकारी **jaankaarii**
8. करना **karnaa**
9. दोस्त **dost**
10. पर **par**

Exercise 2

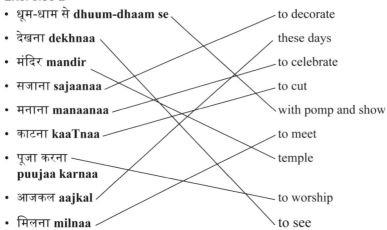

- धूम-धाम से **dhuum-dhaam se**
- देखना **dekhnaa**
- मंदिर **mandir**
- सजाना **sajaanaa**
- मनाना **manaanaa**
- काटना **kaaTnaa**
- पूजा करना **puujaa karnaa**
- आजकल **aajkal**
- मिलना **milnaa**

to decorate
these days
to celebrate
to cut
with pomp and show
to meet
temple
to worship
to see

Exercise 3

1. b. खेलना **khelnaa**
2. d. त्योहार (m) **tyohaar**
3. b. दोस्तों से मिलना **dostoñ se milnaa**
4. d. दिवाली **divaalii**
5. c. आतिशबाज़ी (f) **aatishbaazii**
6. c. आज **aaj**
7. d. चावल (m) **chaaval**
8. d. इसकी क्या ज़रूरत थी। **Is kii kyaa zaruurat thii.**
9. b. छूना **chhuunaa**
10. d. उमर (f) **umar**

Exercise 4

1. T   2. T   3. T   4. F   5. T
6. F   7. T   8. F   9. F   10. T

LESSON 7

Pattern Practice 1

1. यह है तुम्हारा निमंत्रण कार्ड। **Yah hai tumhaaraa nimantraN card.**
2. ज़रूर आना, भूलना नहीं। **Zaruur aanaa, bhuulnaa nahiiñ.**
3. निमंत्रण के लिये शुक्रिया! **NimantraN ke liye shukriyaa!**

Pattern Practice 2

1. किसका/किसकी/किसके **kiskaa/kiskii/kiske**
2. खुश लगना <u>**khush lagnaa**</u>
3. दुल्हन **dulhan**
4. मदद के लिये शुक्रिया **Madad ke liye shukriyaa.**
5. कल **kal**
6. इक्कीस **ikkiis**
7. लाल **laal**

Pattern Practice 3

1. रहा **raha**   2. कर **kar**   3. रहे **rahe**   4. रही **rahii**   5. सीख **siik**

Exercise 1

1. सुनना **sunnaa**
2. क्यों नहीं **kyoñ nahiiñ**
3. मुबारक हो **mubaarak ho**
4. शादी **shaadii**
5. शुक्रवार **Shukrvaar**
6. सुनाना **sunaanaa**

Exercise 2

1. c. निमंत्रण **nimantraN**
2. d. कब **kab**
3. c. ख़ुशी की बात **khushii kii baat**
4. a. ख़ुशी **khushii** (f)
5. d. बहुत **bahut**
6. b. शुक्रिया **shukriyaa**

Exercise 3

1. F   2. T   3. F   4. T   5. T   6. F

LESSON 8

Pattern Practice 1

1. वे हाथों पर मेंहदी लगाते हैं। **Ve hāthoñ par mehandii lagaate haiñ.**
2. वे आग के चारों ओर चक्कर लगाते हैं। **Ve aag ke chaaroñ or saat chakkar lagaate haiñ.**
3. वे नाचती-गाती हैं। **Ve naachtii-gaatii haiñ.**
4. वे शादी जा रहे हैं। **Ve shaadii jaa rahe haiñ.**
5. हिंदू शादी में ख़ास रीति-रिवाज़ होते हैं। **Hinduu shaadii meñ khaas riiti-rivaaz hote haiñ.**

Pattern Practice 2

1. हिंदू शादी में तीन ख़ास रीति-रिवाज़ होते हैं - मेंहदी, महिला संगीत, और फेरे। **Hindu shaadii meñ tiin khaas riiti-rivaaz hote haiñ—mehandii, mahilaa sangiit, aur phere.**
2. ग्यारह, इक्कीस, इक्यावन, एक सौ एक, पाँच सौ एक अच्छा शगुन हैं। **Gyaarah, ikkiis, ikyaawan, ek sau paañch, paañch sau ek, achchha shagun haiñ.**
3. महिला-संगीत में औरतें नाचती-गाती हैं। **Mahilaa sangiit meiñ aurateñ naachtii-gaatii haiñ.**
4. शादी में शगुन के रुपये देना अच्छा है। **Shaadii meñ shagun ke rupaye denaa achchhaa hai.**

Pattern Practice 3

1. Maya is going to Leela's brother's wedding.
2. In a Hindu wedding there are three special customs.
3. Maya is wearing a pink sari.
4. Maya is bringing flowers for the wedding.

Pattern Practice 4

1. Today I am riding a bicycle but I usually drive a car.
2. Our children are playing football.
3. My sisters are watching the news right now.
4. What do women do at the bridal shower?
5. What happens during the "Phere"?

Exercise 1

1. शादी में जा रही है। **Shaadii meñ jaa rahii hai.**
2. गुलाबी साड़ी पहन रही है। **Gulaabii saaRii pehen rahii hai.**
3. ग्यारह, इक्कीस, इक्यावन, एक सौ एक, पाँच सौ एक ठीक हैं। **Gyaarah, ikkiis, ikyaavan, ek sau ek, paach sau ek Thiik haiñ.**
4. लीला व्यस्त है क्योंकि उसके बड़े भाई की शादी है। **Leela vyast hai kyoñki uske baRe bhaaii kii shaadii hai.**
5. लीला के बड़े भाई की शादी है। **Leela ke baRe bhaaii kii shaadii hai.**
6. बीस मार्च को। उस दिन शुक्रवार है। **Biis March ko. Us din shukrvaar hai.**
7. मेंहदी, महिला संगीत, और फेरे। **Mehandii, mahila sangiit aur phere.**
8. मेंहदी में लोग दूल्हा-दुल्हन के परिवार के लोगों को मेंहदी लगाते हैं। **Mehandii meñ log duulha-dulhan ke parivaar ke logoñ ko mehandii lagaate haiñ.**

Exercise 2

1. संगीत **sangiit**
2. नाचना **naachnaa**
3. मेंहदी **mehandii**
4. रीति-रिवाज **riiti-rivaaz**
5. चारों ओर **chaaroñ or**

Exercise 3

1. d. रुपये **rupaye** (m)
2. d. सवाल **savaal** (m)
3. c. शगुन **shagun** (m)
4. c. एक सौ पाँच **ek sau paañch**
5. a. ग्यारह **gyaarah**
6. b. क्या बात है? **Kyaa baat hai?**
7. a. फेरे लगाना **phere lagaanaa**
8. a. रीति **riiti** (f)
9. d. महिला **mahilaa**
10. b. फेरे लगाना **phere lagaanaa**

Exercise 4

1.	F	2.	T	3.	T	4.	T	5.	F
6.	T	7.	T	8.	F	9.	F		

Exercise 5

- कौनसा **kaunsaa** — which (one)
- लिफ़ाफ़ा **lifaafaa** (m) — envelope
- दूल्हा **duulhaa** — groom
- साड़ी **saaRii** (f) — sari
- जितनी आपकी मर्ज़ी **jitnii aapkii marzii** — however much you like
- इक्यावन **ikyaawan** — fifty-one
- पहनना **pehennaa** — to wear
- फेरे **phere** (m) — circles (around holy fire)
- गाना **gaanaa** — to sing
- औरत **aurat** — woman
- मेंहदी लगाना **mehandii lagaana** — to apply henna

LESSON 9

Pattern Practice 1

1. माया दक्षिण भारत में केरल, चैन्नई, और मैसूर जाएगी। **Maya dakshin Bhaarat meñ Kerala, Chennai, aur Mysore jaeegii.**
2. जी हाँ, दक्षिण भारत में देखने लायक़ बहुत जगहें हैं। **Jii haañ, dakshin Bhaarat meñ dekhne laayaq bahut jagaheñ haiñ.**
3. माया केरल, चेन्नई, और मैसूर जाएगी। **Maya Kerala, Chennai, aur Mysore jayegii.**
4. माया आज शाम को होटल बुक करेगी। **Maya aaj shaam ko** *hotel book* **karegii.**
5. वह महारानी होटल में रुकेगी। **Vah Maharani** *Hotel* **me rukegii.**
6. वह तीन दिन रुकेगी, दस दिसंबर से बारह दिसंबर तक। **Vah tiin din rukegii, das DBambar se baarah DBambar tak.**
7. होटल का किराया है आठ सौ रुपये प्रतिदिन। *Hotel* **kaa kiraayaa hai aaTh sau rupaye pratidin.**
8. माया के लिये किराया सात सौ रुपये है। **Maya ke liye** *hotel* **kaa kiraayaa saat sau rupaye hai.**
9. नाश्ता, मुफ़्त इंटरनेट, स्वीमिंग पूल, और जिम भी शामिल हैं। **Naashtaa, muft** *internet, swimming pool,* **aur** *gym* **bhii shaamil haiñ.**

Pattern Practice 2

1. के बारे में **ke baare meñ**
2. देखने लायक़ **dekhne laayaq**
3. दक्षिण भारत **dakshin Bhaarat**
4. छुट्टियों में **chhuTTiyoñ meñ**

Pattern Practice 3

- जगह **jagah** (f) ——————————— to remind
- याद दिलाना **yaad dilaanaa** ——————— place
- शाम को **shaam ko** ————————————— in the evening
- छुट्टी **chhuTTii** (f) ————————————— to think
- मुफ़्त **muft** ——————————————————— included
- शामिल **shaami** ——————————————————— day off, vacation
- सोचना **sochnaa** ——————————————————— free of charge

Pattern Practice 4

1. c. बुक करना *book* **karnaa**   2. c. जगहें **jagaheñ** (f)   3. a. सोचना **sochnaa**

Pattern Practice 5

1. T   2. F   3. F

Pattern Practice 6

1. जाएगी **jaaegii**   2. देखूँगा **dekhuuñgaa**   3. करेंगी **kareñgii**
4. सीखेगी **siikhegii**   5. करोगे **karoge**

Pattern Practice 7

1. मैं लंदन जाऊँगा/जाऊँगी। **Maiñ** *London* **jaauuñgaa/jaauuñgii.**
2. मैं लंदन में मेडम टूसोज़ और टाउर टॉवर लंदन जाऊँगा/जाऊँगी। **Maiñ** *London* **meñ** *Madame Tussauds* **aur** *Tower of London* **jaauuñgaa/jaauuñgii.**
3. मैं रेस्टोरेंट्स में रात का खाना खाऊँगा/खाऊँगी। **Maiñ** *restaurants* **meñ raat kaa khaanaa khaauuñgaa/khaauuñgii.**
4. मैं होटल में ठहरूँगा /ठहरूँगी। **Maiñ** *hotel* **meñ Theheruuñgaa/Theheruuñgii.**

Pattern Practice 8

1. मैं तीन दिन के लिये कमरा बुक करना चाहता/चाहती हूँ। **Maiñ tiin din ke liye kamraa book karnaa caahtaa/caahtii huuñ.**
2. दस दिसंबर से बारह दिसंबर तक। **Das Disambar se baarah Disambar tak.**
3. आपके होटल में कमरे का किराया कितना है? **Aapke hotel meñ kamre kaa kiraayaa kitnaa hai?**
4. किराया ज़रा कम कीजिये। **Kiraayaa zaraa kam kiijiye.**
5. क्या नाश्ता किराये में शामिल है? **Kyaa naashtaa kiraaye meñ shaamil hai?**

Exercise 1

1. सौ **sau**
2. सेवा **sevaa**
3. किराया ज़रा कम कीजिये। **Kiraayaa zaraa kam kiijiye.**
4. यहाँ ... है/हैं। **Yahaañ... hai/haiñ.**
5. क्या सेवा करूँ? **Kyaa sevaa karuuñ?**
6. के लिये **X ke liye**
7. किराया **kiraayaa**
8. आपके लिये **aapke liye**

Exercise 2

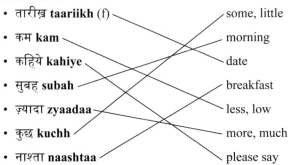

- तारीख़ taariikh (f) ——— some, little
- कम kam ——— morning
- कहिये kahiye ——— date
- सुबह subah ——— breakfast
- ज़्यादा zyaadaa ——— less, low
- कुछ kuchh ——— more, much
- नाश्ता naashtaa ——— please say

Exercise 3

1. a. कुछ ज़्यादा **kuchh zyaadaa**
2. d. शामिल **shaamil**
3. a. प्रतिदिन **pratidin**
4. b. अलग से **alag se**
5. b. तो **to**
6. c. कितना **kitnaa**
7. a. मुफ़्त **muft**

Exercise 4

1. T   2. F   3. T   4. F   5. F
6. T   7. F

LESSON 10

Pattern Practice 1

1. मेरा भाई चाय बनाए। **Meraa bhaaii chaay banaae.** My brother may make tea.
2. वह भी भारत जाए। **Vah bhii bhaarat jaae.** She may also come to India.
3. मैं हिंदी सीखूँ। **Maiñ Hindi siikhuuñ.** I may learn Hindi.

Pattern Practice 2

1. हो सकता है कि वह भी इस साल हिंदी सीखे। **Ho saktaa hai ki vah bhii is saal Hindi siikhe.** She may learn Hindi this year. (She is likely to learn Hindi this year.)
2. आप आज नहीं कल आएँ। **Aap aaj nahiiñ kal aaeñ.** Please come tomorrow, not today.
3. माफ़ कीजिये, लेकिन शायद मैं आज न आ सकूँ। **Maaf kiijiye, lekin shaayad maiñ aaj na aa sakuuñ.** Please excuse me, but I may not be able to come today.
4. इसके बाद मैं क्या करूँ? **Iske baad maiñ kyaa karuuñ?** After this, what shall I do?
5. आप यहाँ बैठें। **Aap yahaañ baitheñ.** (You) Please sit here.

Pattern Practice 3

1. अगर तुम चाय बनाओ तो मैं पीऊँगा। **Agar tum chaay banaao to maiñ piiuuñgaa.**
2. यदि मैं हिन्दी सीखूँ तो मैं भारत जाऊँगा। **Yadi maiñ Hindi siikhuuñ to maiñ Bhaarat jaauuñgaa.**
3. अगर आप दुकान जाएँ तो मैं वहाँ आपसे मिलूँगा। **Agar aap dukaan jaaeñ to maiñ vahaañ aapse miluuñgaa.**
4. अगर तुम उनके घर जाओ तो वे तुम्हारे लिये लिये खाना पकाएँगी। **Agar tum unke ghar jaao to ve tumhaare liye khaanaa pakaaeñgii.**
5. यदि आप भारत जाएँ तो आप ताज महल जा सकेंगे। **Yadi aap Bhaarat jaaeñ to aap Taj Mahal jaa sakeñge.**

Exercise 1

1. मसालेदार **masaaledaar**   2. चाय **chaay**
3. जीरा **jiiraa**   4. पीना **piinaa**
5. माँसाहारी **maañsaahaarii**   6. चीनीवाली चाय **chiiniivaalii chaay**
7. क्रेडिट कार्ड **kreDiT kaarD**   8. कैश, नक़द **kaish, naqd**

Exercise 2

1. A: क्या तुम आज रात को मुझको फ़ोन कर सकते हो? **Kyaa tum aaj raat ko mujhko *phone* kar sakte ho?**
   B: जी हाँ, मैं तुम्हें आज रात को फ़ोन करूँगा। **Jii haañ, maiñ tumheñ aaj raat ko *phone* karuuñgaa.**
2. A: क्या आपको हिंदी आती है? **Kyaa aapko Hindi aatii hai?**
   B: मुझे थोड़ी सी हिंदी आती है। **Mujhe thoRii sii Hindi aatii hai.**
3. A: क्या आप यह खाना खा सकते हैं? मसालेदार है! **Kyaa aap yah khaanaa khaa sakte haiñ? Masaaledaar hai!**

B: मैं यह खा नहीं सकता। बहुत ज़्यादा मसालेदार है। **Maiñ yah khaa nahiiñ saktaa. Bahut zyaadaa masaaledaar hai.**

Exercise 3

1. मैं हिंदुस्तानी खाना खाना चाहता हूँ। **Maiñ Hindustaanii khaanaa khaanaa chaahtaa huuñ.**
2. क्या तुम हिंदुस्तानी खाना खाना चाहती हो? **Kyaa tum Hindustaanii khaanaa khaanaa chaahtii ho?**
3. मैं एक हिंदी फ़िल्म देखना चाहता हूँ। **Maiñ ek Hindi *film* dekhnaa chaahtaa huuñ.**
4. मैं ख़रीददारी करना चाहता हूँ। **Maiñ khariidaarii karnaa chaahtaa huuñ.**
5. मैं ताज महल देखना चाहती हूँ। **Maiñ Taj Mahal dekhnaa chaahtii huuñ.**

LESSON 11

Pattern Practice 1

1. Transitive   2. Transitive   3. Transitive   4. Transitive   5. Intransitive

Pattern Practice 2

1. सीखा **siikha**   2. बोला **bola**   3. सोचा **socha**
4. सोया **soya**   5. आया **aaya**

Exercise 1

1. माया माता-पिता से मिलने के लिये हवाई-अड्डे गयी। **Maya maataa-pitaa se milne ke liye havaaii-aDDe gayii.** Maya went to the airport to meet her parents.
2. माया का सैल-फ़ोन हवाई-अड्डे में कहीं गिर गया। **Maya kaa *cell phone* havaaii-aDDe meñ kahiiñ gir gayaa.** Maya's phone was dropped somewhere in the airport.
3. माया के माता-पिता अमेरिका से भारत आये। **Maya ke maataa-pitaa Amerika se Bhaarat aaye.** Maya's parents came from America to India.
4. नहीं, अभी तक माया ने फ़ोन के खोने की रिपोर्ट दर्ज़ नहीं की है। **Nahiiñ, abhii tak Maya ne *phone* khone kii *report* darz nahiiñ kii hai.** No, Maya has not reported the loss of her phone yet.
5. सैल-फ़ोन के पीछे माया का नाम लिखा है, हिंदी में। **Cell phone ke piichhe Maya kaa naam likhaa hai, Hindi meñ.** Maya's name is written on the back of the phone in Hindi.

Pattern Practice 3

1. हुआ **huaa**   2. आये। **aaye**   3. खो गयी **kho gayii**
4. गये **gaye**   5. देखी **dekhii**

Exercise 2

1. मेरा कंप्यूटर खो गया है! **Meraa *computers* kho goyaa hai!**
2. मैंने यह फ़िल्म दो महीने पहले देखी थी। **Maiñne yah *film* do mahine pehle dekhii thii.**
3. मुझे ऐसा लगता है। **Mujhe aisaa lagtaa hai.**
4. क्या तुमने कंप्यूटर के खोने की रिपोर्ट दर्ज़ की है? **Kyaa tumne *computer* ke khone kii *report* darz kii hai?**
5. मेरे हिसाब से…/मेरे ख़्याल से…/मेरे विचार से… **Mere hisaab se…/mere khayaal se…/mere vichaar se…**
6. आपका विचार बहुत अच्छा है। **Aapkaa vichaar bahut achchhaa hai.**

7. मैं आपके लिये क्या करूँ? **Maiñ aapke liye kyaa karuuñ?**
8. यहाँ बहुत ऐसी किताबें हैं। **Yahaañ bahut aisii kitaabeñ haiñ.**
9. आप अपना आई-कार्ड दिखाइये। **Aap apnaa *I-card* dikhaaiye.**
10. शुक्रिया। **Shukriyaa.**
11. कोई बात नहीं। **Koii baat nahiiñ.**

Exercise 3

1. आप पिछले साल कहाँ गये थे? **Aap pichhle saal kahaañ gaye the?** Where did you go last year?
2. क्या आपने यह फ़िल्म देखी है? **Kyaa aapne yah film dekhii hai?** Have you seen this film?
3. यह फ़िल्म मैंने बचपन में देखी थी। **Yah film maiñne bachpan meñ dekhii thii.** I had seen this film in my childhood.

Exercise 4

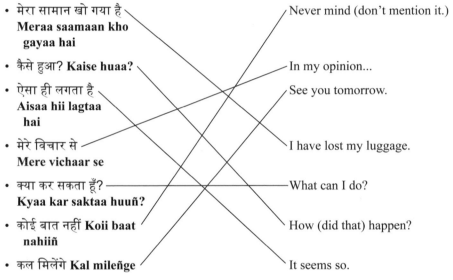

- मेरा सामान खो गया है **Meraa saamaan kho gayaa hai**
- कैसे हुआ? **Kaise huaa?**
- ऐसा ही लगता है **Aisaa hii lagtaa hai**
- मेरे विचार से **Mere vichaar se**
- क्या कर सकता हूँ? **Kyaa kar saktaa huuñ?**
- कोई बात नहीं **Koii baat nahiiñ**
- कल मिलेंगे **Kal mileñge**

- Never mind (don't mention it.)
- In my opinion...
- See you tomorrow.
- I have lost my luggage.
- What can I do?
- How (did that) happen?
- It seems so.

Exercise 5

1. बुरा **buraa**
2. कर्मचारी **kaarmchaarii**
3. जानकारी देना **jaankaarii denaa**
4. जानकारी **jaankaarii**
5. सामान **saamaan**

Exercise 6

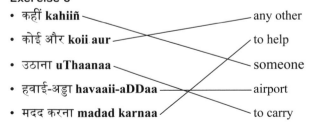

- कहीं **kahiiñ**
- कोई और **koii aur**
- उठाना **uThaanaa**
- हवाई-अड्डा **havaaii-aDDaa**
- मदद करना **madad karnaa**

- any other
- to help
- someone
- airport
- to carry

Exercise 7

1. d. दर्ज़ करना **darz karanaa**
2. b. ऐसा **aisaa**
3. b. गिर जाना **gir jaanaa**
4. a. पहचान **pehchaan**
5. d. भीड़ **bhiiRh**

Exercise 8

1. T   2. F   3. T   4. F   5. F

. . . .

PHOTO CREDITS

Images used in the book come from the following stock libraries:

AdobeStock
gajendra (p 109); michaeljung (p 37)

Shutterstock
Andrey Bayda (p 73); birds friends (p 28 [elephant driver]); chin_2_singh (p 133); Daniel J. Rao (p 170); De Visu (pp 150/151); Dmitry Galanganov (p 163); Don Mammoser (p 45, p 149); Elena Ermakova (pp 18/19); Finn stock (p 53); fizkes (p 5); IndianFaces (p 71); IVASHstudio (p 131); Jayakumar (pp 134/135); JeJai Images (p 168); Joshua Resnick (p 157); Kseniya Pavlenko (p 33 [Michael Jackson]); Mazur Travel (p 43, p 159); MFAHEEM FAHEEM (p 66); Mohammad Shahnawaz (p 162); nevenm (p 28 [black bear]); Pete Burana (p 158); PremiumStock (p 127); Radiokafka (p 35, p 68); rob zs (p 33 [Obama]); Roop_Dey (p 94); saiko3p (p 36, pp 54/55); SGPicture (p 124); small1 (p 65); Sofa Zhuravetc (p 29); Sreeyash Lohiya (p 52); StockImageFactory.com (p 102, p 156); Sudarshan negi (p 126); Susmit Das (p 116, p 129); SyedAliAshraf (p 117, p 132)); The Happy Tag (p 118); Tyshchenko Photography (p 114); V.S Anandhakrishna (p 31); Wanderlust Media (p 44); yurakrasil (p 74); Zvonimir Atletic (p 164)

English–Hindi Dictionary

A

able to, to be (v.i.) **paanaa; saknaa** पाना/सकना

about X (pp) **X ke baare meñ** X के बारे में

above (adv) **uupar** ऊपर

above X (pp) **X ke uupar** X के ऊपर

accelerator (m) **ekselareTar** एक्सेलरेटर

accident (f) **durghaTnaa** दुर्घटना

address, whereabouts (m) **pataa** पता

adjoining (adj) **agal-bagal vaalaa** अगल-बगल वाला

after X (pp) **X ke baad** X के बाद

afternoon (f) **dopahar** दोपहर

afterwards (adv) **baad meñ** बाद में

again (adv) **phir** फिर

age (f) **umr** उम्र

ago; before; previously (adv) **pehle** पहले

ahead (adv) **aage** आगे

ahead of X (pp) **X ke aage** X के आगे

airmail (f) **havaaii Daak** हवाई डाक

airport (m) **havaaii aDDaa** हवाई अड्डा

alcohol; wine (f) **sharaab** शराब

allergy (f) **elarjii** एलर्जी

alone (adj) **akelaa** अकेला

ambulance (m; f) **embulens** एम्बुलेंस

another, second (adj) **duusraa** दूसरा

answer; north (m) **uttar** उत्तर

answer, to (to give an answer) (v.t.) **uttar denaa** उत्तर देना

antibiotics (m) **enTībāyoTik** एंटीबायोटिक

any (pron, adj) **koii** कोई

appear, to (v.i.) (to be visible) **dikhnaa** दिखना

appointment (m) **apaainTmenT** अपॉइंटमेंट

April (m) **Apraił** अप्रैल

area code (m) **eriya koD** एरिया कोड

around X (pp) **X ke aaspaas** X के आसपास

arrival (m) **aagaman** आगमन

arrive, to (v.i.) **pahuñchnaa** पहुँचना

ask, to (v.t.) **puuchhnaa** पूछना

asthma (m) **damaa** दमा

atheist (adj, m) **naastik** नास्तिक

ATM (m) **e. Tii. em.** ए० टी० एम०

attach, to (v.i.) **lagnaa** लगना

attach (v.t.); seem, to **lagaanaa** लगाना

attention; meditation (m) **dhyaan** ध्यान

attention, to give; pay (v.t.) **dhyaan denaa** ध्यान देना

August (m) **agast** अगस्त

auspicious (adj) **shubh** शुभ

auto(rickshaw) (m) **aaTo** ऑटो

available, to be (v.i.) **milnaa** मिलना

B

bad (adj) **kharaab; buraa** ख़राब; बुरा

bag (f) **thailii** थैली

bank (m) **baink** बैंक

barber (m) **naaii** नाई

barfi (a milk-based sweet) (f) **barfii** बर्फ़ी

battery (m); (for car, f) **sel; baiTrii** सेल; बैट्री

beard (f) **daaRhii** दाढ़ी

beautiful (pleasing) (adj) **suhaavnaa** सुहावना; (handsome) (adj) **sundar** सुंदर

beauty salon (m) **sailaan** सैलॉन

become, to (v.i.) (to be made); happen, to **bannaa; honaa** बनना/होना

bed (cot) **caarpaaii (f); palang (m)** चारपाई/पलंग

beef (m) **gaay kaa gosht** गाय का गोश्त

beer (f) **biyar** बियर

before X (pp) **X ke pehle** X के पहले

beginning (m) **shuruu** शुरू

behind (adv) **piichhe** पीछे

behind X (pp) **X ke piichhe** X के पीछे

belief (m) **yaqiin** यक़ीन

believe, to (belief to be) (v.i.) **yaqiin honaa** यक़ीन होना

below (adv) **niiche** नीचे

below X (pp) **X ke niche** X के नीचे

bend (m) **moR** मोड़

berth (m) **barth** बर्थ

best wishes (f, pl.) **shubhkaamnaaeñ** शुभकामनाएँ

bhatura (bread baked on a griddle and deep fried) (m) **bhaTuuraa** भटूरा

big (adj) **baRaa** बड़ा

bill (check) (m) **bil** बिल

biriyani (f) **biryaanii** बिरयानी

birth (m) **janm** जन्म

birthday (m) **janmdin** जन्मदिन

bite, to (v.t.) **kaaTnaa** काटना

bitter (adj) **kaRvaa** कड़वा

black (adj) **kaalaa** काला

blanket (m) **kambal** कम्बल

blood (m) **khuun** ख़ून

blue (adj) **niilaa** नीला

boat (f) **naav** नाव

boil, to (v.t.) **ubaalnaa** उबालना

boiled (adj) **ublaa huaa** उबला हुआ

bother, to (v.t.) **tang karnaa** तंग करना

book (f) **kitaab** किताब

book, to (v.t.) **buuking karaanaa** बुकिंग कराना

booking (f) **buuking** बुकिंग

booking office (m) **buuking aafis** बुकिंग ऑफ़िस

bookstore (f) **kitaab kii dukaan** किताब की दुकान

bottom (adv) (below) **niiche** नीचे

boy (m) **laRkaa** लड़का

brake (m) (car) **brek** ब्रेक

bread (roti) (f) **roTii; chapaatii** रोटी/चपाती

break, to (v.i.) **TuuTnaa** टूटना

break down, to (v.i.) **kharaab honaa** ख़राब होना

breaker (adj) **avarodhak** अवरोधक

breakfast (m) **naashtaa** नाश्ता

breathe, to (v.t.) **saañs lenaa** साँस लेना

breeze (f) **bayaar** बयार

bridge (m) **pul** पुल

bring, to (v.i.) **laanaa** लाना

brochure (m) **broshar** ब्रोशर

brother (m) **bhaaii** भाई

brown (adj) **bhuuraa** भूरा

Buddhism (m) **Bauddh dharm** बौद्ध धर्म

Buddhist (adj, m) **Bauddh** बौद्ध

burn, to (v.i.) **jalnā** जलना

bus (f) **bas** बस

bus terminus (m) **bas kaa aDDaa** बस का अड्डा

businessman; person (m; f) **vyaapaarii** व्यापारी

busy (adj) **vyast** व्यस्त

butter (m) **makkhan** मक्खन

buttermilk (f) **chhaachh** छाछ

button (m) **baTan** बटन

buy, to (v.t.) **khariidnaa** ख़रीदना

by; from; through (pp) **se** से

C

cabbage (f) **band gobhii** बंद गोभी

calculation (m) **hisaab** हिसाब

calculate, to (v.t.) **hisaab lagaanaa** हिसाब लगाना

call, to (X, Y) (v.t.) **X ko Y kehnaa** X को Y कहना

call, to (v.t.) (summon) **bulaanaa** बुलाना

canceled, to have (v.t.) **kainsal karaanaa** कैंसल कराना

car (f) **kaar; gaaRii** कार/गाड़ी

care, to take (v.t.) **khyaal rakhnaa** ख़्याल रखना

carrot (f) **gaajar** गाजर

catch, to (v.t.) **pakaRnaa** पकड़ना

cauliflower (f) **phuul gobhii** फूल गोभी

cell phone (m) **mobaail fon** मोबाइल फ़ोन

century (f) **shatabdii** शताब्दी

certainly (ind) **zaruur** ज़रूर

certificate (m) **pramaan patra** प्रमाण पत्र

chain (f) **zanjiir** ज़ंजीर

chair (f) **kursii** कुरसी

change, to (v.i.; v.t.) **badalnaa** बदलना

charger (m) **chaarjar** चार्जर

chat (spicy fast food) (f) **chaaT** चाट

cheap (adj) **sastaa** सस्ता

check out, to (v.t.) (vacate) **cek aauT karnaa** चेक आउट करना

cheese (m) (*paneer*) **paniir** पनीर

chicken (m) **murgh** मुर्ग़

chickpeas (m, pl.) **chhole** छोले

children (m, pl.) **baal bachche** बाल बच्चे

choose, to (v.t.) **pasand karnaa** पसंद करना

Christian (adj, m) **Iisaaii** ईसाई

Christianity (m) **Iisaaii dharm** ईसाई धर्म

church (m) **girjaa** गिरजा

chutney (f) **chaTnii** चटनी

cinema hall (m) **sinemaahaal** सिनेमाहाल

city (m) **sheher** शहर

class (f) (division) **shreNii** श्रेणी

clean, to (v.t.) **saaf karnaa** साफ़ करना

clear (adj) **saaf** साफ़

close (adj, adv) **nazdiik; paas** नज़दीक/पास

closed (adj) **band** बंद

closed, to be (adj) **band honaa** बंद होना

cloth (m) **kapRaa** कपड़ा

cloth shop (f) **kapRe kii dukaan** कपड़े की दुकान

clothes (m, pl.) **kapRe** कपड़े

cloud (m) **baadal** बादल

clutch (m) (car) **klach** क्लच

coat (m) **koT** कोट

cobbler (m) **mochii** मोची

coffee (f) **kaafii** कॉफ़ी

cold (f) **ThanD** ठंड

cold (adj) **ThanDaa** ठंडा

cold (m) (illness) **zukaam** ज़ुकाम

color (m) **rang** रंग

color, to (v.t.) **rang lagaanaa** रंग लगाना

come, to (v.i.) **aanaa** आना

company (f) **kampanii** कम्पनी

computer (m) **kampyuuTar** कम्प्यूटर

concern (f) **cintaa** चिंता

concern; care (f) **parvaah** परवाह

confirm, to (v.t.) **kanfarm karnaa** कन्फर्म करना

Congratulations! (ind) **Badhaaii ho!; Mubaarak ho!** बधाई हो मुबारक हो

connection (m) **kanekshan** कनेक्शन

contagious (adj) **sankraamak** संक्रामक

contract (m) **anubandh** अनुबंध

cook, to (food) (v.t.) **(khaanaa) pakaanaa** (खाना) पकाना

copy (f) **kaapii** कॉपी

corner (m) **konaa** कोना

cotton (f); cotton (adj); (home-spun, f) **ruii; suutii; khaadii** रुई/सूती/खादी

country (m) **desh** देश

course (m) **kors** कोर्स

credit card (m) **kreDiT kaarD** क्रेडिट कार्ड

cut, to (v.t.) **kaaTnaa** काटना

D

daily (adv) **roz** रोज़

dal (lentil dish) (f) **daal** दाल

danger (m) **khatraa** ख़तरा

dark color (m) **gehraa rang** गहरा रंग

date (f) **taariikh** तारीख़

day (m) **din** दिन

day after tomorrow; day before yesterday (m) **parsoñ** परसों

daughter (f) **beTii** बेटी

December (m) **Disambar** दिसंबर

deep (adj) **gehraa** गहरा

degree (f) **upaadhi** उपाधि

delay (f) **der** देर

delicious (tasty) (adj) **laziiz; svaadiSHT** लज़ीज़/स्वादिष्ट

depart, to (v.i.) **ravaanaa honaa** रवाना होना

depart(ed) (adj) **ravaanaa** रवाना

departure (m) **prasthaan** प्रस्थान

deposit (m) **ḍipaaziT** डिपॉज़िट

descend, to (v.i.) (alight, get down) **utarnaa** उतरना

dew (f) **os; shabnam** ओस/शबनम

diabetes (m) **madhumeh** मधुमेह

dial, to (v.t.) (a number) **(nambar) milaanaa** (नम्बर) मिलाना

diet, to (v.t.) **DaaiTing karnaa** डाइटिंग करना

dining hall (m) **Daaining haal** डाइनिंग हॉल

dinner (m) **raat kaa khaanaa** रात का खाना

dirt-absorbing (adj) **mailkhor** मैलख़ोर

disappear, to (v.i.) **ghaayab honaa** ग़ायब होना

disappeared (adj) **ghaayab** ग़ायब

discount (f) **chuuT; riyaayat** छूट/रियायत

disease (m) **rog** रोग

dissolve, to (v.t.) **gholnaa** घोलना

divorced (adj) **talaaq-shudaa** तलाक़-शुदा

dizzy, to become (v.i.) **cakkar aanaa** चक्कर आना

do, to (v.t.) **karnaa** करना

doctor (m) **DaakTar** डॉक्टर

dog (m) **kuttaa** कुत्ता

domestic (flight) (adj) **antardeshiiya** अंतर्देशीय

don't (ind) **na; mat** न/मत

door (m) **darvaazaa** दरवाज़ा

double (room) (adj) **Dabal** डबल

download (m) **DaauunloD** डाउनलोड

dress (f) **ḍres** ड्रेस

drink, to (v.t.) **piinaa** पीना

drive, to (v.t.); to make move **chalaanaa** चलाना

drive fast, to (v.t.) **tez chalaanaa** तेज़ चलाना

driver (m) **Draaivar** ड्राइवर

drop (f) **buund** बूँद

durable (adj) **Tikaau** टिकाऊ

E

early (f, adv) **jaldii** जल्दी

east (m) **puurv** पूर्व

eastern (adj) **puurvii** पूर्वी

easy (adj) **aasaan** आसान

eat, to (v.t.) **khaanaa** खाना

eggplant (m) **baiñgan** बैंगन

electronic shop (f) **bijlii kii dukaan** बिजली की दुकान

embassy (m) **duutaavas** दूतावास

email (f) **ii-mel** ई-मेल

emergency (m) **aapatkaal** आपातकाल

en route (adv) (in the middle) **biich meñ** बीच में

engine (m) **injan** इंजन

English (f) **Angrezii** अंग्रेज़ी

enjoyable (adj) **mazedaar** मज़ेदार

enjoyment, to come (v.i.) **mazaa aanaa** मज़ा आना

enough (adj) **kaafii** काफ़ी

Enough! (voc) **Bas!** बस

entire (adj) **puuraa** पूरा

evening (f) **shaam** शाम

excellent (adj) **baRhiyaa** बढ़िया

expensive (adj) **mehengaa** महँगा

experience (m) **anubhav** अनुभव

exportation (m) **niryaat** निर्यात

express post (m) **ekspres posT** एक्सप्रेस पोस्ट

express train (f) **ekspres gaaRii** एक्सप्रेस गाड़ी

extra (adj, adv) (more) **zyaadaa** ज़्यादा

eye (f) **aañkh** आँख

F

factory (f) **faikTrii** फ़ैक्टरी

fair (adj) **goraa** गोरा

fake (adj) **naqlii** नक़ली

fall, to (v.i.) **girnaa** गिरना

family (m) **parivaar** परिवार

far (adj, adv) **duur** दूर

fast (for Hindus) (m) **vrat** व्रत

fast (for Muslims) (m) **rozaa** रोज़ा

February (f) **Farvarii** फ़रवरी

feel (X), to (v.i.) **(X kaa) ehsaas honaa** X का एहसास होना

fever (m) **bukhaar** बुख़ार

fill, to (v.i.; v.t.) **bharnaa** भरना

film (f) **film** फ़िल्म

filtered (adj) **filTarD** फ़िल्टर्ड

final (adj) **aakhirii** आख़िरी

fine (adj) **Thiik** ठीक

fine (penalty) (m) **jurmaanaa** जुर्माना

finished, to be (v.i.) **khatm honaa** ख़त्म होना

fire (f) **aag** आग

fire extinguisher (m) **aag bujhaane kaa saadhan** आग बुझाने का साधन

first (adj) **pehlaa** पहला

fish (f) **machhlii** मछली

fish shop (f) **machhlii kii dukaan** मछली की दुकान

flash (f) **flaish** फ़्लैश

flight (f) **flaaiT** फ़्लाइट

flu (m) **fluu** फ़्लू

flyover (m) **flaaii-ovar** फ़्लाइ-ओवर

fog (m) **kuhraa** कुहरा

food (m) **khaanaa** खाना

for (the sake of) X (pp) **X ke liye** X के लिये

forbidden (adj) **niSHedh; manaa** निषेध/मना

foreign tourist quota (m) **TuurisT koTaa** टूरिस्ट कोटा

forget, to (v.i.) **bhuulnaa** भूलना

forgive, to (v.t.) **maaf karnaa** माफ़ करना

fort (m) **qilaa** क़िला

fresh (adj) **taazaa** ताज़ा

Friday (m) **Shukravaar** शुक्रवार
friend (m; f) **dost** दोस्त
from there (adv) **vahaañ se** वहाँ से
fruit (m) **phal** फल

G

game (m) **khel** खेल
garage (m) **gairaaj** गैराज
garden (m) **baghiichaa** बगीचा
garlic (m) **lehsun** लहसुन
gear (m) **giyar** गियर
genuine (adj) **aslii** असली
get; obtain, to (to be obtained) (v.i.) **milnaa** मिलना
get down, to (alight, descend) (v.i.) **utarnaa** उतरना
ghee (m) **ghii** घी
girl (f) **laRkii** लड़की
give, to (v.t.) **denaa** देना
glasses (m) **chashmaa** चश्मा
go, to (v.i.) **jaanaa** जाना
goat's meat (m) **bakre kaa gosht** बकरे का गोश्त
God (for Hindus) (m) **Iishvar; Bhagvaan** ईश्वर/भगवान
God (for Muslims) (m) **Allaah; Khudaa** अल्लाह/खुदा
God (for Christians) (m) **Prabhu; Iishvar** प्रभु/ईश्वर
God (for Sikhs) (m) **Rab** रब
good (adj) **achchhaa** अच्छा
Goodbye (m) **Namaste; Namskaar** नमस्ते/नमस्कार
Good luck (f, pl.) **Shubhkaamnaaeñ** शुभकामनाएँ
good morning (m) **suprabhaat** सुप्रभात
good night (f) **shubh raatri** शुभ रात्रि
goods (m) **saamaan** सामान
gourd (f) **laukii** लौकी
grateful (adj) **ehsaanmand** एहसानमंद
graveyard (m) **qabristaan** क़ब्रिस्तान
gray (adj) **sleTii** स्लेटी
green (adj) **haraa** हरा
grocery (provision) (m) **parchuun** परचून
guide (m) **gaaiD** गाइड

gulab jamun (fried sweet made from milk, served hot in syrup) (m) **gulaab jaamun** गुलाब जामुन
gurudwara (Sikh temple) (m) **gurudvaaraa** गुरुद्वारा

H

hail (stone) (m) **olaa** ओला
hair (m) **baal** बाल
half (adj) **aadhaa** आधा
halva (desserts made with flour or nut butter) (m) **halvaa** हलवा
hand (m) **haath** हाथ
handkerchief (m) **ruumaal** रूमाल
handsome; beautiful (adj) **sundar** सुंदर
happen, to (v.i.) **honaa** होना
happiness (f) **khushii** ख़ुशी
happy (adj) **khush** ख़ुश
harsh (sharp) (adj) **tez** तेज़
headache (m) **sardard** सरदर्द
health (f) (disposition) **tabiyat** तबियत
heart attack (m) **dil ka dauraa** दिल का दौरा
heart condition (f) **dil kii biimaarii** दिल की बीमारी
heat (f) **garmii** गर्मी
heavy rain (f) **muuslaadhaar baarish** मूसलाधार बारिश
hello; goodbye (m) **Namaste; Namaskaar** नमस्ते/नमस्कार
help, to do X's (v.t.) **X kii madad karnaa** X की मदद करना
here (adv) **yahaañ** यहाँ
high (harsh) wind (f) **tez havaa** तेज़ हवा
Hindu (adj, m) **Hinduu** हिन्दू
Hinduism (m) **Hinduu dharm** हिंदू धर्म
historical (adj) **aitihaasik** ऐतिहासिक
hither (adv) **idhar** इधर
hobby (m) **shauq** शौक़
hold, to (v.t.) (to wait on the line) **holḍ karnaa** होल्ड करना
home (m) **ghar** घर
hope (f) **ummiid** उम्मीद
hospital (m) **aspataal** अस्पताल
hot (adj) **garm** गर्म
hot wind (f) **luu** लू

hour; bell (m) **ghaṇTaa** घंटा

how (adj) **kaisaa** कैसा

how much; many (adj) **kitnaa** कितना

humidity (f) **umas** उमस

hundred (m) **sau** सौ

hunger (f) **bhuukh** भूख

hungry, to feel (to X) (v.i.) **(X ko) bhuukh lagnaa** X को भूख लगना

husband (m) **pati** पति

I

ice (f) **barf** बर्फ़

icy wind (f) **barfiilii havaa** बर्फ़ीली हवा

I.D. card (m) **aaii. Dii. kaarD** आई० डी० कार्ड

ill (adj) **biimaar** बीमार

immigration (m) **apravaasan** अप्रवासन

important (adj) **aham** अहम

importation (m) **aayaat** आयात

in (pp) **meñ** में

incline (f) **ḍhalaan** ढलान

in fine fettle (adv) **maze meñ** मज़े में

in the middle (adv) **biich meñ** बीच में

included (adj) **shaamil** शामिल

India (m) **Bhaarat** भारत

infection (m) **infekshan** इन्फ़ेक्शन

information (f) **jaankaarii** जानकारी

injection (f) **suii** सुई

injury (f) **choT** चोट

injured, to become (v.i.) (X) **(X ko) choT lagnaa** (X को) चोट लगना

inside (adv) **andar** अंदर

inside X (adv) **X ke andar** X के अंदर

install (v.t.) **insTaal karnaa** इन्स्टाल करना

insurance (m) **biimaa** बीमा

interpreter (English speaker) (m) **Angrezii bolnevaalaa** अंग्रेज़ी बोलनेवाला

international (adj) **antarraaSHTriiya** अंतर्राष्ट्रीय

Internet (m) **inTarneT; indrajaal** इंटरनेट/इंद्रजाल

Internet café (m) **inTarneT kaife** इंटरनेट कैफ़े

intersection (m) **cauraahaa** चौराहा

Islam (m) **Islaam** इस्लाम

issue (matter) (m) **maamlaa** मामला

issue, to (v.t.) **jaarii karnaa** जारी करना

J

Jain (adj, m) **Jain** जैन

jalebi (fried crisp sweet in syrup) (f) **jalebii** जलेबी

January (f) **Janvarii** जनवरी

jewelry shop (f) **zevarat kii dukaan** ज़ेवरात की दुकान

Jewish (adj, m) **Yahuudii** यहूदी

job (f) **naukrii** नौकरी

job, to do a (for money) (v.t.) **naukrii karnaa** नौकरी करना

journey; trip (f) **yaatraa** यात्रा

Judaism (m) **Yahuudii dharm** यहूदी धर्म

juice (m) **ras; juus** रस/जूस

July (f) **Julaaii** जुलाई

June (m) **Juun** जून

K

keep, to (place) (v.t.) **rakhnaa** रखना

key (f) **chaabii** चाबी

khoya (solidified milk) (m) **khoyaa** खोया

kidney beans (m, pl.) **raajmaa** राजमा

know, to (v.t.) **jaannaa** जानना

know, to (to come to X) (v.i.) **(X ko) aanaa** (X को) आना

know, to (to be known to X) (v.i.) **(X ko) maaluum honaa** (X को) मालूम होना

kulfi (traditional Indian ice cream) (f) **qulfii** कुल्फ़ी

L

laddu (sweet made from chickpea flour) (m) **laDDuu** लड्डू

laneway (f) **galii** गली

laptop (m) **lepTaap** लैपटॉप

lassi (f) **lassii** लस्सी

late (adv) **der se** देर से

late, to be (v.i.) (lateness to happen) **der honaa** देर होना

later (afterwards) (adv) **baad meñ** बाद में

lawyer (m) **vakiil** वकील

leather (m); leather (adj) **camRaa; camRe kaa** चमड़ा/चमड़े का

leave, to (v.t.) (abandon) **chhoRnaa** छोड़ना

left side (adv) **Baayiiñ taraf; or** बायीं तरफ़/ओर

lentils (f) **daal** दाल

letter (m) **patra; chiTThii** पत्र/चिट्ठी

license (m) **laaisens** लाइसेंस

lie down, to (v.i.) **leTnaa** लेटना

light (candle, etc.); traffic light (f) **battii** बत्ती

light color (m) **halkaa rang** हल्का रंग

light rain (f) **buundaabaandii** बूँदाबाँदी

like, to (to be liked, preferred to X) (v.i.) **X ko pasand honaa** X को पसंद होना

like, to (to seem good) to X (v.i.) **X ko achchhaa lagnaa** अच्छा लगना

limit (f) **siimaa** सीमा

line (f) **laain** लाइन

listen, to (v.t.) **sunnaa** सुनना

little (adj) **thoRaa** थोड़ा

live, to (v.i.) **rehnaa** रहना

long (adj) **lambaa** लम्बा

lose, to (v.t.) (an item); lost, to become (v.i.) **khonaa** खोना

lost, to become (v.i.) **khonaa** खोना

love (m) **pyaar** प्यार

love, to (v.t.) **pyaar karnaa** प्यार करना

low beam (m) (car) **ḍipar** डिपर

luggage (m) **saamaan** सामान

lunch (m) **din kaa khaanaa** दिन का खाना

M

machine (f) **mashiin** मशीन

make, to (v.t.) **banaanaa** बनाना

man (m) **aadmii** आदमी

manager (m) **prabandhak** प्रबंधक

map (m) **naqshaa** नक्शा

March (m) **Maarch** मार्च

market (m) **baazaar** बाज़ार

married (adj) **shaadiishudaa; vivaahit** शादीशुदा/विवाहित

massage (f) **maalish** मालिश

massage, to (v.t.) **maalish karnaa** मालिश करना

match (m) **maic** मैच

matter (to discuss; topic) (f) **baat** बात

mausoleum (m) **maqbaraa** मक़बरा

May (f) **Maii** मई

meaning (m) **matlab** मतलब

meanwhile (adv) **biic meñ** बीच में

meat (m) **maañs; gosht** मांस/गोश्त

medication (f) **davaa** दवा

medicine (f) **davaa** दवा

meet, to (v.i.) **milnaa** मिलना

member (m) **membar** मेम्बर

memory card (m) **memarii kaard** मेमरी कार्ड

mend, to (v.t.) **X kii marammat karnaa** X की मरम्मत करना

menstruation (m) **maasik dharm** मासिक धर्म

menu (m) **menuu (kaarD)** मेन्यू कार्ड

meter (m) **miiTar** मीटर

metro (f) **meṭro** मेट्रो

metro station (m) **meTro sTeshan** मेट्रो स्टेशन

midday (f) **dopahar** दोपहर

middle (adv) **biich** बीच

mind; heart (m) **man** मन

minute (m) **minaT** मिनट

mirror (m) **aainaa** आइना

miss, to (the memory to come to) (v.i.) **yaad aanaa** याद आना

mixed (adj) **milaa-julaa** मिला-जुला

mobile phone (m) **mobaail fon** मोबाइल फ़ोन

mobile phone shop (f) **mobaail fon kii dukaan** मोबाइल फ़ोन की दुकान

Monday (m) **Somvaar** सोमवार

money order (m) **manii aarDar** मनी ऑर्डर

monkey (m) **bandar** बंदर

month (m) **mahiinaa** महीना

morning (m) **saveraa**; (f) **subah** सवेरा; सुबह

mosque (f) **masjid** मस्जिद

mosquito (m) **machchhar** मच्छर

mosquito net (f) **machchhardaanii** मच्छरदानी

mouth (m) **muuñh** मुँह

move, to (v.i.) **chalnaa** चलना

movie (f) **film** फ़िल्म
muffler (m) **maflar** मफ़लर
multinational corporation (f)
  bahuraaSHTriiya kampanii बहुराष्ट्रीय
  कम्पनी
muscle (f) **maanspeshii** मांसपेशी
museum (m) **sangrahaalay; myuziyam**
  संग्रहालय/म्यूज़ियम
music (m) **sangiit** संगीत
Muslim (adj, m) **Musalmaan; Muslim**
  मुसलमान/मुसलिम
mustache (f) **muunchh** मूँछ
mutton (m) **bheR kaa gosht** भेड़ का गोश्त

N

name (m) **naam** नाम
nan (f) **naan** नान
nationality (f) **naagriktaa** नागरिकता
necessary (adj) **zaruurii** ज़रूरी
necessity (f) **zaruurat** ज़रूरत
new (adj) **nayaa** नया
next (adj) **aglaa** अगला
next to (adv) **paas** पास
nice (good) (adj) **achchhaa** अच्छा
night (f) **raat** रात
no (adv) **jii nahiiñ** जी नहीं
noise (m) (commotion); (f, sound, voice)
  shorgul; aavaaz शोरगुल/आवाज़
north; answer (m) **uttar** उत्तर
not (ind) **nahiiñ** नहीं
note, to (v.t.) **noṭ karnaa** नोट करना
nothing (pron) **kuchh nahiiñ** कुछ नहीं
November (m) **Navambar** नवम्बर
nowhere (adv) **kahiiñ nahiiñ** कहीं नहीं
number (m) **nambar** नम्बर

O

ocean (m) **samudra** समुद्र
occupation (m) **peshaa** पेशा
o'clock (adv) **baje** बजे
October (m) **Aktuubar** अक्तूबर
office (m) **daftar** दफ़्तर
oil (m) **tel** तेल
ointment (m) **marham** मरहम
old; big (adj) **baRaa** बड़ा

old (adj) (in duration) **puraanaa** पुराना
on (pp) **par; pe** पर/पे
one's own (adj) **apnaa** अपना
one-way (adj) **ek-tarafaa** एक-तरफ़ा
onion (m) **pyaaz** प्याज़
online (adj) **aan-laain** ऑन-लाइन
only (adv+adj) **sirf** सिर्फ़
open (adj) **khulaa** खुला
open, to (v.i.) **khulnaa** खुलना
open, to (v.t.) **kholnaa** खोलना
operation (m) **aapareshan** आपरेशन
opinion (m); (f) **khyaal, vichaar; raay**
  ख़्याल/विचार/राय
optician (optical store) (f) **cashme kii**
  dukaan चश्मे की दुकान
orange (adj, f) **naarangii** नारंगी
orange juice (sweet lime) (m) **mausambii**
  kaa ras मौसंबी का रस
order, to (to give the order) (v.t.) **aarDar**
  denaa ऑर्डर देना
order, to take (to take the order) (v.t.)
  aarDar lenaa ऑर्डर लेना
outside (adv) **baahar** बाहर
outside X (pp) **X ke baahar** X के बाहर
over here (adv) **idhar** इधर
over there (adv) **udhar** उधर
owner (m) **maalik** मालिक

P

pain (m) **dard** दर्द
paisa (m, a hundredth of a rupee) **paisaa**
  पैसा
pants (f) **painṭ** पैंट
paratha (m) (fried bread, unleavened wheat
  flour) **paraañṭhaa** पराँठा
parcel (m) **paarsal** पार्सल
parents (m, pl.) **maataa-pitaa** माता-पिता
park (m) **paark** पार्क
park, to (v.t.) **gaaRī lagaanaa** गाड़ी लगाना
partner (m) **saathii** साथी
passport (m) **passport** पासपोर्ट
path (m) **raastaa** रास्ता
pay, to (v.t.) **bhugtaan karnaa** भुगतान करना
pay the bill, to (v.t.) **bil chukaanaa** बिल
  चुकाना

pea (f) **maTar** मटर
pedal (m) (car; bike) **paiDal** पैडल
perhaps (ind) **shaayad** शायद
permission, to give (v.t.) **ijaazat denaa** इजाज़त देना
permit (m) **parmiT** परमिट
person (man) (m) **aadmii** आदमी
petrol (m) **peṭrol; tel** पैट्रोल/तेल
pharmacy (m) **davaakhaanaa** दवाख़ाना
phone, to (v.t.) **fon karnaa** फ़ोन करना
phone card (m) **fon kaarD** फ़ोन कार्ड
photo (f) **tasviir** (m; f)**; foTo** तस्वीर/फ़ोटो
pickle (m) **achaarr** अचार
pick up, to (v.t.) **uThaanaa** उठाना
piece (m) **piis; ṭukRaa** पीस/टुकड़ा
pill (f) **golii** गोली
pink (adj) **gulaabii** गुलाबी
place (m) **sthaan** स्थान
place (f) **jagah** जगह
play, to (v.i.; v.t.) **khelnaa** खेलना
pneumonia (m) **nimoniyaa** निमोनिया
police (f) **pulis** पुलिस
police station (m) **thaanaa** थाना
polish, to (v.t.) **chamkaanaa** चमकाना
pollution (m) **praduuSHaṇ** प्रदूषण
pool (m) **puul** पूल
pond (m) **taalaab** तालाब
porter (m) **porTar** पोर्टर
postcard (m) **posTkaarD** पोस्टकार्ड
post office (m) **Dakkhaanaa** डाकख़ाना
potato (m) **aaluu** आलू
prayer (for Hindus and Christians) (f) **praarthnaa** प्रार्थना
prayer (for Muslims) (f) **namaaz** (formal); **duaa** नमाज़/दुआ
preferred (adj) **pasand** पसंद
pregnant (adj) **garbhvatii** गर्भवती
prescription (m) **nuskhaa** नुस्ख़ा
pressure (m) **preshar** प्रेशर
previous (adj) **pichhlaa** पिछला
price (m) **daam** दाम
printer (m) **priṇTar** प्रिंटर
profession (m) **peshaa** पेशा
professional (adj) **peshevar** पेशेवर
properly (adv) **Thiik se** ठीक से

provision (grocery) (m) **parchuun** परचून
public (adj) **saarvajanik** सार्वजनिक
pumpkin (m) **kadduu** कद्दू
pure (adj) **shudh** शुद्ध
puri (fried bread) (f) **puuṛii** पूड़ी
purple (adj) **baiganii** बैगनी
purse; wallet (m) **baTuaa** बटुआ
put; pour, to (v.t.) **Daalnaa** डालना
pyjama (m) (type of pant) **paijaamaa** पैजामा

Q

qualified (adj) **dakSH** दक्ष
quickly (adv) **jaldii** जल्दी

R

radiator (m) (car) **reDiyeTar** रेडियेटर
rain (f) **bArish** बारिश
rain, to (v.i.) **baarish honaa** बारिश होना
raincoat (f) **barsaatii** बरसाती
rainy season (m, pl.) **barsaat ke din** बरसात के दिन
rape (m) **balaatkaar** बलात्कार
rasmalai (sweet dish, made of cream, milk and syrup) (f) **rasmalaaii** रसमलाई
read; study, to (v.t.) **paRhnaa** पढ़ना
ready (adj) **taiyaar** तैयार
real (adj) **aslii** असली
receipt (f) **rasiid** रसीद
red (adj) **laal** लाल
reduce, to (v.t.) **kam karnaa** कम करना
registered post (m) **rejisTarD posT** रेजिस्टर्ड पोस्ट
relate, to (v.t.) **sunaanaa** सुनाना
religion (for Hinduism and others) (m) **dharm** धर्म
religion (for Islam) (m) **mazhab** मज़हब
religious (adj) **dhaarmik** धार्मिक
religious site (m) **dhaarmik sthal** धार्मिक स्थल
remain, to (stay, live) (v.i.) **rehnaa** रहना
remember, X to; to be remembered) (v.i.) **X ko yaad honaa** X को याद होना
rent, to (to take on rent) (v.t.) **kiraaye par lenaa** किराये पर लेना

rental (m) **kiraayaa** किराया

reservation, to make (have done) (v.t.)
aarakSHaṇ karaanaa आरक्षण कराना

reserve, to (v.t.) **aarakSHaṇ karnaa**
आरक्षण करना

restaurant (m) **resTaraañ**; *restaurant*
रेस्ट्राँ/रेस्टोरेंट

return, to (v.i.) (come back); return
something, to **vaapas aanaa**; **vaapas
karnaa** वापस आना/वापस करना

return(ed) (adj) **vaapas** वापस

return ticket (m; f) **vaapasii TikaT** वापसी
टिकट

rice (m) **chaaval** चावल

rice pudding (f) **khiir** खीर

right now (adv) **abhii** अभी

right side (adv) **daahinii taraf**; **or** दाहिनी
तरफ़/ओर

road (path) (m) **maarg** मार्ग

robbery (f) **chorii** चोरी

robbery, to happen (v.i.) **chorii honaa** चोरी
होना

room (m) **kamraa** कमरा

roti (bread) (f) **roTii** रोटी

rouse, to (v.t.) **uThaanaa** उठाना

rupee (m) **rupayaa** रुपया

S

sad (adj) **dukhii** दुखी

sadness (m) **dukh** दुख

safe (for valuables) (f) **tijorii** तिजोरी

safely (adv) **sahii-salaamat** सही-सलामत

salary (m) **vetan** वेतन

salt (m) **namak** नमक

salty (adj) **namkiin** नमकीन

salwar (type of pant) (f) **salvaar** सलवार

sambhar (m; lentil based vegetable stew)
saanbhar साँभर

samosa (m) **samosaa** समोसा

sandals (f) **chappal** चप्पल

sari (f) **saaRii** साड़ी

Saturday (m) **Shanivaar**; **Shanishchar**
शनिवार/शनिश्चर

savory (adj) **namkiin** नमकीन

say, to (v.t.) **kehnaa** कहना

scan, to (v.t.) **skain karna** स्कैन करना

scanner (m) **skainar** स्कैनर

scarf (m) **dupaTTaa** दुपट्टा

search, to (v.t.) **talaash karnaa** तलाश करना

season (m) **mausam** मौसम

seat (f) **siT**; **kursii** सीट/कुर्सी

second (other) (adj) **duusraa** दूसरा

second time (adv) **dobaaraa** दोबारा

see; watch, to (v.t.) **dekhnaa** देखना

seem right, to (v.i.) **Thiik lagnaa** ठीक लगना

sell, to (v.t.) **bechnaa** बेचना

send, to (v.t.) **bhejnaa** भेजना

senior (elder) (adj) **buzurg** बुज़ुर्ग

September (m) **Sitambar** सितम्बर

serious (adj) **gabhiir** गंभीर

sex (male; female) (m) **ling (puruSH; strii)**
लिंग (पुरुष/स्त्री)

sharp (adj) **tiivra** तीव्र

shave a beard, to (v.t.) **daaRhii banaanaa**
दाढ़ी बनाना

shave a mustache, to (v.t.) **muuñchheñ
kaaTnaa** मूँछें काटना

shawl (m) **shaal** शॉल

sheet (bed) (f) **chaadar** चादर

Shia (adj, m) (one of the two major sects of
Islam) **Shiyaa** शिया

shiny (adj) **camkiilaa** चमकीला

shirt (f) **kamiiz**; **kurtaa** कमीज़/कुरता

shoe (m) **juutaa** जूता

shoelace (m) **fiitaa** फ़ीता

shop, to (to do shopping) (v.t.) **shaaping
karnaa** शॉपिंग करना

show (m) **sho** शो

show, to (v.t.) **dikhaanaa** दिखाना

sick (adj) **biimaar** बीमार

side (m) **kinaaraa**; (f) **taraf** किनारा/तरफ़

sign (m) **nishaan** निशान

sign, to (v.t.) **hastaakSHar karnaa** हस्ताक्षर
करना

signature (m, pl.) **hastaakSHar** हस्ताक्षर

Sikh (adj, m) **Sikh** सिक्ख

Sikhism (m) **Sikh dharm** सिक्ख धर्म

silk (m); silk (adj) **resham**; **reshmii**
रेशम/रेशमी

SIM card (m) **sim kaarD** सिम कार्ड

single (room) (adj) **singal** सिंगल
Sir (m) **(Bhaaii) saahab** (भाई) साहब
sister (f) **behen** बहन
sit, to (v.i.) **baiThnaa** बैठना
site (m) (place) **sthaan** स्थान
skin (f) **khaal** खाल
sky (m) **asmaan** आसमान
sleep, to (v.i.) **sonaa** सोना
slope (f) **Dhalaan** ढलान
slow (adj) **dhiimaa** धीमा
slowly (adv) **dhiire** धीरे
small; young (adj) **choTaa** छोटा
smile (f) **muskaan** मुस्कान
smoking (m) **dhuumrapaan** धूम्रपान
snack (m) **namkiin** नमकीन
snow (f) **barf** बर्फ़
soap (m) **saabun** साबुन
socks (m, pl.) **moze** मोज़े
soda (m) **soDaa** सोडा
sole (m) **talaa** तला
some, something (pron, adj) **kuchh** कुछ
some more (adj) **kuchh aur** कुछ और
somewhere (adv) **kahiiñ** कहीं
so much (adj) **itnaa** इतना
son (m) **beTaa** बेटा
sorrow (m) **afsos** अफ़सोस
sour (adj) **khaTTaa** खट्टा
south (m) **dakSHiN** दक्षिण
spam (m) **spaim** स्पैम
speak, to (v.i.; v.t.) **bolnaa** बोलना
speed (f) **gati** गति
speed, to (v.t.) **tez gati se gaaRii chalaanaa** तेज़ गति से गाड़ी चलाना
spicy (adj) **tiikhaa** तीखा
spinach (m) **paalak** पालक
spoon (m) **chammach** चम्मच
sports store (f) **khel-kuud ke saamaan** खेल के सामान का विक्रेता
sprain, to come (v.i.) **moch aanaa** मोच आना
stale (adj) **baasii** बासी
stamp (m; f) **TikaT** टिकट
statement (m) **bayaan** बयान
station (m) **sTeshan** स्टेशन
statue (f) **muurti** मूर्ति

stay, to (v.i.) (remain, live); (to stop) **rehnaa; Thehrnaa** रहना/ठहरना
stay away, to (v.i.) **duur rehnaa** दूर रहना
STD (m) **gupt rog** गुप्त रोग
stomach (m) **peT** पेट
stool (f) (feces) **TaTTii** टट्टी
stop; wait, to (v.i.) **ruknaa** रुकना
store (f) **dukaan** दुकान
storm (f) **aañdhii** आँधी
straight (adj) **siidhaa** सीधा
straight ahead (adv) **siidhe** सीधे
street (f) **saRak** सड़क
strike, to (v.i.) **bajnaa** बजना
stroll, to (v.i.) **Tehalnaa** टहलना
stuck, to become (v.i.) **phañsnaa** फँसना
student (m) **chaatra** (f); **chaatraa** छात्र/छात्रा
study; read, to (v.t.) **paRhnaa** पढ़ना
suit (m) **suuT** सूट
summer (m, pl) **garmii ke din** गर्मी के दिन
Sunday (m) **Ravivaar; Itvaar** रविवार/इतवार
sunlight (f) **dhuup** धूप
Sunni (adj, m) (one of the two major sects of Islam **Sunnii** सुन्नी
supermarket (m) **suparmaarkeT** सुपरमार्केट
swallow, to (v.t.) **nigalnaa** निगलना
sweater (m) **sveTar** स्वेटर
sweet (taste) (adj) **miiThaa** मीठा
sweet shop (f) **miThaaii kii dukaan** मिठाई की दुकान
swim, to (v.i.; v.t.) **tairnaa** तैरना
switch off, to (v.t.) **band karnaa** बंद करना
synthetic (adj) **banaavaTii** बनावटी

T
table (f) **mez** मेज़
tablet (f) **golii** गोली
tailor (m) **darzii** दर्ज़ी
take, to (v.t.) **lenaa** लेना
take a photo, to (v.t.) **foTo; tasviir khiiñchnaa** फ़ोटो/खींचना
take off, to (v.t.) **utaarnaa** उतारना
talk, to (v.t.) (to X) **(X se) baat karnaa** (X से) बात करना

tasty (delicious) (adj) **laziiz; svaadiSHT** लज़ीज़/स्वादिष्ट

tax (m) **shulk** शुल्क

taxi (f) **Taiksii** टैक्सी

tea (f) **chaii** चाय

teacher (m; f) **Tiichar** टीचर

tell, to (v.t.) **bataanaa** बताना

temperature (m) **taapmaan** तापमान

temple (m) **mandir** मंदिर

testing (f) (examination) **jaañch** जाँच

Thank you (m) **Shukriyaa** शुक्रिया

that (pron) **voh** वह

there (adv) **vahaañ** वहाँ

these (pron) **ye** ये

these days (adv) **aajkal** आजकल

thief (m) **chor** चोर

thing (f); material object **baat; chiiz** बात/चीज़

think, to (v.t.) **sochnaa** सोचना

thirst (f) **pyaas** प्यास

thirsty, to feel (v.i.) **pyaas lagnaa** प्यास लगना

this (pron) **yeh** यह

thither (adv) **udhar** उधर

those (pron) **vo** वे

thousand (m) **hazaar** हज़ार

Thursday (m) **Guruvaar; Brihaspativar** गुरुवार; बृहस्पतिवार

ticket (m; f) **TikaT** टिकट

time (m) **samay; Taaim** समय/टाइम

timetable (f) **samay saarNii** समय सारणी

tip (f) **bakhshish** बरूशीश

tire, tyre (m) **pahiyaa** पहिया

tobacconist (f) **paan kii dukaan** पान की दुकान

today (adv) **aaj** आज

toilet (m) **shaucaalay; TayleT** शौचालय/टॉयलेट

toilet paper (m) **TaayleT pepar** टॉयलेट पेपर

tomorrow (m); yesterday **kal** कल

tonight (f) **aaj raat** आज रात

top (adv) (above) **uupar** ऊपर

touch, to (v.t.) **chhuunaa** छूना

tour (m) **Tuur** टूर

tourist (m) **paryaTak** पर्यटक

town (m) **nagar** नगर

train (f) **Tren; relgaaRii; gaaRii** ट्रेन/रेलगाड़ी/गाड़ी

training (m) **prashikSHaN** प्रशिक्षण

transfer (m) **sthaanaantaraN** स्थानांतरण

trapped, to become (v.i.) **phañsnaa** फँसना

travel; wander, to (v.i.) **ghuumnaa** घूमना

travel, to (v.t.) **yaatraa karnaa** यात्रा करना

traveler (m) **yaatrii** यात्री

trunk (f) (car) **Dikkii** डिक्की

t-shirt (f) **Tii sharY** टी शर्ट

Tuesday (m) **Mangalvaar** मंगल(वार)

turn, to (v.i.) **muRnaa** मुड़ना

twenty-four hours (adv) **chaubiis ghaNTe** चौबीस घंटे

Twitter (m) **TviTar** ट्विटर

two-way (adj) **do-tarafaa** दो-तरफ़ा

U

ulcer (m) **alsar** अलसर

understand, to (v.t.) **samajhnaa** समझना

unemployed (adj) **berozgaar** बेरोज़गार

unleaded (petrol) (adj) **anleDeD** अनलेडेड

unmarried (adj) **avivaahit** अविवाहित

until, up to (pp) **tak** तक

urinate, to (v.t.) **peshaab karnaa** पेशाब करना

use (X), to (v.t.) **(X kaa) istemaal karnaa** (X का) इस्तेमाल करना

V

vacate, to (v.t.) **khaalii karnaa** ख़ाली करना

valuable (adj) **beshqiimatii** बेशक़ीमती

vegetable (dish) (f) **sabzii** सब्ज़ी

vegetarian (adj) **shaakaahaarii** शाकाहारी

very (adj, adv) **bahut** बहुत

via (adv) X **X se ho kar** X से होकर

vigilance (f) **saavadhaanii** सावधानी

virus (m) **vaairas** वाइरस

visible, to be (v.i.) **dikhaaii denaa** दिखाई देना

vomit, to (v.i.) **ulTii honaa** उल्टी होना

W

wait; stop, to (v.i.) **ruknaa** रुकना

wait, to (for X) (v.t.) **X kaa intazaar karnaa** X का इंतज़ार करना

want to, to (v.t.) **chaahnaa** चाहना

want; need (an object) (v.i.) **chaahiye** चाहिये

wash, to (v.t.) **dhonaa** धोना

water (m) **paanii** पानी

way (m) (path) **rāstā** रास्ता

wear, to (v.t.) **pehennaa** पहनना

weather (m) **mausam** मौसम

web browser (m) **veb braauzar** वेब ब्राउज़र

wedding (f) **shaadii** शादी

Wednesday (m) **Budhvaar** बुधवार

week (m) **haftaa** हफ़्ता

Well done! (ind) **Shaabaash!** शाबाश

west (m) **pashchim** पश्चिम

western (adj) **pashchimii** पश्चिमी

what (pron) **kyaa** क्या

when (adv) **kab** कब

where (adv) **kahaañ** कहाँ

which (adj) **kaun-saa** कौन-सा

whiskey (f) **whiskii** ह्विस्की

white (adj) **safed** सफ़ेद

who (pron) **kaun** कौन

why (adv) **kyoñ** क्यों

widow (f) **vidhvaa** विधवा

widower (m) **vidhur** विधुर

wife (f) **patnii** पत्नी

wind (f) **havaa** हवा

window (f) **khiRkii** खिड़की

windshield (glass) (m) **shiishaa** शीशा

winter (m, pl.) **ThaND ke din** ठंड के दिन

with (pp) X **X ke saath** X के साथ

witness (m) **gavaah** गवाह

woman (f) **aurat** औरत

wood (f); wooden (adj) **lakRii; lakRii kaa** लकड़ी/लकड़ी का

wool (m); woollen (adj) **uun; uunii** ऊन/ऊनी

work, to (do) (v.t.) **kaam karnaa** काम करना

worried (adj) **fikramand** फ़िक्रमंद

worth (adj) **laayaq** लायक़

wrap, to (v.t.) **lapeTnaa** लपेटना

write, to (v.t.) **likhnaa** लिखना

wrong (adj) **ghalat** ग़लत

Y

year (m) **saal** साल

yellow (adj) **piilaa** पीला

yes (adv) **jii haañ** जी हाँ

yoghurt (m) **dahii** दही

you (pron, polite) **aap** आप; (pron, informal) **tuu** तू; (very informal; intimate) **Tum** तुम;तू

Z

zero (adj, m) **shuunyaa** शून्य

Hindi–English Dictionary

A

aadhaa आधा half (adj)

aadmii आदमी person (man) (m)

aag आग fire (f)

aag bujhaane kaa saadhan आग बुझाने का सामान fire extinguisher (m)

aagaman आगमन arrival (m)

aage आगे ahead (adv)

aaii. Dii. kaarD आई॰ डी॰ कार्ड I.D. card (m)

aainaa आइना mirror (m)

aaj आज today (adv)

aaj raat आज रात tonight (f)

aajkal आजकल these days (adv)

aakhirii आख़िरी final (adj)

aaluu आलू potato (m)

aan-laain ऑन-लाइन online (adj)

aanaa आना to come (v.i.)

aañdhii आँधी storm (f)

aañkh आँख eye (f)

aap आप you (pron, polite)

aapareshan आपरेशन operation (m)

aapatkaal आपत्काल emergency (m)

aarakSHaṇ karaanaa आरक्षण कराना to make (have done) reservation (v.t.)

aarakSHaṇ karnaa आरक्षण करना reserve, to (v.t.)

aarDar denaa ऑर्डर देना to order (to give the order) (v.t.)

aarDar lenaa ऑर्डर लेना to take order (to take the order) (v.t.)

aasaan आसान easy (adj)

aaTo ऑटो auto(rickshaw) (m)

aayaat आयात importation (m)

abhii अभी right now (adv)

achaarr अचार pickle (m)

achchhaa अच्छा good; nice (adj)

afsos अफ़सोस sorrow (m)

agal-bagal vaalaa अगल-बगल वाला adjoining (adj)

Agast अगस्त August (m)

aglaa अगला next (adj)

aham अहम important (adj)

aitihaasik ऐतिहासिक historical (adj)

akelaa अकेला alone (adj)

Aktuubar अक्तूबर October (m)

Allaah; Khudaa अल्लाह/ख़ुदा God (for Muslims) (m)

alsar अलसर ulcer (m)

andar अंदर inside (adv)

Angrezii अंग्रेज़ी English (f)

Angrezii bolnevaalaa अंग्रेज़ी बोलनेवाला interpreter (English speaker) (m)

anleDeD अनलेडेड unleaded (petrol) (adj)

antardeshiiya अंतर्देशीय domestic (flight) (adj)

antarraaSHTriiya अंतर्राष्ट्रीय international (adj)

anubandh अनुबंध contract (m)

anubhav अनुभव experience (m)

apaainTmenT अपॉइंटमेंट appointment (m)

apnaa अपना one's own (adj)

Aprail अप्रैल April (m)

apravaasan अप्रवासन immigration (m)

aslii असली genuine; real (adj)

asmaan आसमान sky (m)

aspataal अस्पताल hospital (m)

aurat औरत woman (f)

avarodhak अवरोधक breaker (adj)

avivaahit अविवाहित unmarried (adj)

B

baad meñ बाद में later (afterwards) (adv)

baadal बादल cloud (m)

baahar बाहर outside (adv)

baal बाल hair (m)

baal bachche बाल बच्चे children (m, pl.)

baarish बारिश rain (f)

baarish honaa बारिश होना to rain (v.i.)

baasii बासी stale (adj)

baat बात matter (to discuss; topic) (f)

baat; chiiz बात/चीज़ thing (f); material object

Baayiiñ taraf; or बायीं तरफ़/ओर left side (adv)

baazaar बाज़ार market (m)

badalnaa बदलना   to change (v.i.; v.t.)

Badhaaii ho!; Mubaarak ho! बधाई हो/
मुबारक हो   Congratulations! (ind)

baghiichaa बगीचा   garden (m)

bahuraaSHTriiya kampanii बहुराष्ट्रीय
कम्पनी   multinational corporation (f)

bahut बहुत   very (adj, adv)

baiganii बैगनी   purple (adj)

baiñgan बैंगन   eggplant (m)

baink बैंक   bank (m)

baiThnaa बैठना   to sit (v.i.)

baje बजे   o'clock (adv)

bajnaa बजना   to strike (v.i.)

bakhshish बख़्शीश   tip (f)

bakre kaa gosht बकरे का गोश्त   goat's meat
(m)

balaatkaar बलात्कार   rape (m)

banaanaa बनाना   to make (v.t.)

banaavaTii बनावटी   synthetic (adj)

band बंद   closed (adj)

band gobhii बंद गोभी   cabbage (f)

band honaa बंद होना   to be closed (adj)

band karnaa बंद करना   to switch off (v.t.)

bandar बंदर   monkey (m)

bannaa बनना   to become (v.i.) (to be made)

baRaa बड़ा   big; old (adj)

barf बर्फ़   ice; snow (f)

barfii बर्फ़ी   barfi (a milk-based sweet) (f)

barfiilii havaa बर्फ़ीली हवा   icy wind (f)

baRhiyaa बढ़िया   excellent (adj)

barsaat ke din बरसात के दिन   rainy season
(m, pl.)

barsaatii बरसाती   raincoat (f)

barth बर्थ   berth (m)

bas बस   bus (f)

bas kaa aDDaa बस का अड्डा   bus terminus
(m)

Bas! बसढ   Enough! (voc)

bataanaa बताना   to tell (v.t.)

baTan बटन   button (m)

battii बी   light (candle, etc.); traffic light (f)

baTuaa बटुआ   purse; wallet (m)

Bauddh बौद्ध   Buddhist (adj, m)

Bauddh dharm बौद्ध धर्म   Buddhism (m)

bayaan बयान   statement (m)

bayaar बयार   breeze (f)

bechnaa बेचना   to sell (v.t.)

behen बहन   sister (f)

berozgaar बेरोज़गार   unemployed (adj)

beshqiimatii बेशक़ीमती   valuable (adj)

beTaa बेटा   son (m)

beTii बेटी   daughter (f)

bhaaii भाई   brother (m)

Bhaaiisaahab भाईसाहब   Sir (m)

Bhaarat भारत   India (m)

bharnaa भरना   to fill (v.i.; v.t.)

bhaTuuraa भटूरा   bhatura (bread baked on
a griddle and deep fried) (m)

bhejnaa भेजना   to send (v.t.)

bheR kaa gosht भेड़ का गोश्त   mutton (m)

bhugtaan karnaa भुगतान करना   to pay (v.t.)

bhuukh भूख   hunger (f)

bhuulnaa भूलना   to forget (v.i.)

bhuuraa भूरा   brown (adj)

biic meñ बीच में   meanwhile (adv)

biich बीच   middle (adv)

biich meñ बीच में   en route (adv) (in the
middle)

biimaa बीमा   insurance (m)

biimaar बीमार   ill; sick (adj)

bijlii kii dukaan बिजली की दुकान
electronic shop (f)

bil बिल   bill (check) (m)

bil chukaanaa बिल चुकाना   to pay the bill
(v.t.)

biryaanii बिरयानी   biriyani (f)

biyar बियर   beer (f)

bolnaa बोलना   to speak (v.i.; v.t.)

brek ब्रेक   break (m) (car)

broshar ब्रोशर   brochure (m)

budhvaar बुधवार   Wednesday (m)

bukhaar बुख़ार   fever (m)

bulaanaa बुलाना   to call (v.t.) (summon)

buuking बुकिंग   booking (f)

buuking aafis बुकिंग ऑफ़िस   booking office
(m)

buuking karaanaa बुकिंग कराना   to book (v.t.)

buund बूँद   drop (m)

buundaabaandii बूँदाबाँदी   light rain (f)

buzurg बुज़ुर्ग   senior (elder) (adj)

C

caarpaaii (f); **palang** (m) चारपाई/पलंग bed (cot)

cakkar aanaa चक्कर आना to become dizzy (v.i.)

camkiilaa चमकीला shiny (adj)

camRaa; camRe kaa चमड़ा/चमड़े का leather (m); leather (adj)

cashme kii dukaan चश्मे की दुकान optician (optical store) (f)

cauraahaa चौराहा intersection (m)

cek aauT karnaa चेक आउट करना to check out (v.t.) (vacate)

chaabii चाबी key (f)

chaadar चादर sheet (bed) (f)

chaahiye चाहिये to want; need (an object) (v.i.)

chaahnaa चाहना to want to (v.t.)

chaarjar चार्जर charger (m)

chaaT चाट *chat* (spicy fast food) (f)

chaatra (f) **chaatraa** छात्र/छात्रा student (m)

chaaval चावल rice (m)

chaii चाय tea (f)

chalaanaa चलाना to drive (v.t.); to make move

chalnaa चलना to move (v.i.)

chamkaanaa चमकाना to polish (v.t.)

chammach चम्मच spoon (m)

chappal चप्पल sandals (f)

chashmaa चश्मा glasses (m)

chaTnii चटनी chutney (f)

chaubiis ghaNTe चौबीस घंटे 24 hours (adv)

chhaachh छाछ buttermilk (f)

chhole छोले chickpeas (m, pl.)

chhoRnaa छोड़ना to leave (abandon) (v.t.)

chhuunaa छूना to touch (v.t.)

chor चोर thief (m)

chorii चोरी robbery (f)

chorii honaa चोरी होना robbery to happen (v.i.)

choT चोट injury (f)

choTaa छोटा small (adj); young

chuuT; riyaayat छूट/रियायत discount (f)

cintaa चिंता concern (f)

D

daahinii taraf; or दाहिनी तरफ़/ओर right side (adv)

Daaining haal डाइनिंग हॉल dining hall (m)

DaaiTing karnaa डाइटिंग करना to diet (v.t.)

DaakTar डॉक्टर doctor (m)

daal दाल *dal* (lentil dish); lentils (f)

Daalnaa डालना to put; pour (v.t.)

daam दाम price (m)

daaRhii दाढ़ी beard (f)

daaRhii banaanaa दाढ़ी बनाना to shave a beard (v.t.)

DaauunloD डाउनलोड download (m)

Dabal डबल double (room) (adj)

daftar दफ़्तर office (m)

dahii दही yoghurt (m)

Dakkhaanaa डाकख़ाना post office (m)

dakSH दक्ष qualified (adj)

dakSHiN दक्षिण south (m)

damaa दमा asthma (m)

dard दर्द pain (m)

darvaazaa दरवाज़ा door (m)

darzii दर्ज़ी tailor (m)

davaa दवा medication; medicine (f)

davaakhaanaa दवाख़ाना pharmacy (m)

dekhnaa देखना to see; watch (v.t.)

denaa देना to give (v.t.)

der देर delay (f)

der honaa देर होना to be late (v.i.) (lateness to happen)

der se देर से late (adv)

desh देश country (m)

dhaarmik धार्मिक religious (adj)

dhaarmik sthal धार्मिक स्थल religious site (m)

Dhalaan ढलान slope; incline (f)

dharm धर्म religion (for Hinduism and others) (m)

dhiimaa धीमा slow (adj)

dhiire धीरे slowly (adv)

dhonaa धोना to wash (v.t.)

dhuumrapaan धूम्रपान smoking (m)

dhuup धूप sunlight (f)

dhyaan ध्यान attention; meditation (m)

dhyaan denaa ध्यान देना to give/pay attention (v.t.)

dikhaaii denaa दिखाई देना to be visible (v.i.)

dikhaanaa दिखाना to show (v.t.)

dikhnaa दिखना to appear (v.i.) (to be visible)

Dikkii डिक्की trunk (f) (car)

dil ka dauraa दिल का दौरा heart attack (m)

dil kii biimaarii दिल की बीमारी heart condition (f)

din दिन day (m)

din kaa khaanaa दिन का खाना lunch (m)

DipaaziT डिपॉज़िट deposit (m)

Dipar डिपर low beam (m) (car)

Disambar दिसंबर December (m)

do-tarafaa दो-तरफ़ा two-way (adj)

dobaaraa दोबारा second time (adv)

dopahar दोपहर midday (f); afternoon (f)

dost दोस्त friend (m; f)

Draaivar ड्राइवर driver (m)

Dres ड्रेस dress (f)

dukaan दुकान store (f)

dukh दुख sadness (m)

dukhii दुखी sad (adj)

dupaTTaa दुपट्टा scarf (m)

durghaTnaa दुर्घटना accident (f)

duur दूर far (adj, adv)

duur rehnaa दूर रहना to stay away (v.i.)

duusraa दूसरा another, second (other) (adj)

duutaavas दूतावास embassy (m)

E

e. Tii. em. ए० टी० एम० ATM (m)

ehsaanmand एहसानमंद grateful (adj)

ek-tarafaa एक-तरफ़ा one-way (adj)

ekselareTar एक्सेलरेटर accelerator (m)

ekspres gaaRii एक्सप्रेस गाड़ी express train (f)

ekspres posT एक्सप्रेस पोस्ट express post (m)

elarjii एलर्जी allergy (f)

embulens एम्बुलेंस ambulance (m; f)

enTiibaayoTik एंटीबायोटिक antibiotics (m)

F

faikTrii फ़ैक्टरी factory (f)

Farvarii फ़रवरी February (f)

fiitaa फ़ीता shoelace (m)

fikramand फ़िक्रमंद worried (adj)

film फ़िल्म film; movie (f)

filTarD फ़िल्टर्ड filtered (adj)

flaaii-ovar फ़्लाइ-ओवर flyover (m)

flaaiT फ़्लाइट flight (f)

flaish फ़्लैश flash (f)

fluu फ़्लू flu (m)

fon kaarD फ़ोन कार्ड phone card (m)

fon karnaa फ़ोन करना to phone (v.t.)

foTo; tasviir khiiñchnaa फ़ोटो खींचना to take a photo (v.t.)

G

gaaiD गाइड guide (m)

gaajar गाजर carrot (f)

gaaRī lagaanaa गाड़ी लगाना to park (v.t.)

gaay kaa gosht गाय का गोश्त beef (m)

gabhiir गंभीर serious (adj)

gairaaj गैराज garage (m)

galii गली laneway (f)

garbhvatii गर्भवती pregnant (adj)

garm गर्म hot (adj)

garmii गर्मी heat (f)

garmii ke din गर्मी के दिन summer (m, pl.)

gati गति speed (f)

gavaah गवाह witness (m)

gehraa गहरा deep (adj)

gehraa rang गहरा रंग dark color (m)

ghaayab ग़ायब disappeared (adj)

ghaayab honaa ग़ायब होना to disappear (v.i.)

ghalat ग़लत wrong (adj)

ghanTaa घंटा hour; bell (m)

ghar घर home (m)

ghii घी ghee (m)

gholnaa घोलना to dissolve (v.t.)

ghuumnaa घूमना travel; to wander (v.i.)

girjaa गिरजा church (m)

girnaa गिरना to fall (v.i.)

giyar गियर gear (m)

golii गोली pill; tablet (f)

goraa गोरा fair (adj)

gulaab jaamun गुलाब जामुन *gulab jamun* (fried sweet made from milk, served hot in syrup) (m)

gulaabii गुलाबी   pink (adj)

gupt rog गुप्त रोग   STD (m)

gurudvaaraa गुरुद्वारा *gurudwara* (Sikh temple) (m)

Guruvaar; Brihaspativar गुरुवार बृहस्पतिवार   Thursday (m)

H

haath हाथ   hand (m)

haftaa हफ़्ता   week (m)

halkaa rang हल्का रंग   light color (m)

halvaa हलवा *halva* (desserts made with flour or nut butter) (m)

haraa हरा   green (adj)

hastaakSHar हस्ताक्षर   signature (m, pl.)

hastaakSHar karnaa हस्ताक्षर करना   to sign (v.t.)

havaa हवा   wind (f)

havaaii aDDaa हवाई अड्डा   airport (m)

havaaii Daak हवाई डाक   airmail (f)

hazaar हज़ार   thousand (m)

Hinduu हिन्दू   Hindu (adj, m)

Hinduu dharm हिंदू धर्म   Hinduism (m)

hisaab हिसाब   calculation (m)

hisaab lagaanaa हिसाब लगाना   to calculate (v.t.)

holḍ karnaa होल्ड करना   to hold (v.t.) (to wait on the line)

honaa होना   to become; happen (v.i.)

I

idhar इधर   hither; over here (adv)

ii-mel ई-मेल   email (f)

Iisaaii ईसाई   Christian (adj, m)

Iisaaii dharm ईसाई धर्म   Christianity (m)

Iishvar; Bhagvaan ईश्वर/भगवान   God (for Hindus) (m)

ijaazat denaa इजाज़त देना   to give permission (v.t.)

infekshan इन्फ़ेक्शन   infection (m)

injan इंजन   engine (m)

insTaal karnaa इन्स्टाल करना   to install (v.t.)

inTarneT kaife इंटरनेट कैफ़े   Internet café (m)

inTarneT; indrajaal इंटरनेट/इंद्रजाल   Internet (m)

Islaam इस्लाम   Islam (m)

itnaa इतना   so much (adj)

J

jaanaa जाना   to go (v.i.)

jaañch जाँच   testing (f) (examination)

jaankaarii जानकारी   information (f)

jaannaa जानना   to know (v.t.)

jaarii karnaa जारी करना   to issue (v.t.)

jagah जगह   place (f)

Jain जैन   Jain (adj, m)

jaldii जल्दी   early; quickly (f, adv)

jalebii जलेबी *jalebi* (fried crisp sweet in syrup) (f)

jalnā जलना   to burn (v.i.)

janm जन्म   birth (m)

janmdin जन्मदिन   birthday (m)

Janvarii जनवरी   January (f)

jii haañ जी हाँ   yes (adv)

jii nahiiñ जी नहीं   no (adv)

Julaaii जुलाई   July (f)

jurmaanaa जुर्माना   fine (penalty) (m)

Juun जून   June (m)

juutaa जूता   shoe (m)

K

kaafii कॉफ़ी   coffee (f); enough (adj)

kaalaa काला   black (adj)

kaam karnaa काम करना   to work (do) (v.t.)

kaapii कॉपी   copy (f)

kaar; gaaRii कार/गाड़ी   car (f)

kaaTnaa काटना   to bite; cut (v.t.)

kab कब   when (adv)

kadduu कद्दू   pumpkin (m)

kahaañ कहाँ   where (adv)

kahiiñ कहीं   somewhere (adv)

kahiiñ nahiiñ कहीं नहीं   nowhere (adv)

kainsal karaanaa कैंसल कराना   to have canceled (v.t.)

kaisaa कैसा   how (adj)

kal कल   tomorrow; yesterday (m)

kam karnaa कम करना   to reduce (v.t.)

kambal कम्बल   blanket (m)

kamiiz; kurtaa कमीज़/कुरता   shirt (f)

kampanii कम्पनी   company (f)

kampyuuTar कम्प्यूटर   computer (m)

kamraa कमरा   room (m)

kanekshan कनेक्शन   connection (m)

kanfarm karnaa कन्फ़र्म करना   to confirm
(v.t.)

kapRaa कपड़ा   cloth (m)

kapRe कपड़े   clothes (m, pl.)

kapRe kii dukaan कपड़े की दुकान   cloth
shop (f)

karnaa करना   to do (v.t.)

kaRvaa कड़वा   bitter (adj)

kaun कौन   who (pron)

kaun-saa कौन-सा   which (adj)

kehnaa कहना   to say (v.t.)

khaal ख़ाल   skin (f)

khaalii karnaa ख़ाली करना   to vacate (v.t.)

khaanaa ख़ाना   eat, to (v.t.); food (m)

(khaanaa) pakaanaa ख़ाना। पकाना
to cook (food) (v.t.)

kharaab honaa ख़राब होना   to break down
(v.i.)

kharaab; buraa ख़राब बुरा   bad (adj)

khariidnaa ख़रीदना   to buy (v.t.)

khatm honaa ख़त्म होना   to be finished (v.i.)

khatraa ख़तरा   danger (m)

khaTTaa खट्टा   sour (adj)

khel खेल   game (m)

khel-kuud ke saamaan खेल-कूद के सामान
sports store (f)

khelnaa खेलना   to play (v.i.; v.t.)

khiir खीर   rice pudding (f)

khiRkii खिड़की   window (f)

kholnaa खोलना   to open (v.t.)

khonaa खोना   to become lost (v.i.); to lose
(v.t.) (an item)

khoyaa खोया   *khoya* (solidified milk) (m)

khulaa खुला   open (adj)

khulnaa खुलना   to open (v.i.)

khush खुश   happy (adj)

khushii खुशी   happiness (f)

khuun ख़ून   blood (m)

khyaal rakhnaa ख़्याल रखना   to take care (v.t.)

khyaal, vichaar; raay ख़्याल/विचार/राय
opinion (m); (f)

kinaaraa (f); **taraf** (m) किनारा/तरफ़   side

kiraayaa किराया   rental (m)

kiraaye par lenaa किराये पर लेना   to rent
(to take on rent) (v.t.)

kitaab किताब   book (f)

kitaab kii dukaan किताब की दुकान
bookstore (f)

kitnaa कितना   how much; many (adj)

klach क्लच   clutch (m) (car)

koD कोड   area code (m)

koii कोई   any (pron, adj)

konaa कोना   corner (m)

kors कोर्स   course (m)

koT कोट   coat (m)

kreDiT kaarD क्रेडिट कार्ड   credit
card (m)

kuchh कुछ   some, something (pron, adj)

kuchh aur कुछ और   some more (adj)

kuchh nahiiñ कुछ नहीं   nothing (pron)

kuhraa कुहरा   fog (m)

kursii कुर्सी   chair (f)

kuttaa कुत्ता   dog (m)

kyaa क्या   what (pron)

kyoñ क्यों   why (adv)

L

laain लाइन   line (f)

laaisens लाइसेंस   license (m)

laal लाल   red (adj)

laanaa लाना   to bring (v.i.)

laayaq लायक़   worth (adj)

laDDuu लड्डू   *laddu* (sweet made from
chickpea flour) (m)

lagaanaa लगाना   to attach (v.t.)

lagnaa लगना   to attach; seem (v.i.)

lakRii; lakRii kaa लकड़ी/लकड़ी का   wood
(f); wooden (adj)

lambaa लम्बा   long (adj)

lapeTnaa लपेटना   to wrap (v.t.)

laRkaa लड़का   boy (m)

laRkii लड़की   girl (f)

lassii लस्सी   *lassi* (f)

laukii लौकी   gourd (f)

laziiz; svaadiSHT लज़ीज़/स्वादिष्ट delicious
(tasty) (adj)

lehsun लहसुन garlic (m)

lenaa लेना to take (v.t.)

lepTaap लैपटॉप laptop (m)

leTnaa लेटना to lie down (v.i.)

likhnaa लिखना to write (v.t.)

ling (puruSH; strii) लिंग (पुरुष/स्त्री) sex
(male; female) (m)

luu लू hot wind (f)

M

maaf karnaa माफ़ करना to forgive (v.t.)

maalik मालिक owner (m)

maalish मालिश massage (f)

maalish karnaa मालिश करना to massage
(v.t.)

maamlaa मामला issue (matter) (m)

maañs; gosht मांस/गोश्त meat (m)

maanspeshii मांसपेशी muscle (f)

Maarch मार्च March (m)

maarg मार्ग road (path) (m)

maasik dharm मासिक धर्म menstruation (m)

maataa-pitaa माता-पिता parents (m, pl.)

machchhar मच्छर mosquito (m)

machchhardaanii मच्छरदानी mosquito net
(f)

machhlii मछली fish (f)

machhlii kii dukaan मछली की दुकान fish
shop (f)

madhumeh मधुमेह diabetes (m)

maflar मफ़लर muffler (m)

mahiinaa महीना month (m)

maic मैच match (m)

Maii मई May (f)

mailkhor मैलख़ोर dirt-absorbing (adj)

makkhan मक्खन butter (m)

man मन mind; heart (m)

mandir मंदिर temple (m)

Mangalvaar मंगल(वार) Tuesday (m)

manii aarDar मनी ऑर्डर money order (m)

maqbaraa मक़बरा mausoleum (m)

marham मरहम ointment (m)

mashiin मशीन machine (f)

masjid मस्जिद mosque (f)

maTar मटर pea (f)

matlab मतलब meaning (m)

mausam मौसम season; weather (m)

mausambii kaa ras मौसंबी का रस orange
juice (sweet lime) (m)

mazaa aanaa मज़ा आना enjoyment to
come (v.i.)

maze meñ मज़े में in fine fettle (adv)

mazedaar मज़ेदार enjoyable (adj)

mazhab मज़हब religion (for Islam) (m)

mehengaa महँगा expensive (adj)

memarii kaarD मेमरी कार्ड memory card
(m)

membar मेम्बर member (m)

meñ में in (pp)

menuu (kaarD) मेनू कार्ड menu (m)

meṭro मेट्रो metro (f)

meTro sTeshan मेट्रो स्टेशन metro station
(m)

mez मेज़ table (f)

miiTar मीटर meter (m)

miiThaa मीठा sweet (taste) (adj)

milaa-julaa मिला-जुला mixed (adj)

milnaa मिलना to be available; to get,
obtain (to be obtained); to meet (v.i.)

minaT मिनट minute (m)

miThaaii kii dukaan मिठाई की दुकान
sweet shop (f)

mobaail fon मोबाइल फ़ोन cell phone;
mobile phone (m)

mobaail fon kii dukaan मोबाइल फ़ोन की
दुकान mobile phone shop (f)

moch aanaa मोच आना sprain to come
(v.i.)

mochii मोची cobbler (m)

moR मोड़ bend (m)

moze मोज़े socks (m, pl.)

murgh मुर्ग़ chicken (m)

muRnaa मुड़ना to turn (v.i.)

Musalmaan; Muslim मुसलमान/मुसलिम
Muslim (adj, m)

muskaan मुस्कान smile (f)

muunchh मूँछ mustache (f)

muuñchheñ kaaTnaa मूँछें काटना to shave
a mustache (v.t.)

muuñh मुँह   mouth (m)

muurti मूर्ति   statue (f)

muuslaadhaar baarish मूसलाधार बारिश बारिश   heavy rain (f)

N

na; mat न/मत   don't (ind)

naagriktaa नागरिकता   nationality (f)

naaii नाई   barber (m)

naam नाम   name (m)

naan नान   *nan* (f)

naarangii नारंगी   orange (adj, f)

naashtaa नाश्ता   breakfast (m)

naastik नास्तिक   atheist (adj, m)

naav नाव   boat (f)

nagar नगर   town (m)

nahiiñ नहीं   not (ind)

namaaz (formal); duaa नमाज़/दुआ   prayer (for Muslims) (f)

namak नमक   salt (m)

Namaste; Namskaar नमस्ते/नमस्कार Goodbye (m)

nambar नम्बर   number (m)

(nambar) milaanaa (नम्बर) मिलाना   to dial (v.t.) (a number)

namkiin नमकीन   salty; savory; snack (adj)

naqlii नक़ली   fake (adj)

naqshaa नक़्शा   map (m)

naukrii नौकरी   job (f)

naukrii karnaa नौकरी करना   to do a job (for money) (v.t.)

Navambar नवम्बर   November (m)

nayaa नया   new (adj)

nazdiik; paas नज़दीक/पास   close (adj, adv)

nigalnaa निगलना   to swallow (v.t.)

niiche नीचे   below; bottom (adv)

niilaa नीला   blue (adj)

nimoniyaa निमोनिया   pneumonia (m)

niryaat निर्यात   exportation (m)

nishaan निशान   sign (m)

niSHedh; manaa निषेध/मना   forbidden (adj)

noṭ karnaa नोट करना   to note (v.t.)

nuskhaa नुस्ख़ा   prescription (m)

O

olaa ओला   hail (stone) (m)

os; shabnam ओस/शबनम   dew (f)

P

paalak पालक   spinach (m)

paan kii dukaan पान की दुकान tobacconist (f)

paanaa; saknaa पाना/सकना   to be able to (v.i.)

paanii पानी   water (m)

paark पार्क   park (m)

paarsal पार्सल   parcel (m)

paas पास   next to (adv)

pahiyaa पहिया   tire, tyre (m)

pahuñchnaa पहुँचना   to arrive (v.i.)

paiDal पैडल   pedal (m) (car; bike)

paijaamaa पैजामा   pyjama (m) (type of pant)

painṭ पैंट   pants (f)

paisaa पैसा   *paisa* (m, a hundredth of a rupee)

pakaRnaa पकड़ना   to catch (v.t.)

paniir पनीर   cheese (m) (*paneer*)

par; pe पर/पे   on (pp)

paraañṭhaa पराँठा   *paratha* (m) (fried bread, unleavened wheat flour)

parchuun परचून   grocery (provision) (m)

paRhnaa पढ़ना   to read; study (v.t.)

parivaar परिवार   family (m)

parmiT परमिट   permit (m)

parsoñ परसों   day after tomorrow; day before yesterday (m)

parvaah परवाह   concern; care (f)

paryaTak पर्यटक   tourist (m)

pasand पसंद   preferred (adj)

pasand karnaa पसंद करना   to choose (v.t.)

pashchim पश्चिम   west (m)

pashchimii पश्चिमी   western (adj)

passport पासपोर्ट   passport (m)

pataa पता   address, whereabouts (m)

pati पति   husband (m)

patnii पत्नी   wife (f)

patra; chiTThii पत्र/चिट्ठी   letter (m)

pehennaa पहनना   to wear (v.t.)

pehlaa पहला   first (adj)

pehle पहले   ago; before; previously (adv)

peshaa पेशा occupation; profession (m)

peshaab karnaa पेशाब करना to urinate (v.t.)

peshevar पेशेवर professional (adj)

peT पेट stomach (m)

peṭrol; tel पेट्रोल/तेल petrol (m)

phal फल fruit (m)

phañsnaa फँसना to become stuck (v.i.)

phir फिर again (adv)

phuul gobhii फूल गोभी cauliflower (f)

pichhlaa पिछला previous (adj)

piichhe पीछे behind (adv)

piilaa पीला yellow (adj)

piinaa पीना to drink (v.t.)

piis; ṭukRaa पीस/टुकड़ा piece (m)

porTar पोर्टर porter (m)

posTkaarD पोस्टकार्ड postcard (m)

praarthnaa प्रार्थना prayer (for Hindus and Christians) (f)

prabandhak प्रबंधक manager (m)

Prabhu; Iishvar प्रभु/ईश्वर God (for Christians) (m)

praduuSHaṇ प्रदूषण pollution (m)

pramaan patra प्रमाण पत्र certificate (m)

prashikSHaN प्रशिक्षण training (m)

prasthaan प्रस्थान departure (m)

preshar प्रेशर pressure (m)

prinṭar प्रिंटर printer (m)

pul पुल bridge (m)

pulis पुलिस police (f)

puraanaa पुराना old (adj) (in duration)

puuchhnaa पूछना to ask (v.t.)

puul पूल pool (m)

puuraa पूरा entire (adj)

puuṛii पूड़ी puri (fried bread) (f)

puurv पूर्व east (m)

puurvii पूर्वी eastern (adj)

pyaar प्यार love (m)

pyaar karnaa प्यार करना to love (v.t.)

pyaas प्यास thirst (f)

pyaas lagnaa प्यास लगना to feel thirsty (v.i.)

pyaaz प्याज़ onion (m)

Q

qabristaan क़ब्रिस्तान graveyard (m)

qilaa क़िला fort (m)

qulfii क़ुल्फ़ी *kulfi* (traditional Indian ice cream) (f)

R

raajmaa राजमा kidney beans (m, pl.)

raastaa रास्ता path (m)

raat रात night (f)

raat kaa khaanaa रात का खाना dinner (m)

Rab रब God (for Sikhs) (m)

rakhnaa रखना keep to (place) (v.t.)

rang रंग color (m)

rang lagaanaa रंग लगाना to color (v.t.)

ras; juus रस/जूस juice (m)

rasiid रसीद receipt (f)

rasmalaaii रसमलाई *rasmalai* (sweet dish, made of cream, milk and syrup) (f)

rāstā रास्ता way (m) (path)

ravaanaa रवाना depart(ed) (adj)

ravaanaa honaa रवाना होना to depart (v.i.)

Raviivaar; Itvaar रविवार इतवार Sunday (m)

reDiyeTar रेडियेटर radiator (m) (car)

rehnaa; Thehrnaa रहना/ठहरना to stay (v.i.) (remain, live); (to stop)

rejisTarD posT रेजिस्टर्ड पोस्ट registered post (m)

resham; reshmii रेशम/रेशमी silk (m); silk (adj)

resTaraañ रेस्ट्राँ/रेस्टोरेंट restaurant (m)

rog रोग disease (m)

roTii रोटी *roti* (bread) (f)

roTii; chapaatii रोटी/चपाती bread (*roti*) (f)

roz रोज़ daily (adv)

rozaa रोज़ा fast (for Muslims) (m)

ruii; suutii; khaadii रुई/सूती/खादी cotton (f); cotton (adj); (home-spun, f)

ruknaa रुकना to stop; wait (v.i.)

rupayaa रुपया rupee (m)

ruumaal रूमाल handkerchief (m)

S

saabun साबुन soap (m)

saaf साफ़ clear (adj)

saaf karnaa साफ़ करना to clean (v.t.)

saal साल year (m)

saamaan सामान   goods; luggage (m)

saanbhar साँभर   *sambhar* (m; lentil based vegetable stew)

saañs lenaa साँस लेना   to breathe (v.t.)

saaRii साड़ी   sari (f)

saarvajanik सार्वजनिक   public (adj)

saathii साथी   partner (m)

saavadhaanii सावधानी   vigilance (f)

sabzii सब्ज़ी   vegetable (dish) (f)

safed सफ़ेद   white (adj)

sahii-salaamat सही-सलामत   safely (adv)

sailaan सैलॉन   beauty salon (m)

samajhnaa समझना   to understand (v.t.)

samay saarNii समय सारणी   timetable (f)

samay; Taaim समय/टाइम   time (m)

samosaa समोसा   *samosa* (m)

samudra समुद्र   ocean (m)

sangiit संगीत   music (m)

sangrahaalay; myuziyam संग्रहालय/म्यूज़ियम   museum (m)

sankraamak संक्रामक   contagious (adj)

saRak सड़क   street (f)

sardard सरदर्द   headache (m)

sastaa सस्ता   cheap (adj)

sau सौ   hundred (m)

saveraa; (f) subah सवेरा; सुबह   morning (m)

se से   by; from; with (through) (pp)

sel; baiTrii सेल बैट्री   battery (m); (for car, f)

Shaabaash! शाबाश   Well done! (ind)

shaadii शादी   wedding (f)

shaadiishudaa; vivaahit शादीशुदा/विवाहित   married (adj)

shaakaahaarii शाकाहारी   vegetarian (adj)

shaal शॉल   shawl (m)

shaam शाम   evening (f)

shaamil शामिल   included (adj)

shaaping karnaa शॉपिंग करना   to shop (to do shopping) (v.t.)

shaayad शायद   perhaps (ind)

shalwaar सलवार   *shalwar* (type of pant) (f)

Shanivaar; Shanishchar शनिवार/शनिश्चर   Saturday (m)

sharaab शराब   alcohol; wine (f)

shatabdii शताब्दी   century (f)

shaucaalay; TayleT शौचालय/टॉयलेट   toilet (m)

shauq शौक़   hobby (m)

sheher शहर   city (m)

shiishaa शीशा   windshield (glass) (m)

Shiyaa शिया   Shia (adj, m) (one of the two major sects of Islam)

sho शो   show (m)

shorgul; aavaaz शोरगुल/आवाज़   noise (m) (commotion); (f, sound, voice)

shreNii श्रेणी   class (f) (division)

shubh शुभ   auspicious (adj)

shubh raatri शुभ रात्रि   good night (f)

Shubhkaamnaaeñ शुभकामनाएँ   Best wishes; Good luck (f, pl.)

shudh शुद्ध   pure (adj)

Shukravaar शुक्रवार   Friday (m)

Shukriyaa शुक्रिया   Thank you (m)

shulk शुल्क   tax (m)

shuruu शुरू   beginning (m)

shuunyaa शून्य   zero (adj, m)

siidhaa सीधा   straight (adj)

siidhe सीधे   straight ahead (adv)

siimaa सीमा   limit (f)

Sikh सिक्ख   Sikh (adj, m)

Sikh dharm सिक्ख धर्म   Sikhism (m)

sim kaarD सिम कार्ड   SIM card (m)

sinemaahaal सिनेमाहाल   cinema hall (m)

singal सिंगल   single (room) (adj)

sirf सिर्फ़   only (adv+adj)

siT; kursii सीट/कुरसी   seat (f)

Sitambar सितम्बर   September (m)

skain karna स्कैन करना   to scan (v.t.)

skainar स्कैनर   scanner (m)

sleTii स्लेटी   gray (adj)

sochnaa सोचना   to think (v.t.)

soDaa सोडा   soda (m)

Somvaar सोमवार   Monday (m)

sonaa सोना   to sleep (v.i.)

spaim स्पैम   spam (m)

sTeshan स्टेशन   station (m)

sthaan स्थान   site (m) (place)

sthaanaantaraN स्थानांतरण   transfer (m)

suhaavnaa; sundar सुहावना/सुंदर   beautiful (pleasing; handsome) (adj)

suii सुई   injection (f)

sunaanaa सुनाना   to relate (v.t.)

sundar सुंदर   handsome; beautiful (adj)

sunnaa सुनना   to listen (v.t.)

Sunnii सुन्नी   Sunni (adj, m) (one of the two major sects of Islam)

suparmaarkeT सुपरमार्केट   supermarket (m)

suprabhaat सुप्रभात   good morning (m)

suuT सूट   suit (m)

sveTar स्वेटर   sweater (m)

T

taalaab तालाब   pond (m)

taapmaan तापमान   temperature (m)

taariikh तारीख़   date (f)

TaayleT pepar टॉयलेट पेपर   toilet paper (m)

taazaa ताज़ा   fresh (adj)

tabiyat तबियत   health (f) (disposition)

Taiksii टैक्सी   taxi (f)

tairnaa तैरना   to swim (v.i.; v.t.)

taiyaar तैयार   ready (adj)

tak तक   until, up to (pp)

talaa तला   sole (m)

talaaq-shudaa तलाक़-शुदा   divorced (adj)

talaash karnaa तलाश करना   to search (v.t.)

tang karnaa तंग करना   to bother (v.t)

tasviir (m; f); **foTo** तस्वीर/फ़ोटो   photo (f)

TaTTii टट्टी   stool (f) (feces)

Tehelnaa टहलना   to stroll (v.i.)

tel तेल   oil (m)

tez तेज़   harsh (sharp) (adj)

tez chalaanaa तेज़ चलाना   to drive fast (v.t.)

tez gati se gaaRii chalaanaa तेज़ गति से गाड़ी चलाना   to speed (v.t.)

tez havaa तेज़ हवा   high (harsh) wind (f)

thaanaa थाना   police station (m)

thailii थैली   bag (f)

ThanD; ThanDaa ठंड/ठंडा   cold (f); (adj)

ThanD ke din ठंड के दिन   winter (m, pl.)

Thiik ठीक   fine (adj)

Thiik lagnaa ठीक लगना   to seem right (v.i.)

Thiik se ठीक से   properly (adv)

thoRaa थोड़ा   little (adj)

Tii sharY टी शर्ट   t-shirt (f)

Tiichar टीचर   teacher (m; f)

tiikhaa तीखा   spicy (adj)

tiivra तीव्र   sharp (adj)

tijorii तिजोरी   safe (for valuables) (f)

Tikaau टिकाऊ   durable (adj)

TikaT टिकट   stamp; ticket (m; f)

Tren; relgaaRii; gaaRii ट्रेन/रेलगाड़ी/गाड़ी   train (f)

Tum; tuu तुम/तू   you (pron, informal); you (very informal; intimate)

Tuur टूर   tour (m)

TuurisT koTaa टूरिस्ट कोटा   foreign tourist quota (m)

TuuTnaa टूटना   to break (v.i.)

TviTar ट्विटर   Twitter (m)

U

ubaalnaa उबालना   to boil (v.t.)

ublaa huaa उबला हुआ   boiled (adj)

udhar उधर   over there; thither (adv)

ulTii honaa उल्टी होना   to vomit (v.i.)

umas उमस   humidity (f)

ummiid उम्मीद   hope (f)

umr उम्र   age (f)

upaadhi उपाधि   degree (f)

utaarnaa उतारना   to take off (v.t.)

utarnaa उतरना   to descend (alight, get down) (v.i.)

uThaanaa उठाना   to pick up (v.t.)

uttar उत्तर   north; answer (m)

uttar denaa उत्तर देना   to answer (to give an answer) (v.t.)

uun; uunii ऊन/ऊनी   wool (m); woollen (adj)

uupar ऊपर   top (adv) (above)

V

vaairas वाइरस   virus (m)

vaapas वापस   return(ed) (adj)

vaapas aanaa; vaapas karnaa वापस आना/वापस करना   to return (v.i.) (come back); to return something

vaapasii TikaT वापसी टिकट   return ticket (m; f)

vahaañ वहाँ   there (adv)

vahaañ se वहाँ से   from there (adv)

vakiil वकील   lawyer (m)

vetan वेतन   salary (m)

vidhur विधुर   widower (m)

vidhvaa विधवा widow (f)

vo वे those (pron)

voh वह that (pron)

vrat व्रत fast (for Hindus) (m)

vyaapaarii व्यापारी businessman; person (m; f)

vyast व्यस्त busy (adj)

W

whiskii ह्विस्की whiskey (f)

X

(X kaa) ehsaas honaa (X का) एहसास होना to feel (X) (v.i.)

X kaa intazaar karnaa X का इंतज़ार करना to wait (for X) (v.t.)

(X kaa) istemaal karnaa (X का) इस्तेमाल करना to use (X) (v.t.)

X ke aage X के आगे ahead of X (pp)

X ke aaspaas X के आसपास around X (pp)

X ke andar X के अंदर inside X (adv)

X ke baad X के बाद after X (pp)

X ke baahar X के बाहर outside X (pp)

X ke baare meñ X के बारे में about X (pp)

X ke liye X के लिये for (the sake of) X (pp)

X ke niche X के नीचे below X (pp)

X ke pehle X के पहले before X (pp)

X ke piichhe X के पीछे behind X (pp)

X ke saath X के साथ with X (pp)

X ke uupar X के ऊपर above X (pp)

X kii madad karnaa X की मदद करना help, to do X's (v.t.)

X kii marammat karnaa X की मरम्मत करना to mend (v.t.)

(X ko) aanaa (X को) आना to know (to come to X) (v.i.)

X ko achchhaa lagnaa अच्छा लगना to like (to seem good) to X (v.i.)

(X ko) bhuukh lagnaa (X को) भूख लगना to feel hungry (to X) (v.i.)

(X ko) choT lagnaa (X को) चोट लगना to become injured (v.i.) (X)

(X ko) maaluum honaa (X को) मालूम होना to know (to be known to X) (v.i.)

X ko pasand honaa X को पसंद होना to like (to be liked, preferred to X) (v.i.)

X ko Y kehnaa X को Y कहना to call (X to Y) (v.t.)

X ko yaad honaa X को याद होना X to remember (to be remembered) (v.i.)

(X se) baat karnaa (X से) बात करना to talk (v.t.) (to X)

X se ho kar X से होकर via (adv) X

Y

yaad aanaa याद आना to miss (the memory to come to) (v.i.)

yaatraa यात्रा journey; trip (f)

yaatraa karnaa यात्रा करना to travel (v.t.)

yaatrii यात्री traveler (m)

yahaañ यहाँ here (adv)

Yahuudii यहूदी Jewish (adj, m)

Yahuudii dharm यहूदी धर्म Judaism (m)

yaqiin यक़ीन belief (m)

yaqiin honaa यक़ीन होना to believe (belief to be) (v.i.)

ye ये these (pron)

yeh यह this (pron)

Z

zanjiir ज़ंजीर chain (f)

zaruur! ज़रूर certainly (ind)

zaruurat ज़रूरत necessity (f)

zaruurii ज़रूरी necessary (adj)

zevarat kii dukaan ज़ेवरात की दुकान jewelry shop (f)

zukaam जुकाम cold (m) (illness)

zyaadaa ज़्यादा extra (adj, adv) (more)

"Books to Span the East and West"

Tuttle Publishing was founded in 1832 in the small New England town of Rutland, Vermont [USA]. Our core values remain as strong today as they were then—to publish best-in-class books which bring people together one page at a time. In 1948, we established a publishing outpost in Japan—and Tuttle is now a leader in publishing English-language books about the arts, languages and cultures of Asia. The world has become a much smaller place today and Asia's economic and cultural influence has grown. Yet the need for meaningful dialogue and information about this diverse region has never been greater. Over the past seven decades, Tuttle has published thousands of books on subjects ranging from martial arts and paper crafts to language learning and literature—and our talented authors, illustrators, designers and photographers have won many prestigious awards. We welcome you to explore the wealth of information available on Asia at **www.tuttlepublishing.com.**

Published by Tuttle Publishing, an imprint of Periplus Editions (HK) Ltd.

www.tuttlepublishing.com

Copyright © 2024 Periplus Editions (HK) Ltd.

Library of Congress Control Number is in process

ISBN: 978-0-8048-5747-5

First edition

27 26 25 24 23   6 5 4 3 2 1
Printed in China   2311CM

Distributed by

North America, Latin America & Europe
Tuttle Publishing
364 Innovation Drive,
North Clarendon,
VT 05759-9436, USA
Tel: 1 (802) 773 8930
Fax: 1 (802) 773 6993
info@tuttlepublishing.com
www.tuttlepublishing.com

Asia Pacific
Berkeley Books Pte. Ltd.
3 Kallang Sector #04–01
Singapore 349278
Tel: (65) 6741 2178
Fax: (65) 6741 2179
inquiries@periplus.com.sg
www.tuttlepublishing.com

TUTTLE PUBLISHING® is a registered trademark of Tuttle Publishing, a division of Periplus Editions (HK) Ltd.

How to Stream the Audios and Flash Cards of this Book.

1. Make sure you have an Internet connection.
2. Type the URL below into your web browser.
   https://www.tuttlepublishing.com/learning-hindi

For support, you can email us at info@tuttlepublishing.com.